LIFE'S GREATEST JOURNEY

HOW TO BE HEAVENLY MINDED *AND* OF EARTHLY GOOD

DOUG McINTOSH

MOODY PRESS
CHICAGO

Library of Congress Cataloging-in-Publication Data

McIntosh, Doug.
    Life's greatest journey / by Doug McIntosh.
        p. cm.
    Includes bibliographical references (p.).
    ISBN 0-8024-6648-6 (trade pbk.)
    1. Christian life. 2. Church and the world. I. Title

BV4509.5 .M344 2000
248.4–dc21

00-025756

1 3 5 7 9 10 8 6 4 2

Printed in the United States of America

*To the missionaries of the Cross
scattered abroad in God's world,
emissaries of the great King,
pilgrims twice over;
and especially to those sent out by
Stone Mountain Community Church:*

Cliff and Judy Anderson
Bob and Julie Barber
Dick and Pat Beller
Peter and Iko Blank
Boyden and Lois Donmoyer
Ben Gaines
Juanita Goodall
Rick and Mary Harbin
Dick and Betty Kay
Don and Ruth May
Amy Miller
Dan and Tricia Miller
Howard and Trudy Owens
Gene and Martha Purvis
Mike and Jan Rogers
Paul and Kathy Schmidt
Mary Ann Steffy
Lawrence and Barbara Trumbower

CONTENTS

ACKNOWLEDGMENTS

T hanks are due to many who assisted me in putting this book together. In particular, I am grateful to Jo Ann Jones, who checked my Scripture references for accuracy; to Karen Bouchard, Kay Himmel, and Emmie Loften, who read the manuscript and offered a variety of suggestions for improvement; and to Karen Hutto, whose encouragements and editorial insights were both thoughtful and useful. I also am grateful to Tim Crater, who provided several suggestions (and some of the text) for chapter 8.

My thanks also to Jim Bell, editorial director of Moody Press, for his suggestions and vision for the project as well as contributing the study questions for "On the Journey," the response section that concludes each chapter. And thanks to Jim Vincent for his counsel during the editing of the manuscript.

May their efforts and these words serve as an encouragement to those on the road to the New Jerusalem.

THE TRIP
OF A LIFETIME

*A*s I write these words, the Thanksgiving holiday is fast approaching. Images readily spring to mind connected with this special day: turkey, the gathering of family members, football, pumpkin pie, and perhaps above all, the pilgrims. It is difficult not to smile as we think of them, for we visualize quite easily their quaint forms of dress and recall their Elizabethan language, characteristics that seem nearly as foreign to modern Americans as if the pilgrims had been space invaders.

The pilgrims would have seemed even stranger, of course, to the native inhabitants of the region that came in time to be called New England. I remember seeing a cartoon some years back. It showed two native Americans standing on the shore as people approach in a rowboat from the *Mayflower*. One native turns to the other and says, "Oh, no. Boat people!"

The pilgrims maintained their identity in the new land even when the existing culture resisted them. In doing so, they stamped their mark on an entire civilization, and exhibited a key quality of the spiritual pilgrim—an idea found in Scripture centuries before it was ever applied to those English Separatists who founded the Plymouth Colony.

In the Bible, in fact, God characterizes the whole of Christian living as a pilgrimage—not a journey to a shrine, but to a heavenly city, an ultimate reality that will outlast the ages. The biblical notion of being one of God's pilgrims includes three critical parts. First of all, God creates pilgrims by enrolling those who trust in Christ on His personal census. We are told that our citizenship is in heaven, that our names are written there, and that one day our heavenly city will descend to a renewed earth to inaugurate an unending age.

Second, those who have been transferred into God's kingdom —God's pilgrims, if you will—still have to live in the present world. We have a job to do here as His representatives. "We are ambassadors for Christ," Paul wrote (2 Corinthians 5:20). Representatives of foreign powers must never lose their distinctive links with their homeland.

Third, because our ultimate loyalty lies with our homeland and its all-powerful Sovereign, our pilgrimage through the present age will often bring us into conflict with this world's values and philosophies. From these conflicts we must not retreat. Our Master did not when He was an earthly Pilgrim, and He calls us to imitate Him.

Being such a pilgrim calls for a paradoxical attitude. On the one hand, we must be gracious and loving, patient with people and sympathetic to their concerns in order to properly represent Him to the world. On the other hand, we must be unbending in our commitments to integrity and righteousness—again, just as the Master was. We are never to jettison truth because of its inconvenience, but we are always to speak it in love and demonstrate it in life.

The people at Plymouth understood that a commitment to integrity isn't cheap. They had a successful growing season only in their third year. Then, in two successive years, they filled the hold of a visiting vessel, bound for England, with their produce in payment of their debt. Both times pirates hijacked the cargo, and all the results of their labors were stolen. Only after another growing season did their crops make it to England.

Yet many of us today find it less threatening and much simpler to let the world squeeze us into its mold. That's a blunder the apostle Paul warned the Romans so forcibly against. He wrote, "Do not be conformed to this world, but be transformed by the renewing of your mind, that you may prove what is that good and acceptable and perfect will of God" (Romans 12:2). If we would resist conformity to the values and lifestyle of a decaying age, we must begin with mind renewal.

As we will see in the upcoming chapters, learning to treasure the heavenly Jerusalem above our chief earthly joys does not happen spontaneously. Nearly as soon as we discover the identity of our homeland, we must begin the process of pondering its realities and learning to love it and its King.

Having a mind saturated with the great truths of Scripture forms the best guarantee that a believer will not suffer the conformity to the world that is so common to our age. God's truth will help us know Him, and "the people who know their God shall be strong, and carry out great exploits" (Daniel 11:32). As I will show, modern Christians suffer from an extraordinary ignorance of Scripture. More than any other factor, it is this biblical illiteracy that makes us so anemic in the modern world, for it guarantees that our affection for and knowledge of our Sovereign and His government will be limited and superficial.

Our consequent lack of attachment to the City of God makes us susceptible to the myriad attractions of our pragmatic age. The degree to which we have succumbed and allowed the world to shape us—and the results of that surrender—will form the subject of the first few chapters of this book. Afterward, I will attempt to present how the notion of being a pilgrim works out in the realms of work, ethics, and politics, and how it gives believers hope and a calm attitude during suffering.

My purpose in writing is to help you consider what being one of God's pilgrims means in your own life. I will urge you in the chapters ahead to think of yourself in a distinctive and biblical way. I argue that basic to being a serious pilgrim is a determination, built on biblical theology, to delight in being different.

As pilgrims, we walk along a path that is delightful yet demanding. Delightful because the Master walks with us, demanding because suffering and unexpected turns await. But it is life's greatest journey, one well worth trodding. As we will see, the rewards await at the end, yet along the way there is great satisfaction and purpose in what we do and who we are.

Before proceeding, however, we must turn our attention to the somber realities of the church in the Western world, and the degree to which modern Christians have surrendered the distinctive behavior that ought to serve as the chief commendation of our faith.

1

LEANING AND MEANING

---

*We live in a world of appearances
trying to pass for reality.*

—VACLAV HAVEL[1]

Several years ago, one of the television networks offered a children's news show with brief items of interest for the Saturday morning cartoon crowd. One video feature called attention to Italy's Leaning Tower of Pisa and noted that the historic structure was tilting so severely that it was in danger of falling. The network invited young viewers to send in suggestions about how to repair the tower, and the responses were illuminating.

One boy suggested that caretakers pull the tower back with a cable and then freeze the ground beneath it with refrigeration coils. Another youthful viewer thought authorities should abandon attempts to pull the building upright and just lay it down gently instead. Someone proposed building a museum next to the tower and connecting the two with supporting braces. Perhaps the most revealing, however, was the suggestion of the young man who said, "Just build the buildings around it the same way and nobody will notice!"

Many Christians take a similar approach when it comes to getting along in the world. They observe that the world is crooked, and their solution to living in a crooked world is to build their lives alongside it so that they simply blend in. Some do so to accomplish social or business objectives; others apparently in the hope that by being like the world no one will notice them. The tragedy is that often no one does.

The moral slide that so dominates Western culture has exerted a powerful influence on the values of Christians. The evidence for this decay is not hard to find.

For example, in October of 1998, thousands of people across America found large envelopes tucked in their mailboxes. They appeared to be the kind of urgent overnight letters delivered by companies like Federal Express, bearing labels like "worldwide express—urgent" and exhibiting bar codes, "airbills," and important-looking identification numbers.

People opened them, however, to discover that the codes and numbers were bogus. These compelling communications proved to be deceptively dressed appeals for funds from conservative Christian organizations. The ministries that sent them were seeking, among other things, financial assistance for congressional candidates who would turn the U.S. Congress in a new moral direction.

That this worthy purpose was being pursued via deceptive advertising seemed not to bother the leaders of those organizations. When one Christian writer privately called the practice into question, the leader of the fund-raising ministry countered that the mailing in question produced double the usual response rate. "We've been able to pass on millions of dollars to good candidates, and I can almost guarantee you that by the end of this [election] day, we will have elected enough new good people to the Senate to overturn the partial-birth abortion veto." Other leaders defended the practice by saying, "You've got to understand how wonderfully effective for good these methods have proven to be."[2]

Effective methods are not always righteous ones, however.

As a recipient of one of the fund-raising letters, I began to wonder about a couple of issues. First, I pondered how Christian organizations could afford to risk offending their supporters with such (obviously, it seemed to me) deceptive material. Evidently they had little to fear; at least the people who responded apparently did not entertain doubts, as I did, about the character of the leaders of these ministries. I also found myself contemplating how Christians could hope to elect public officials with integrity when our own methods lack it.

Those misleading "urgent mail" advertisements reflect an underlying condition in Western Christendom that is disturbing. Many Christians—even those in leadership positions—appear to be deeply committed to the moral pragmatism that is so common in today's world. A concerned Christian asks about the morality of a practice and receives an answer describing the effectiveness of it. The test of Christian behavior has shifted from "Is it right?" to "Does it work?" We appear to subscribe to moral values that are virtually indistinguishable from those of the society around us.

LIFE IN TWO WORLDS

What complicates matters is that Christians inhabit one world but belong to another. Though our bodies may live in this visible and fallen universe, the unseen kingdom of God owns exclusive rights to our hearts, loyalties, and values. The Bible says that we are "sojourners and pilgrims (1 Peter 2:11). Peter urged his readers to recognize that they were temporary residents—"sojourners and pilgrims," to use his expression—in this world and to behave accordingly. The common denominator of the great heroes of the faith, according to the writer of Hebrews, was their confession "that they were strangers and pilgrims on the earth" (Hebrews 11:13). We are, in effect, "resident aliens" with the responsibility of representing our homeland while living in a culture that is fundamentally hostile to its ideals. When we allow the kingdom of God to dictate what we believe, say, and do in this world, we become walking advertising for our homeland. On the other hand, when we slant our lives so that we imitate the culture, we are betraying our eternal city and its Sovereign. Even worse, when we abandon biblical loyalties in an effort to find acceptance or anonymity, we do our neighbors little good and our own souls great harm.

God calls Christians to take the issue of ultimate allegiance seriously. That means, according to Peter, turning away from that "aimless conduct received by tradition" (1 Peter 1:18) and living in ways that would engage our world without being conformed to it. The apostle noted, "We have spent enough of our past lifetime in doing the will of the Gentiles—when we walked in lewdness, lusts, drunkenness, revelries, drinking parties, and abominable idolatries" (1 Peter 4:3). "The will of the Gentiles" was merely Peter's way of describing the culture his readers lived in, an environment not unlike our own, filled with tensions, conflicting worldviews, distractions, and temptations.

I . . . grieve when [I] compare the influence that Western Christians presently have in their environment compared to what we could have.

How tense and distracting is it? Witness the bumper stickers on our automobiles. Not long ago, someone handed me a list containing the text of several of the most popular signs adorning today's chrome:

- *Warning: Dates in calendar are closer than they appear.*
- *Give me ambiguity or give me something else.*
- *Always remember: You're unique, just like everyone else.*
- *Hard work has a future payoff. Laziness pays off now.*
- *Change is inevitable—except from a vending machine.*
- *I don't suffer from insanity. I enjoy every minute of it.*
- *Forget world peace: visualize using your turn signal.*
- *All generalizations are false.*

At the risk of producing a falsehood, I'm now going to generalize: *Conformity with the world's way of thinking is the curse of Christianity in the Western world.* I'll defend that assertion in chapter 2, but for the moment I want to explore it a bit further.

Though many churches and church leaders sustain highly visible public ministries, when it comes to the mind-set of individual believers, we blend too readily with the neopagan culture that surrounds us. Sometimes our behavior suggests that we long more for the approval of our culture than for its spiritual transformation.

Don't misunderstand. I'm not among those alarmists who think that the church is in danger of disappearing altogether. Nor do I place myself among the Pollyannas who are sure that with one more evangelistic push unbelief will become a historical curiosity.

I do number myself, however, among the many who grieve when we compare the influence that Western Christians presently have in their environment compared to what we could have. We possess nothing like the influence of Christians in colonial America, for example, or that exerted by the Korean church in the first half of the twentieth century, or the present impact of believers in China, or the influence of apostolic and postapostolic Christianity on the Roman world. Should some historian take pen in hand to characterize our present situation, it would be unlikely that he would write anything like what appeared in the early second-century letter known as *The Epistle to Diognetus*. In a chapter called "The Manners of the Christians," the author, who is unknown but claims to have studied under the apostles, wrote that the Christians of his era

> display to us their wonderful and confessedly striking method of life. They dwell in their own countries, but simply as sojourners. As citizens, they share in all things with others, and yet endure all things as if foreigners. Every foreign land is to them as their native country, and every land of their birth as a land of strangers. They marry, as do all [others]; they beget children; but they do not destroy their offspring. They have a common table, but not a common bed. They are in the flesh, but they do not live after the flesh. They pass their days on earth, but they are citizens of heaven. They obey the prescribed laws, and at the same time surpass the laws by their lives. They love all men, and are persecuted by all. They are unknown and condemned; they are put to death, and restored to life. They are poor, yet make many rich; they are in lack of all things, and yet abound in all; they are dishonored, and yet in their very dishonor are glorified. They are evil spoken of, and yet are justified; they are reviled, and bless; they are insulted, and repay the insult with honor; they do good, yet are punished as evil-doers. When punished, they rejoice

as if quickened into life; they are assailed by the Jews as foreigners, and are persecuted by the Greeks; yet those who hate them are unable to assign any reason for their hatred.[3]

By the time our Diognetus received his epistle in A.D. 130, the Christian faith, which started as an obscure Jewish sect in Palestine in A.D. 33, had penetrated the outposts of the Roman Empire in every direction. Its handful of converts had grown into the hundreds of thousands. By contrast, American Christianity is either stagnant or perhaps declining slightly in the number of its adherents. The difference between the early church's phenomenal growth and its modern counterpart's shaky condition calls for an explanation, which will serve as the subject of chapter 2.

One clue to why those believers left such a mark on their era can be found in *The Epistle to Diognetus*'s reference to the early Christians' attachment to another world. The writer of the letter thought he had discerned in the believers' way of thinking like foreigners a key to their impact: "They dwell in their own countries, but simply as sojourners. As citizens, they share in all things with others, and yet endure all things as if foreigners."

PILGRIM JOURNEYS

It is a mentality easily lost. We are pilgrims on a journey. It is life's greatest journey, yet often we pilgrims have forgotten that truth.

God has gone to considerable lengths, however, to keep His people conscious of their pilgrim status; He's done so through the ages. For example, in ancient Israel every family was expected to celebrate annually the Feast of Tabernacles. They were instructed to dwell in temporary shelters ("booths" or "tabernacles") to remind themselves that they were once sojourners in Egypt: "You shall dwell in booths [tents] for seven days. All who are native Israelites shall dwell in booths, that your generations may know that I made the children of Israel dwell in booths when I brought them out of the land of Egypt" (Leviticus 23:42–43). The feast was sort of a mass backyard camping experience. It kept the people in touch with their nomadic origins and their dependence on God.

Likewise, each year at harvesttime, Israelites were expected to bring the firstfruits of their crops to the temple in Jerusalem. Each person was to present this fresh evidence of God's kindness to the priest and repeat the words of a confession:

> My father was a Syrian, about to perish, and he went down to Egypt and dwelt there, few in number; and there he became a nation, great, mighty, and populous. But the Egyptians mistreated us, afflicted us, and laid hard bondage on us. Then we cried out to the Lord God of our fathers, and the Lord heard our voice and looked on our affliction and our labor and our oppression. (Deuteronomy 26:5–7)

The confession began with this reminder of Jacob and Israel's four centuries of slavery, and then recalled God's kindness: "So the Lord brought us out of Egypt with a mighty hand and with an outstretched arm, with great terror and with signs and wonders. He has brought us to this place and has given us this land, 'a land flowing with milk and honey'" (Deuteronomy 26:8–9).

Then there is that group of Psalms (120–134), each of which begins with the words "A Song of Ascents." The plural provides a clue to the "ascents" the writer had in mind. These psalms were not written to be used once, but many times, in many ascents— probably the annual pilgrimages to Jerusalem to keep the three major festivals of Israel: Passover, Pentecost, and Tabernacles. We know that the pilgrims did customarily sing on their way to these festivals. Isaiah 30:29 explains: "You shall have a song as in the night when a holy festival is kept, and gladness of heart as when one goes with a flute, to come into the mountain of the Lord."

Christian believers are likewise pilgrims, walking . . . toward the world that Jesus promised, a land that often seems far away.

No matter where they come from, inside or outside the Land of Promise, the pilgrims had to walk uphill to reach the city of Jerusalem, which rests atop the mountain ridge running down the center of Palestine. In Scripture, people spoke consistently of "going up" to Jerusalem.

This view of the songs' purpose is supported by the progress that is made from one to the next. The worshipers start in Psalm 120 in the distant lands of Meschech and Kedar and continue through the mountains of Judah in Psalm 121 to arrive in Jerusalem. Then in Psalm 122, pilgrims are in the city at last: "Our feet have been standing within your gates, O Jerusalem!" (Psalm 122:2).

In Psalm 132, worshipers arrive on Mount Zion, the center of worship. The final song in the series, Psalm 134, finds believers inside God's sanctuary itself: "Lift up your hands in the sanctuary, and bless the Lord" (Psalm 134:2). So these psalms together represent the movement of obedient believers who are making their way through the workaday world to a holiday festival of the people of God.

Christian believers are likewise pilgrims, walking along the highway toward the world that Jesus promised, a land that often seems far away. We walk with others like us who share the same concerns and weaknesses. We are headed toward a bright and happy time, filled with rejoicing in which our hearts will be united in our love of the true and living God. Getting there while influencing this world for good—without losing our distinctiveness as pilgrims—is the challenge we face.

DANIEL AND HIS KIN

Daniel knew about walking the pilgrim way. Forcibly removed from Jerusalem as a teenager, he walked to Babylon along with many of his contemporaries. Though not personally involved in bowing down to idols, he was part of a nation that had been guilty of it for centuries. So Daniel found himself in Babylon, and entered a culture that was overtly hostile to his values.

Babylon embraced religious pluralism, but only to a point. The Babylonians were always ready to close ranks in opposition to God's truth. They did not believe in peaceful coexistence with people who claimed to worship the only true God.

Against their will, Daniel and his friends were given names that associated them with pagan deities. Because they formed part of a nation that had been defeated militarily, they were subjected to scorn and humiliation. Psalm 137, written by one of the captives, recalls the cruel taunts of the Babylonians: "Those who carried us away captive asked of us a song, and those who plundered us requested mirth, saying, 'Sing us one of the songs of Zion!' How shall we sing the Lord's song in a foreign land?" (Psalm 137:3–4).

How, indeed? Yet that remains one of the challenges of living as a Christian pilgrim in a hostile culture. The Lord's song must be sung—not to entertain the culture, but to bear witness to it that a better land exists.

The first hurdle, however, is to ensure we are identifiable as aliens. Sinclair Ferguson, a professor at Westminster Theological Seminary in Philadelphia, put the question accurately: "How are we to function here in such a way that we influence our society without being corrupted by it?"[4]

The answer is one that the psalmist knew well: We must keep our homeland uppermost in our affections: "If I forget you, O Jerusalem, let my right hand forget its skill! If I do not remember you, let my tongue cling to the roof of my mouth—if I do not exalt Jerusalem above my chief joy" (Psalm 137:5–6). Such an attachment to our distant homeland will keep us from drifting into a wholesale allegiance to the present Babylonianism. The way we think, in short, constitutes both our protection and our potential for ministry. The moment we begin to lose our delight in the City of God, distant and unattainable though it may seem at present, we take our first step into a comfortable accommodation of this world's attractions. As soon as we settle into that cozy condition, we lose our ability to speak to this age effectively.

Daniel never made that mistake. As a teenager in the king's court, he distinguished himself as a person of principle and integrity. During adulthood, he became a treasured counselor to the kings of Babylon; yet, even at the risk of his neck, he never shrank from speaking the truth to them.

Instead of providing such living examples of resistance to cultural decay and conformity, however, Western Christians in large measure have joined the culture's slow but steady march into oblivion. Unlike Daniel, we seem to have lost touch with the grand reality of our homeland.

THE PATRIARCHS' CITY

The prototypical sojourner, Abraham, understood that his true homeland was afar. The New Testament records how he "dwelt in the land of promise as in a foreign country, dwelling in tents with

Isaac and Jacob, the heirs with him of the same promise" (Hebrews 11:9). God had promised him all the land in due course, yet he owned almost no property in it and lived in a tent instead of a mansion. He dwelt "as in a foreign country." He refused to plant his tent stakes too deeply, recognizing that his true possessions lay in a future time, beyond his physical life: "He waited for the city which has foundations, whose builder and maker is God" (Hebrews 11:10).

The letter to the Hebrews tells how the patriarchs "confessed that they were strangers and pilgrims on the earth" (Hebrews 11:13). "Confessed" suggests a tension in which it would have been easier to keep quiet, a scenario that is always true for a foreigner. The writer characterized the faith heroes of the past as people gripped by a certainty of future reward that went far beyond merely escaping condemnation. Those people of faith knew—as they knew little else—that the city to come constituted ultimate reality. Their hopes were fixed on a place and a Ruler they could not see.

Yet the heroes of Hebrews 11 powerfully influenced this world for good. The way they carried off the challenge proves that a balance can be struck between an impassioned attachment to a future world and a profound influence on this one. It is, however, a knife-edge balance that is easily lost, and with fearful consequences. If we become preoccupied with the world to come to the exclusion of the present, we slip into monastic tendencies, retreat into the bliss of our tight little corporate endeavors, and lose our audience. If we become too attached to this world, we blend into the cultural paganism around us and lose the distinctiveness of our message.

Both errors are committed in Western Christendom, but it is the latter that dominates the spiritual environment at the turn of the millennium. We need to regain that way of thinking that drove Abraham, Jacob, Joseph, and Moses to make hard choices for the sake of maintaining a distinctive testimony. Their pilgrim mind-set formed the heart of the way they behaved. The New Testament writers repeatedly extolled their way of thinking and called believers to imitate it.

NOW LIVING IN A NEW KINGDOM

Take the apostle Paul, for example. He often wrote of those unseen changes that God effects in the life of a Christian, dramatic alterations that take place at the moment of conversion entirely apart from sense experience. They are known to us only because God tells us they happened. One important example: "He has delivered us from the power of darkness and conveyed us into the kingdom of the Son of His love" (Colossians 1:13). The use of the past tense is noteworthy. We who are Christians *have been transferred* from one kingdom to another. That was done apart from our experiential awareness, on the basis of our faith in Christ.

This transfer is the most important characteristic of the Christian, yet one which, because it is unseen and unnoticed with the physical senses, is often unappreciated. Many believers conceive of themselves as people with roots in this world who are headed for a future, better one. God conceives of us in just the opposite way. Our new birth marks us as people whose citizenship and affections lie in the other world, but whose temporary assignment is to live in the visible world as His representatives. C. S. Lewis traded on this notion when he said that Christianity is the story of how earth's rightful King has landed here in disguise and is calling on His people to join Him in a grand campaign of sabotage.[5]

The challenges of such a campaign are great. For one thing, as citizens of His kingdom, we are obliged to live under a set of laws that often conflict with those of our earthly homeland. To cite a rough parallel: When the United States sends ambassadors to foreign lands, they live in embassies, which are regarded as "mini-states" within the countries where they are placed. Inside American embassy compounds, the laws of America prevail. During the 1920s, prohibition was the law of the United States. That law prohibited American citizens from drinking or selling alcoholic beverages. It meant that, in London, for example, Americans could not drink alcohol inside the embassy compound. They could do so in English pubs or in their flats; but when they imbibed they were expressing disapproval, however mild, of their homeland and its laws.

In a similar way, believers are ambassadors for Christ. We are to forego liberties allowed to others because we are loyal to our homeland and to its King. The Lord Jesus has purchased us by the blood of His cross. We are His. As a result, our loyalty belongs to Him. If we belong to His "country," then by definition we are foreigners in our own, regardless of where it is. That profound fact, if taken seriously, guarantees that we will experience what foreigners routinely endure in every culture: a measure of both contempt and suspicion. Those discomforts are small pains that ought to be borne cheerfully for the sake of our King; yet many find them all too heavy.

Timid believers soon discover the way to avoid such discomforts, of course—merely downplay those differences in allegiance and lifestyle that are part of living as a pilgrim. Those differences that make the world uncomfortable go unseen, and Christians lose their "foreignness." Unfortunately, they also lose the distinctives that would cause non-Christians to be attracted to this new homeland and its glorious King.

The introduction of the Susan B. Anthony dollar some years ago produced widespread public resistance. This small coin was designed primarily to be a durable and lightweight alternative to its paper equivalent. Its size, however, created problems, because it was easily confused with a quarter. Legally it was worth a dollar, but practically, many people considered it a nuisance because of its confusing appearance. It was not distinctive. The same thing happens when the unbelieving world encounters Christian pilgrims who cannot be distinguished from the society in which they live. We are foreigners and need to keep our distinctiveness, or we become merely confusing.

AN APPEALING DIFFERENCE

Peter, like his colleague Paul, knew that Christians need to keep their sense of foreignness near the front of their thinking. He wrote: "Beloved, I beg you as sojourners and pilgrims, abstain from fleshly lusts which war against the soul" (1 Peter 2:11). And what is the solution to such temptation? To have fleshly behavior replaced; "[Have] your conduct honorable among the Gentiles, that when they speak against you as evildoers, they may, by your good works which they observe, glorify God in the day of visitation" (1 Peter 2:12).

Peter's words give the antidote to an easily absorbed poison. It is not merely what we avoid that sets us apart. Good works mark the distinctive lifestyle of God's pilgrims. His sojourners, convinced of the realities of their unseen homeland, refuse to give their neighbors any valid reason to criticize it. Your neighbors will find fault anyway, Peter said, just because you are different; but as they observe what you do to commend your home country and your King, they may be won to Jesus Christ themselves. Even if they are not, in the end they will be forced to glorify God that He placed you in their midst as His ambassador.

Remember, the promises of God were so real to the patriarchs that they *embraced* them. Though they "died in faith, not having received the promises, [yet] having seen them afar off were assured of them, [they] embraced them and confessed that they were strangers and pilgrims on the earth" (Hebrews 11:13). Nowadays, however, it has become unfashionable (at least openly) to find delight in the promise of an age to come, though such pleasure forms the core of thinking like a pilgrim. Many Christians prefer not to endure such labels as *fanatic* or politically irresponsible *misfit* (dismissing the realities of the present world), and as a result they simply keep quiet about their faith.

C. S. Lewis insisted, however, that "a continual looking forward to the eternal world is not (as some modern people think) a form of escapism or wishful thinking, but one of the things a Christian is meant to do." In fact, Lewis was careful to point out that those who have done the most for the visible world have been those who were most attracted to the world to come. In his words, "The Apostles themselves, who set on foot the conversion of the Roman Empire, the great men who built up the Middle Ages, the English Evangelicals who abolished the Slave Trade, all left their mark on Earth, precisely because their minds were occupied with Heaven. It is since Christians have largely ceased to think of the other world that they have become so ineffective in this."[6]

[Our] commitment to the unseen world . . . tells us that our souls are infinitely worthy—not only into the ages to come, but right now.

Christians are supposed to behave differently because we have an unbreakable commitment to the unseen world, an engagement that makes sense out of the world that we do see. That commitment tells us that we are to behave in ways that reflect our belief that we will outlive the physical world. It informs us that we live in the context of the eternal. It tells us that our souls are infinitely worthy—not only into the ages to come, but right now.

In the rain forest of Brazil, there lives a plant which the locals call a "matador" or "murderer" plant. The matador sends out slender vines in all directions, looking for a tree. When it finds one, it begins wrapping itself around the trunk of its host, sending out tendrils that surround the tree and begin to squeeze the life out of it. Finally, as if in celebration, it sends a head filled with flowers above the topmost branches of its victim, scattering seeds to continue its murderous cycle.

The world behaves similarly toward the Christian. Paul gave the Ephesians—and us—a way to oppose such slow strangulation. He explained that Christian living involves a three-step process. He wrote them, "Put off, concerning your former conduct, the old man which grows corrupt according to the deceitful lusts, and be renewed in the spirit of your mind, and . . . put on the new man which was created according to God, in true righteousness and holiness" (Ephesians 4:22–24). Did you catch the key phrases? "Put off . . . renew your mind . . . put on." Christians cannot walk righteously without their minds being engaged any more than they can walk physically without their brains being involved.

In the chapters ahead, we will attempt some mind renewal. Having a mind saturated with the great truths of Scripture forms the best guarantee that a believer will not suffer the conformity to the world that is so common to our age. God's truth will help us know Him. We will examine what the Scripture says about pilgrim behavior in a number of key areas. We will consider what it means to sing the Lord's song in a foreign land. It's all part of life's greatest journey.

First, however, we must explore the degree to which the minds of Western Christians have been conformed to the thinking of the age.

ON THE JOURNEY

1. As you reread *The Epistle to Diognetus,* what types of behavior on the part of Christians in the early church are rare or would be considered radical today? Which ones would you like to see in greater supply in your life?

2. Of the following pilgrim journeys, whose are you most impressed with: Abraham's, Joseph's, Moses', or Daniel's? Which of these pilgrims speaks to you most about his different quality of life from that of the world?

2
BLENDED PILGRIMS

If you were arrested for being a Christian,
would there be enough evidence to convict you?

—GRAFFITI ON SEMINARY BULLETIN BOARD

Not long ago, I was interviewed on a Christian radio station about my book *God Up Close*. During a commercial break, I was chatting off the air with the host, who told me that (based on the station's market studies) about 30,000 people were probably tuned in. "Almost all our listeners are professing Christians," he explained, "and about 80 percent of them attend church." When I expressed surprise at the incongruity of those two percentages, he assured me that the numbers were accurate, adding, "We consider one of our ministry objectives to be getting that other 20 percent back in contact with the local church."

Church attendance is the one characteristic that, in most

people's minds, marks out Christians by definition; but we are gradually surrendering even that part of our distinctiveness. A cultural situation in which one out of five Christians doesn't attend church at all might be expected to exhibit other odd phenomena, and it does. Research conducted by the Barna Research Group found that, among other things, even among people who describe themselves as born-again, only about half say they attend church virtually every week.[1] We may be converted, but we try not to be religious about it.

We certainly can't be numbered with the elderly gentleman who lost his hearing late in life. In spite of being unable to comprehend a single word said or sung in the services, he could be found in church every week. When asked why he continued to attend when his ability to participate was so limited, he simply replied, "I want people to know whose side I'm on."

We Christians today have trouble partaking of the pilgrim journey because, in most areas of values and thought, we blend with our pagan environment too easily. Our commitment and our knowledge of Scripture are among several areas in which we strangely parallel the unbelieving community. With certain exceptions, our stands on issues and what we consider true virtues have been more heavily influenced by our culture than we realize.

In addition to spotty church attendance, "fewer than 10 percent of Americans are deeply committed Christians," according to George Gallup. He noted, however, that those who are committed believers "are far, far happier than the rest of the population." Committed Christians, Gallup found, are more tolerant than the average American, more involved in charitable activities, and are "absolutely committed to prayer." While many more Americans than this 10 percent profess to be Christians, most actually know little or nothing of Christian beliefs, and act no differently than non-Christians. "Overall," says Gallup, "the Sunday School and religious education system in this country is not working."[2]

KNOWLEDGE OF SCRIPTURE

Our loss of identity may go much deeper, however, than a technical deficiency in educational methods.

For one thing, our values certainly do not appear to be coming from the Scriptures. Though nine out of ten American households possess a Bible and most have two or more, people's views on critical issues of truth are not being shaped by the Word of God. For example, while the Bible teaches that God gives His blessings to be shared so that the world can know Him (Genesis 12:1–3), 72 percent of American adults think that God blesses people "so that they can enjoy life as much as possible."[3]

Even the simplest facts of Scripture are foreign to us. A high school teacher in Massachusetts quizzed a group of students in the mid-1980s on their knowledge of some particulars of Scripture. These boys and girls were all juniors and seniors, headed for college, attending one of the better public schools in the area. His diagnostic test yielded the following discoveries:

- Sodom and Gomorrah were lovers.
- Jezebel was Ahab's donkey.
- The four horsemen appeared on the Acropolis.
- Eve was created from an apple.
- Jesus was baptized by Moses.
- Golgotha was the giant who slew the apostle David.[4]

Today those students have joined the widening stream of America's biblically illiterate adults. Nowadays even Christians display only a vague familiarity with the content of Scripture. One group of poll respondents was asked whether "God helps those who help themselves" was a quotation from the Bible. Among those who were regular church attenders, 60 percent thought it was. That is grievous enough, but there was worse to come. Among people who *didn't* attend church, only 53 percent thought the quotation came from Scripture. In that sample, at least, you stood a better chance of recognizing Scripture if you were not a churchgoer.

Even the most basic questions seemed to baffle believers. Most of the Christian respondents, for example, didn't know that Jonah is a book of the Bible. Most did not know that Jesus preached the Sermon on the Mount. Some thought He did, but nearly as many suspected that Billy Graham preached it. A number believed it was delivered by someone on horseback.[5]

VIEWS OF DOCTRINE

We do little better when it comes to the simplest matters of doctrine. One group of respondents was asked whether Satan was a living person or only a symbol of evil. Fifty-six percent of church attenders voted for the "symbol" option.[6] Satan, named as the tempter in the Garden of Eden, the oppressor of God's people through the ages, the agent in the temptation of Christ, and the archenemy of God, no longer exists as a living person in the minds of most churchgoers. Having concluded that no real enemy exists to trouble us, perhaps it is not surprising that we neither see nor resist his faith-wrecking temptations.

The doctrinal weakness of the modern church doesn't just touch the edges of our faith. According to a Barna survey of people claiming to be born-again, nearly one-third agree with the statement that "when He lived on earth, Jesus Christ was human and committed sins, like other people." Four in ten also maintain that "if a person is generally good, or does enough good things for others during their life, they will earn a place in heaven."[7]

Perhaps that is why we feel little urgency about sharing the gospel of Christ. Or it could be because 70 percent of those attending mainline Protestant churches believe that Christians, Jews, Muslims, Buddhists, and others all pray to the same God and merely use different names for Him.[8]

CULTURAL ATTITUDES

The last percentage suggests that the one supreme virtue of Western culture, "tolerance," has slimed its way to the front of the Christian value parade as well. Whatever else we do, we must exhibit an enlightened, unqualified acceptance of the views of everyone. That means denying the basic motivation for the gospel itself, namely, the lostness of humanity. If we don't believe that the Hindu next door is lost, we are certainly unlikely to think that the college-educated pagan down the street is. After all, he looks and acts even more like us.

The exaltation of tolerance (falsely so called) has emerged in lockstep with a corresponding discouragement about the modern world and its institutions. During the Gulf War, a number of people in the military made news when they expressed their resentment against being sent into a combat zone. I saw one such person interviewed on a news broadcast. He was asked if the army's mission was a worthy one. He replied that he didn't think *any* cause was worth dying for. It seemed an odd viewpoint for a soldier.

Such declarations seem strange to many, but in reality they merely mark an outgrowth of the modern indifference to true virtue. Dorothy Sayers observed, "In the world it is called Tolerance, but in hell it is called Despair: the sin that believes in nothing, cares for nothing, seeks to know nothing, interferes with nothing, enjoys nothing, hates nothing, finds purpose in nothing, lives for nothing, and remains alive because there is nothing for which it will die."[9]

In jettisoning God's truth, modern society seems to have lost the ability to distinguish between tolerance of people—respecting them as made in the image of God, a biblically necessary virtue —and approval of their ideas and convictions. Our culture insists that we regard the two as inseparable, thus putting us in the position of choosing between forbearance and evangelism. Astonishingly, Christians have largely bought such a position, one that brings with it a resultant loss of true concern for lost people.

According to George Gallup, "We find there is very little difference in ethical behavior between churchgoers and those who are not active religiously. . . . The levels of lying, cheating, and stealing are remarkably similar in both groups." He observed that "eight out of ten Americans consider themselves Christians, yet only . . . two in ten said they would be willing to suffer for their faith."[10]

Even our voting habits and choices of candidates at the polls reflect the similarities between Christians and non-Christians. In the November 1998 elections, for example, one analyst noted the pathetic percentages of evangelicals voting. Then he consoled himself with the observation, "Exit polls suggest that even among conservative Christians who did go to the polls, their votes on several telling issues were only marginally different from the population at large."[11] Sometimes you have to find your consolation where you can.

MARRIAGE AND FAMILY LIFE

The blending of Christians' lives with those of the surrounding culture now extends to family life. When I began my ministry in the late 1960s, divorce among Christians was comparatively rare, and divorce in conservative evangelical churches was almost nonexistent. The same was true of out-of-wedlock pregnancies. They didn't happen often. Having the community know that you had conceived outside of marriage was simply too shameful.

I still remember the experience of a neighbor who came home after work to find his house deserted. Both his wife and daughter were missing. At first he thought they might have been the victims of foul play, but their clothes and personal effects were gone, too. Months passed before the truth came out—at least the version I heard. His daughter had conceived a child out of wedlock, and rather than simply send her away to have the baby with distant relatives, her mother had gone with her. She felt the dissolution of her marriage less of a problem than facing the disapproval of her husband, church, and community over her daughter's pregnancy.

The daughter was a friend of mine. She and I had had a conversation a week or so before the disappearance in which, I came to realize later, she had tried to tell me in veiled terms of her plight, but I was too dense at the time to recognize that she was describing herself. It simply didn't occur to me that she could be pregnant.

I don't need to tell you that things are different now. Divorce in evangelical churches is as common as in the general population, according to Dennis Rainey, author and radio host of *Family Life Today*.[12] Nor are evangelical Christians far behind in out-of-wedlock pregnancies; and those are simply two of the most obvious ways that we are imitating the culture.

Not surprisingly, the next generation appears to be sliding still further in family morals. In a major study of 3,795 youth, all of whom attended evangelical churches, researchers discovered a series of sobering statistics:

- 66 percent had lied to their parents within the past three months.
- 57 percent of evangelical youth cannot affirm that an objective standard of right and wrong exists (among the parents: 53 percent).
- 36 percent had cheated on school exams in the past three months.
- 55 percent have engaged in sexual activity by age 18.[13]

Clearly, the families of Christians are in close pursuit of the moral decay of Western culture. When "tolerance" rises, shame—with its attached brake on sinful indulgence—disappears.

PERSONAL ETHICS

And what about Christian morality in the workplace? One Gallup poll surveyed adults about their behavior in moral situations at work: for example, whether they used the company phone for personal long-distance calls; whether they brought office supplies home; whether they put in a full day's work. They were also asked their religious preference.

Most of the responses were not too surprising. The pollsters found a lot of invalid absenteeism; they learned employees do use company phones for personal long-distance calls, and so on. What was shocking to many, however, was that there was *no significant statistical difference* between those calling themselves Christians and those not doing so. The Christians were within a point or two of the non-Christians on almost every question. In the workplace, at least, Christian pilgrims have become indistinguishable from the general population.

Gallup noted that church attendance made little difference in people's ethical views and behavior with respect to lying, cheating, pilfering, and not reporting theft. He also observed that equal proportions of churched and unchurched admit to understating income on federal tax forms.[14]

The shift to the ethics of expedience is discussed in depth in chapter 5, but we should note that the quest for self-fulfillment has been common since the 1970s. In a landmark study published in 1982 and entitled *New Rules: Searching for Self-Fulfillment in a World Turned Upside Down* 1982, Daniel Yankelovich documented a shift in social values that had taken place in the late 1960s and early 1970s in America. Yankelovich, a sociologist at New York University, asserted that the old rules of social ethics no longer apply. Formerly, society insisted on the fulfillment of responsibility and duty to others, notably one's family. When a person gave in to personal temptation and was exposed, he often experienced shame and embarrassment and the rejection of his social circle.

Today, that fundamental standard has been replaced with what Yankelovich calls the "duty to self ethic," the idea that one's supreme duty is to oneself. Though Yankelovich is sympathetic to the new ethic—as are 83 percent of the American public—he admits that his questionnaire work shows that for all of modern man's striving few seem to find it fulfilling.[15] In fact, the trend seems to have produced just the opposite effect. Man is more alienated and adrift than ever.

Yet, according to subsequent research done by James Davison Hunter, who used Yankelovich's surveys in sixteen leading evangelical colleges and seminaries, young evangelical believers are *more* committed to the self-fulfillment ethic than the general public: "The percentage of evangelical students agreeing with these statements far exceeded the corresponding percentage of the general population. Self-fulfillment is no longer a natural by-product of a life committed to higher ideals, but rather is a goal, pursued rationally and with calculation as an end in itself."[16]

VIEWS OF TRUTH

In no area, however, have pilgrims blended with the culture more than in their attitudes toward the concept of absolute truth. George Barna asked a group of poll respondents to react to this sentence: "There is no such thing as absolute truth; different people can define truth in conflicting ways and still be correct." It would be hard to devise a more obvious renunciation of Christian faith. If the statement were true, all our disputes about the value of Scripture would be irrelevant. It would make little difference if the Bible is "inspired" if by definition what it teaches may be dismissed or ignored according to individual opinion.

Yet among church attenders, 59 percent agreed with the above statement. That means that six out of ten people sitting in pews on Sunday morning nod their heads and issue an occasional "amen," all the while subscribing to the position that there is no standard outside of themselves to which they yield a willing submission. Amazingly, among those attending mainline Protestant churches, 74 percent do not believe in absolute truth—7 percent *more* than the general population. Churches are not merely participants in the cultural parade into the darkness, they are the marching band. Even among evangelicals, 53 percent reject the concept of absolute truth.[17] *Fifty-three percent.*

Modern education has exerted a considerable influence in the march toward ambiguity, with its refusal to teach values at school, or among school systems that do, its use of "values clarification" classes that make every child's interpretation of right and wrong equally valid. Such is the moral environment that molds young believers today: Teachers and school officials no longer argue that there is a right and wrong.

The setting aside of absolutes in the culture has come to affect, among other things, the way Christians approach the Bible. Walt Russell, an associate professor at the Talbot School of Theology in La Mirada, California, described in a *Christianity Today* article not long ago what has become a cliché in Christian circles: a group of believers in a Bible study, with the leader asking, "What does this verse mean to you?" In response, participants contribute a series of assertions and defenses, ending in a disagreement, which the leader "resolves" by saying, "'Well, this is another example of how reading the Bible is a matter of personal interpretation and how a verse can mean one thing to one person and something else to another.' The group members . . . leave with a vague, hollow feeling in their chests."[18]

Meaning, however, does not come from consensus. The meaning of the text is what the author intends, not what the readers discern. The postmodern Christian makes a virtue out of vagueness in order to avoid unpleasantness in the form of disagreement. Can you imagine Peter standing before the assembly in Jerusalem at Pentecost trying to resolve the disparate opinions about the reason for the empty tomb by asking people what it meant to them?

By adopting practices like these, Christians join the pageant of the indeterminate. The culture sneers at certainties, so we abandon the certainties that launched our faith. As G. K. Chesterton once observed, however, "Having an open mind is nothing; the object of opening the mind, as of opening the mouth, is to shut it again on something solid."[19]

THE PRACTICES OF CHRISTIAN LEADERS

We now face a bizarre combination in Western Christianity. The person in the pew has blended into the ethical woodwork of his generation, while the person in the pulpit often stands out— but for all the wrong reasons. We find ourselves in the position of the church of the sixteenth century, when Raphael was working his artistic wonders in the Vatican. Once, while painting a biblical scene, he was critiqued by a couple of church dignitaries. One observed of his work, "The face of the Apostle Paul is too red."

Raphael curtly answered: "He blushes to see into whose hands the church has fallen."[20]

Modern preachers, too, have cast aside biblical ethics repeatedly in attempts to build empires and feather their financial nests. For example, many news services followed the February 1999 trial of the Reverend Henry Lyons as he was convicted in Florida of an assortment of state charges including racketeering and grand theft. Lyons at the time was president of the National Baptist Convention USA (NBCUSA).

Dr. Lyons, on behalf of his denomination, entered into an agreement with the Union Planters Bank to supply the names of church members so that the bank could solicit credit card business from them. Unfortunately, the denomination had no such list. No problem. According to sworn testimony, Lyons simply invented state-by-state estimates of church members to present to the bank and other large corporations. "I would say a state and he would give me a figure," Lynda Shorter, his administrative assistant, testified. "At first I thought he was really intelligent. He had a really great memory." When Lyons began to smile as they continued to compile estimates, Shorter concluded, "I realized he was making it up."

The bank eventually loaned the NBCUSA $300,000 to help market the credit card scheme (money it later sued to recover, since the bank never received anything in return). Prosecutors asserted that much of the money went into Lyons's pocket. Shorter explained that the denomination had no financial controls. When prosecutors asked, "What was the name of your bookkeeper?" she replied, "There was no bookkeeper."

"What was the name of your accountant?"

"There was no accountant."[21]

Not long after being elected to his post as denominational president, Lyons opened a bank account over which he had sole control. The account, which during a two-year period saw more than five million dollars pass through it, was used to launder money to be placed in personal accounts of Mr. Lyons and his mistress. (Unbeknownst to her, Lyons also used the account to provide $800,000 to two former lovers as well.) When church officials were asked to comment on Lyons's financial actions, they made matters worse by noting that the denomination gave a great deal of freedom to its president, and that as far as they could tell Lyons had violated no church financial practice—observations that may, astonishingly, be true.

The bank, at any rate, thought their arrangement with Mr. Lyons a secure one, since he had claimed an NBCUSA membership of 8.5 million people. (Best estimates place the actual number at between 500,000 and one million.) The pact was authorized by a resolution signed by the denomination's general secretary, Roscoe Cooper. The signature, however, was bogus; prosecutors said that Lyons forged it. Lyons is now serving a prison term for violation of both state and federal statutes.

The Florida pastor is hardly alone, however, in dubious moral practices among Christian leaders. A regional magazine in the Southwest recently included an article entitled "Thy Neighbors' Wives," describing the sexual waywardness of a megachurch pastor. One of the church's deacons noted, "One beautiful woman was not enough," referring to his pastor's wife. "He was set up as an ideal man. He was adored and he ate it up."[22]

The pastor of one of the fastest-growing churches in the South was arrested not long ago for drug smuggling. He confessed to bringing cocaine into the United States from Colombia for $50,000 and was sentenced to three years in prison. His church had led the denomination in his home state in the number of baptisms that year.[23]

Several years ago, one prominent minister sent out a folksy letter to supporters, explaining his personal plight. He was writing, he said, on Christmas Eve, sitting in his study, facing the unpleasant prospect of ruining his family's holiday by going downstairs and revealing to them just how broke his ministry was: Could the reader please respond right away and keep the work afloat?

Unfortunately, someone in the mailroom had gotten overeager and the letters arrived two or three days *before* Christmas. Since his ministry continues today in apparent prosperity, I can only conclude that not many people were disturbed by his lying in the interests of fund-raising.

Meanwhile, the support letters of Christian organizations are often written not by those in ministry but by public relations professionals, raising other ethical issues we will look at in detail in chapter 5.

The key words of such appeals are often underlined in blue

so the readers won't have to waste all that time reading the whole letter. It rarely seems to dawn on readers that these letters occur with predictable frequency, or that they especially seem to be concentrated around Christmas. We apparently never wonder why it is that the disintegration of a great ministry repeatedly coincides with the season when charitable giving tends to increase.

Whether the Christian leader directs an organization or a church, his practices should be above reproach. Indeed, the first measure of one who models biblical ethics ought to be his willingness to subject his own moral choices to his theology.

Since so many in public ministry have abandoned this part of the pilgrim way, it ought not to surprise us that large numbers in the pew have also failed to pursue it. We fail as well to attract people outside the faith to a better world, often because we know so little of it ourselves.

OUT OF THE SALTSHAKER?

Several years ago, in an effort to assist my busy wife, I asked her to teach me some of the rudiments of cooking. I had been doing the outdoor grilling for many years, but as every homemaker knows, you take the game to a new level when you move into the kitchen. She started me off by teaching me how to make mashed potatoes. Naturally, I learned to make the real thing—no dehydrated spuds for yours truly. Being a quick study, I learned to peel, slice, and boil potatoes to just the right level of softness, to push them through a ricer, then use a mixer to whip them to a fluffy perfection.

I also learned about the key ingredient: just the right amount of salt. Potatoes without salt aren't very appealing, as some of my early products demonstrated. (My culinary career is now on probation.)

Neither is an environment without a savory Christian testimony appealing. In fact, a culture in which the Christians have been largely assimilated—something perilously close to reality in the West—can be a downright inhospitable place. Many a sermon today exalts the need for Christians to get out of the saltshaker and into the world. Yet these observations I have been discussing suggest a more critical need—to have the salt become salty again. Jesus spoke of this in the famous Sermon on the Mount: "You are the salt of the earth; but if the salt loses its flavor, how shall it be seasoned? It is then good for nothing but to be thrown out and trampled underfoot by men" (Matthew 5:13). In the quotation, "loses its flavor" comes from a Greek verb that in other contexts means "to act the fool."

I fear that is what we have done. We have played the fool in losing our distinctiveness. It is not merely that we are not influencing the culture in significant ways; we are not even identifiable in it. We hold its views, praise its virtues, shrink away from its sins, and subscribe to its panaceas. Our salt has lost its flavor, and we aren't even sure how it happened.

ON THE JOURNEY

1. To what degree does your knowledge of Christian doctrine affect your everyday behavior? Has God's holiness and His commands put a holy fear in you of violating His laws?

2. On a more subtle level, how have the attitudes of your heart and mind been affected in areas such as lust, pride, envy, etc.? Would a greater knowledge of truth at least begin a process of recovery? How about discipleship and accountability?

3
THE VALUES
OF A PILGRIM

I have now disposed of all my property to my family.
There is one thing more I wish I could give them
and that is faith in Jesus Christ.
If they had that
and I had not given them a single shilling,
they would have been rich;
and if they had not that,
and I had given them all the world,
they would be poor indeed.

—PATRICK HENRY[1]

The social impulse to conformity is uncommonly strong, as was demonstrated some years ago when psychologist Ruth Berenda performed an experiment with teens. She divided her subjects into groups of ten, bringing each group into a room for a test. The students were told that they should raise their hands when the teacher pointed to the longest line (out of three) on a wall chart. Pretty simple—except that the experiment was loaded. Nine members of each group had been told ahead of time to point to the *second*-longest line instead of the longest. There was one "victim" in each group of ten.

You can guess what happened. The victim consistently voted

against the obvious evidence of his own mind. Better than 75 percent of the time, the stooge lacked the confidence to go against the group even when he could see for himself that they were mistaken. Adults usually show more confidence in similar experiments, but still go along with the group about 40 percent of the time.[2]

Christian believers suffer from a more significant set of pressures. The world seems to scream its godless views into the faces of pilgrims. Living distinctively requires objectives and priorities that set the believer apart; it also calls for an awareness that pilgrims are the primary targets of the world's push to assimilate us.

When the Babylonians gave Daniel and his friends new, pagan names, they were only doing overtly what the world system has always done more subtly. The enemy of souls knows that if he can persuade God's sojourners to be like everyone else when it comes to their values, he has things going his way.

When the devil sought to discredit Jesus, he said to Him, "All this authority I will give You, and their glory; for this has been delivered to me, and I give it to whomever I wish. Therefore, if You will worship before me, all will be Yours" (Luke 4:6–7). If the devil has been granted temporary authority of this world, then the pilgrim is living in enemy-occupied territory. That makes it imperative that Christians know what they are about. We dare not spend our creative energies in pursuit of details without appreciation of the whole of human life; and without a standard by which to eliminate the extraneous from our schedules, we can overlook the beautiful in pursuit of the trivial.

As Alexander the Great's army was fighting the Persians, his soldiers overran the palace of Darius, the Persian king. Seeking items to steal, one soldier discovered a leather bag containing the crown jewels of Persia. The stones were worth millions; however, they didn't seem that impressive to the ignorant man who found them. He dumped them and saved only the leather container, going around the camp later in the day gleefully telling his comrades about the marvelous bag he had found in which to carry his food.

We laugh at his ignorance, but today people seem equally dense when it comes to their priorities, as exemplified in the silly story that circulated during the 1980s. It seems that a state trooper found a battered Yuppie lying by the roadside next to his demolished automobile. The crash victim was moaning, "My BMW! My BMW!"

The trooper observed, "Never mind the car, man. You've lost your left arm."

The Yuppie looked at his bleeding shoulder and cried, "My Rolex! I've lost my Rolex!"

The story would be funnier if it were not so close to reality.

A CENTRAL FOCUS: KNOWING GOD

Some time ago, psychologist William Moulton Marston asked three thousand people in a survey, "What have you to live for?" The overwhelming majority of his respondents, 94 percent, were simply enduring the present while waiting for the future. They were waiting for "something" to happen—for children to grow up and leave home, for next year, for a time to start a new business or take a college course, or just for tomorrow.[3] Modern culture is five billion characters trying to ignore the Author while in search of the plot.

The apostle Paul, though incarcerated in a Roman prison, never lacked a central focus to his life. As a pilgrim, he expressed his values lucidly in his letter to the Philippians. His declaration of purpose is all the more forceful because it was issued at a time when he seemed to have little freedom to achieve anything. Yet Paul knew that despite his external restraints he was truly free in Christ.

According to Paul, *the first priority of a pilgrim—his central focus—is to be constantly advancing in the knowledge of Christ.* A man of considerable accomplishment prior to his conversion, the apostle realized the true value of what he had achieved: "What things were gain to me, these I have counted loss for Christ. Yet indeed I also count all things loss for the excellence of the knowledge of Christ Jesus my Lord" (Philippians 3:7–8).

The pilgrim experience begins with a transaction: repudiating personal accomplishments and trusting in Christ alone. As Paul put it, "not having my own righteousness, which is from the law, but that which is through faith in Christ, the righteousness which is from God by faith" (Philippians 3:9). If he could not base his hope of eternity on his obedience, no one can.

Remember, Paul had several impressive accomplishments. First of all, he was a Pharisee, with all the devotion to God that that implies. He was meticulous in his observance of the Old Testament. He thought about the Law day and night, studying under the man who was one of the greatest teachers of his era, the rabbi Gamaliel.

Yet Paul knew that his own record of obedience suffered from one great problem: It wasn't perfect. People are impressed with how good other people are; God is not. People accept relative goodness; God does not. Men know that if a professional baseball player can hit the ball three out of ten times, he will make it to the Hall of Fame. God says if you hit the ball nine out of ten times when it comes to righteousness, your efforts don't measure up.

So who can be right with God? No one can on the basis of obedience. Paul recognized this: "Not having my own righteousness, which is from the law." The alternative? Paul wanted that righteousness "which is through faith in Christ, the righteousness which is from God by faith" (Philippians 3:9). How does one get it? By trusting what Christ has already done.

A pilgrim can possess Christ's righteousness without knowing Him well.

He says that it is "the righteousness which is from God." That is, God has it, and He gives it to those who place their trust in His Son. We can know we have it on the authority of His Word: "These things I have written to you who believe in the name of the Son of God, that you may know that you have eternal life" (1 John 5:13).

However, the apostle was not satisfied simply to possess a standing in the family of God. A pilgrim can possess Christ's righteousness without knowing Him well. A case in point is the apostle Philip, to whom Jesus said on the night of the Last Supper, "Have I been with you so long, and yet you have not known Me, Philip?" (John 14:9). He asked this question even though Philip was one of the first disciples to believe in the Lord Jesus. The Bible uses the expression "knowing the Lord" in the same way we refer to knowing someone today. "I know a person" may mean anything from "We've been introduced" to "We're close friends" depending on the context.

The difference between the two is similar to the experience of being part of a family. When we are born into a family, we have all the standings and privileges that go with being a member of our households. Our parents will defend, provide for, and protect us; yet we don't truly know them. Only after we mature do we know them well. Being born takes only a few minutes; really knowing our parents takes much longer, and in a sense is never complete.

Naturally, complications arise when the One we long to know well is not physically present. However, His reality can be confirmed in a very personal way.

KNOW CHRIST THROUGH
HIS SUPERNATURAL POWER

Paul said he wanted to know "the power of His resurrection" (Philippians 3:10). Note that the resurrection in question is Christ's; Paul wanted to know its power in a personal way *right then*. That is possible for the pilgrim, because the power that brought Christ out of the grave—the limitless power of heaven—is that which enables the believer in Christ to overcome spiritual obstacles and please God. Whenever we turn away from satisfying the impulses of the "old man" and embrace the values of the age to come, that choice is animated by the resurrection power of Christ within us.

The apostle talked about this in Romans 6:8–10 as well: "If we died with Christ, we believe that we shall also live with Him, knowing that Christ, having been raised from the dead, dies no more. Death no longer has dominion over Him. For the death that He died, He died to sin once for all; but the life that He lives, He lives to God." "We shall also live with Him" refers not to the day of resurrection in the future, but to the experience of walking with God in the process of overcoming sin by the power that brought Christ out of the grave.

That is what pilgrims are supposed to be about. As far as God is concerned, we died when Christ did. We rose when Christ did. And just as sin has no dominion over Christ, sin should have no dominion over us. The sins that would trip us on the pilgrim road require us to lean on the resurrection power of Christ personally. When you walk away from temptation, you exhibit—you "know," to use Paul's term—the power of His resurrection life. He lives today to make the believer equal to the challenge of resisting sin and producing righteousness.

KNOW CHRIST BY SHARING HIS SUFFERINGS

Knowing Christ also means sharing His sufferings: "that I may know . . . the fellowship of His sufferings" (Philippians 3:10). Paul did not, of course, refer to the substitutionary sufferings of Christ on the cross. We can't enter into those agonies, which were His alone. However, we can know the present suffering which He experiences when a member of His body experiences pain or sorrow. In that sense, Christ is still suffering today.

In fact, that was the very subject of discussion between Paul and Jesus on the day Paul (then known as Saul) was converted. He was on his way to Damascus to have believers locked up and persecuted. Then a bright light shone out of heaven and he found himself blinded and heard a voice saying, "Saul, Saul, why are you persecuting Me?" (Acts 9:4). As far as Saul was concerned, he was persecuting the church. As far as the Lord Jesus was concerned, when a believer felt pain under Saul's treatment, Christ Himself experienced the pain.

The apostle referred to this when he wrote the Colossian believers later, "I now rejoice in my sufferings for you, and fill up in my flesh what is lacking in the afflictions of Christ, for the sake of His body, which is the church" (Colossians 1:24). Paul did not shrink from taking abuse for his faith.

Disobedience—in the form of spiritual cowardice—keeps us from knowing Christ well. He refuses to allow those people to become His intimate associates who will not share in His sufferings. This is one area where we have undergone an overhaul of values in the Western church. In the Bible, suffering with Christ is considered a privilege. Today, suffering is considered an admission that you aren't sufficiently spiritual to get what you want out of God. If you're ill, if you're in financial distress, you are told you need to get closer to God so that these bad things won't happen to you. Christianity has become in some circles a prophylactic—an umbrella to keep out the rain of pain. The God of the apostle Paul, by contrast, was One who walked with Paul through stonings, shipwreck, floggings, and persecutions. The apostle held to a rather different definition of "success" than is common in Western Christendom. He knew that it was not his accomplishments but his sufferings that gave him a platform from which to speak.

With . . . the Christian celebrity syndrome,
we [try] to find people who have
the public's eye and ear and [sell] the faith
through their endorsements.

By contrast, it would be hard to find a more evident example of our blended values today than what some call the Christian celebrity syndrome. We seem to have a virtual obsession with trying to find people who have the public's eye and ear and "selling" the faith through their endorsements. We parade athletes and beauty queens, millionaires and TV stars, one after another, in front of our cameras or before our pulpits much in the same way that advertising agencies use them to sell tuna or automobiles. A.W. Tozer used to scornfully refer to this practice as "Wheaties evangelism."

The modern church adopts this questionable methodology despite the apostle Paul's rebuke of the Corinthians about their own lack of prominence. When they were claiming allegiance to teacher-celebrities, Paul told them to drop it: "For you see your calling, brethren, that not many wise according to the flesh, not many mighty, not many noble, are called. But God has chosen the foolish things of the world to put to shame the wise, and God has chosen the weak things of the world to put to shame the things which are mighty" (1 Corinthians 1:26–27).

The apostle himself briefly flirted with the celebrity syndrome. Shortly after his conversion, God informed Paul that his own Jewish nation would not respond to Paul's testimony. Paul argued that he stood in a unique position with regard to Jewish evangelism: "I said, 'Lord, they know that in every synagogue I imprisoned and beat those who believe on You. And when the blood of Your martyr Stephen was shed, I also was standing by consenting to his death, and guarding the clothes of those who were killing him'"(Acts 22:19–20). In other words: "They'll be impressed when they discover that I, the persecutor of Christians, have undergone conversion. They will see the folly of their own ways and believe my testimony."

God remained unpersuaded, as Paul remembered: "[God] said to me, 'Depart, for I will send you far from here to the Gentiles'" (Acts 22:21). He did not call Paul because of his qualifications; He called him in order to provide him with qualifications: a knowledge of Himself, gained in part through what Paul endured. One analyst described how Christians have turned away from such notions and conformed to the world's values:

> The church has been mesmerized by power. We stand in awe of the beauty queen, the pro football player, the wealthy businessman, and we willingly pay millions of dollars to anyone who will take our money and prove to us that we are the majority; that we are respectable; that we are the winners. We gladly allow these personages of power to travel in their private jets with their loyal platoon of executive assistants and press secretaries. We gladly give our substance to vicariously share with them as they wine and dine with presidents, scurry from one TV studio to the next, and whisk in and out of airports in long, black limousines. These power personalities have become our evangelical gigolos. We gladly prostitute our money, our time, and all that we have, so that we can flaunt them in front of those who do not believe that we are, in fact, winners. And it isn't their fault. It's ours.[4]

Among other things, when the celebrity steps in a moral hole, the name of Christ is dragged through the mud along with him. The night before the 1999 Super Bowl, an All-Pro Atlanta Falcon defensive back, an outspoken Christian, was arrested while soliciting sex from an undercover vice officer in Miami. Because he had assumed such a prominent position of Christian leadership on the team and in the community, great harm was done to the cause of Christ. Christian organizations who had thrust the man forward as a spokesman to the community found themselves backpedaling to keep from being associated with him. The embarrassment could have been avoided if the Christian community could and would count on the ordinary believer to commend its virtues and its Lord—and if that typical believer accepted the responsibility.

KNOW CHRIST BY
ENTERING INTO HIS MOTIVES

Still another part of knowing Christ is "being conformed to His death" (Philippians 3:10). This expression does not, of course, mean dying on a cross as Christ did. Instead, it involves spending our lives so that we enter into—at least in a faint way—the motives that drove the Lord Jesus to the cross. He did nothing to bring it on. His hands were clean. He spent his life for the benefit of others, and so should we.

When James Calvert went out as a missionary to the cannibals of the Fiji Islands, the captain of his ship warned him that his ministry might be brief and painful. The mariner tried to discourage Calvert from going by saying, "You will lose your life and the lives of those with you if you go among such savages." Calvert's reply demonstrated the meaning of Philippians 3:10. He said, "We died before we came here."[5] The freedom to attempt significant work for Christ begins where our desperate self-obsession stops.

A SECOND FOCUS:
HAVING THE APPROVAL OF CHRIST

The second supreme value of the pilgrim is to achieve the approval of Christ. Paul stated this goal—the approval of Christ—in Philippians 3:11, and it was the focus of his life that "by any means, I may attain to the resurrection from the dead." Paul wanted to achieve a distinctive resurrection life—a new life that stood out from the rest.

Let me explain how I come to this understanding. First, whatever Paul meant by "the resurrection from the dead," he was unsure that he would gain it. That is the only way the text can possibly be understood here. "If, by any means" does not sound as though he was speaking of what was inevitable. In view of Paul's great confidence—indeed, his certainty—that he had already been justified by faith and that he now possessed eternal life, it is hard to avoid the notion that he was thinking of something different here.

That conclusion is buttressed by the term translated "resurrection" in Philippians 3:11. It is not the normal Greek term for resurrection, which is *anastasis*. Here he used instead the unusual word *exanastasis,* a term that appears in Greek literature only here. Paul's word adds a suggestive prefix, *ex,* which means "out of." His hope was not simply to be resurrected, but to gain what he called the "out-resurrection"—a resurrection which stands out from the rest.

This "out-resurrection," according to Paul, remained to be earned. Knowing Christ and the power of His resurrection is required. Sharing His sufferings is required. Conforming oneself to His death by serving others is required. Paul even described his objective as a "prize" (Philippians 3:14). The Greek word used for "prize" occurs in only one other part of the New Testament—in another classic statement of a goal: "Do you not know that those who run in a race all run, but one receives the *prize?* Run in such a way that you may obtain it. And everyone who competes for the *prize* is temperate in all things. Now they do it to obtain a perishable crown, but we for an imperishable crown" (1 Corinthians 9:24–25, italics added). Paul spoke of competing in a race to gain a crown, a prize that symbolized the approval and commendation of the Lord Jesus.

Paul had as one of his life goals the distinctive resurrection life—a new life that stood out. His words call to mind Hebrews 11:35, which says, "Others were tortured, not accepting deliverance, that they might obtain a better resurrection." The writer of Hebrews was not thinking of a different model of a resurrection body, but a better quality of resurrection life. It was not merely being resurrected that he was trying to gain, but being distinctively resurrected—resurrected to stand approved and commended before Christ in the age to come.

The wording of Philippians 3:14 supports that conclusion: "I press toward the goal for the prize of *the upward call of God* in Christ Jesus" (italics added). The apostle likely had in mind the parable Jesus once told as He watched the guests at a dinner party jockey for position for the places of honor near the host. He told them that they would do better for themselves by seeking out the humblest places: "Do not sit down in the best place, lest one more honorable than you be invited by him; and he who invited you and him come and say to you, 'Give place to this man,' and then you begin with shame to take the lowest place" (Luke

14:8–9). On the contrary, the Lord Jesus said, sit at the end of the table, the humblest position. Then the host can exalt you, or to put it in His terms: "Go and sit down in the lowest place, so that when he who invited you comes he may say to you, 'Friend, *go up higher*'" (Luke 14:10, italics added).

Such an invitation to intimacy with Christ was one of Paul's life goals; it was the prize he longed for. It guided his choices. Charles Brent once observed, "If every call to Christ . . . is a call to suffering, the converse is equally true—every call to suffering is a call to Christ, a promotion, an invitation to come up higher."[6]

The values of the pilgrim require making hard choices as well as taking risks. Several years ago, a group of courageous individuals attempted to achieve the first crossing of the Atlantic in a hot air balloon. They had almost made it when the balloon began to lose altitude. Since they were still miles from the coast of France, it became apparent that they were not going to make it without lightening their craft. All their ballast was already tossed overboard, so they began to look for other items to jettison.

They tried chopping away part of the gondola, but the effort was taking too long, so they had no choice. They began to throw away items that would ordinarily be considered essential. They tossed out their navigational computers, then jettisoned the radio they had been using to stay in touch with friends. Cameras, clothes, food, and valuable equipment—all sank beneath the waves because the presence of these items interfered with the gaining of their objective—which had necessarily shifted to survival.

---

*Pilgrims [can] rejoice in the knowledge
that they possess the life of God.*

When the goal is clear, the choices become easier, though still painful. Unfortunately, Christian pilgrims don't always see the urgency and importance of some of their own spiritual decisions, in spite of the fact that God has gone to great lengths to give us reasons to think clearly in this regard.

Pilgrims can proceed with confidence toward the gaining of eternal values because the Lord Jesus has already promised exemption from judgment. We are not to be people who go through life obsessed with survival, much less with our comforts. In John 5:24, Jesus promised, "Most assuredly, I say to you, he who hears My word and believes in Him who sent Me has everlasting life, and shall not come into judgment, but has passed from death into life." This judgment, from which Christians have escaped, is the awful time described in Revelation 20:11–15, when those outside of Christ are brought face-to-face with the outcome of their deeds.

The lovely assurance of John 5:24 allows pilgrims to rejoice in the knowledge that they possess the life of God. Ignoring Jesus' words—or failing to take them as a solemn declaration of reality—cripples Christian living almost before it begins. After hearing Dwight L. Moody preach in Chicago, Wilbur Chapman felt honored when following the meeting, the evangelist came and sat down next to him. Moody asked him if he was a Christian. He said, "Mr. Moody, I am not sure whether I am a Christian or not."

Moody asked whether Chapman was a church member, and he said he was, but was not always sure about his standing with God. Moody slowly took out his Bible, turned to John 5:24, and read the words of Jesus: "Most assuredly, I say to you, he who hears My Word and believes in Him who sent Me has everlasting life, and shall not come into judgment, but has passed from death into life."

Chapman read it through, and then Moody said, "Do you believe it?"

"Yes," Chapman answered.

"Do you accept it?"

"Yes."

"Well, are you a Christian?" Moody asked.

"Mr. Moody, I sometimes think I am, and sometimes I am afraid I am not."

"Read it again," Moody kindly said, and Chapman did. Then Moody said, "Do you believe it?"

"Yes."

"Do you accept it?" Moody asked. "Do you receive Him?"

"Yes," Chapman replied.

Moody asked, "Do you then have eternal life? Are you a Christian?"

Chapman started to give the same reply, and he got about as

far as "Sometimes I think I am . . ." when Moody interrupted him and said, "See here, my friend. Whom are you doubting?"[7]

Even when Jesus' promise of life isn't doubted, however, there still remains a time of examination when believers will have their values weighed and either approved or disapproved. Paul called it the "judgment seat of Christ" (Romans 14:10). The issue at that judgment is not *where* we spend eternity but *how* we spend it. The results will largely issue from our values, for they invariably determine how we behave.

Those who would honor Jesus Christ as sojourners in this foreign land we call the world will never find right choices effortlessly. Godly pilgrim living will issue in direct proportion to the strength of our convictions. Do you believe that the highest of all values is to know Christ and to gain His approval? If and only if you do, you have something to say to this generation that it desperately needs to hear; and Jesus Christ will reward you openly when you stand before Him.

On the other hand, no amount of present success and approval will compensate for experiencing the disapproval of the King of Kings when He sits as the believer's judge: "We must all appear before the judgment seat of Christ, . . . *Knowing, therefore, the terror of the Lord,* we persuade men" (2 Corinthians 5:10–11, italics added). And with confidence in Jesus' words that everlasting life is ours, we continue on life's greatest journey.

ON THE JOURNEY

1. How can both the death and resurrection of Christ be demonstrated in our lives at the same time? What things do you need to die to in order to experience the true resurrection life of Christ in your life?

2. How can you choose to "lighten your load" or give up those things that keep you from growing closer to God—to live a simpler, more focused life?

4

THE VISION
OF A PILGRIM

Elisha prayed, and said,
"Lord, I pray, open his eyes that he may see."
Then the Lord opened the eyes of the young man,
and he saw. And behold, the mountain was
full of horses and chariots of fire all around Elisha.

—2 KINGS 6:17

One of my most valued possessions is a piece of the Berlin Wall, a small chunk of pink concrete given to me by a Spanish evangelist. To me, that concrete represents the bankruptcy of modern man's attempts to deny his longings for spiritual realities.

Many observers have written about the destruction of the wall and the apparently abrupt fall of European communism in the late 1980s. Strangely, secular writers tended to attribute the event to widespread anger at the shortage of consumer goods in communist countries at the time. Most people, however, will not place themselves in front of tanks and machine guns or risk trial at the accusations of a government informant because they desperately want a microwave oven. Communism, in my judgment, failed as a political system largely because it denied the reality of man's most basic inner need, a need for a spiritual connection that nothing native to this world can provide.

The communists' denials of that unseen reality sometimes took absurd forms. During one space flight, for example, a Soviet cosmonaut was asked if he could see any indications in the exosphere of the existence of God. He grandly reported that God was nowhere to be seen, thus expressing utter contempt for the intelligence of the world in general and for that of the Soviet people in particular. Many noted at the time that if the cosmonaut had decided to step outside his spacecraft without his gear he would have met God soon enough.

Prior to the collapse of Soviet communism and the Berlin Wall, there were clues that the communist world was not the monolith that it appeared to be. Well before the fall, Western analysts were noting that the Soviet Union held more professing Christians—some 97 million[1]—than any country on the globe. This, in spite of seven decades of wholesale persecutions and labor camps, ought to have suggested that the communist system was like a dying oak whose impressive looks harbored a hollow interior.

Even in those prison camps, people were thinking about spiritual matters. Several who wrote of life in the gulag noted that decisions about one's inner life were required. For example, before an inmate became an informant—and many sadly did—there was a cost to consider. Spy on fellow prisoners and you could receive extra food by being transferred to kitchen detail—but the extra food was taken from that of one of the other prisoners. So the spy could exercise "self" interest only at the expense of his conscience and soul. Even in the harsh environs of Siberian gulags, men have souls, and souls have needs just as vital as those of the body.

Man—even communist man—knows intuitively that he is incomplete in himself. C. S. Lewis noted the best explanation of man's quest: "If I find in myself a desire which no experience in this world can satisfy, the most probable explanation is that I was made for another world."[2]

THINGS THAT ARE UNSEEN

The "other world" to which Lewis referred is not simply a heavenly city the pilgrim hopes to see one day when Christ returns.

It is that, to be sure—but it is also an alternate reality that exists now alongside the world that his eyes see: "We do not look at the things which are seen, but at the things which are not seen. For the things which are seen are temporary, but the things which are not seen are eternal" (2 Corinthians 4:18). "Looking" at realities that are "not seen" is what pilgrim living is all about.

All spiritual accomplishment, in fact, is built on the ability of the individual believer to see spiritually. God calls us to see things that are real (if He can be trusted), yet cannot be observed with the senses. These invisible realities have to be revealed by Him to fall within the scope of our vision. When God does reveal them, they often fly in the face of everything our senses and our memories tell us.

The pilgrim's mind must engage the visible world by using the weapons of its invisible counterpart. The fundamentals upon which godly living depend are constructed upon an invisible grid of pilgrim realities. Here are some examples; each is a direct biblical assertion addressed to Christians:

• You were crucified (Galatians 2:20).
• You died (Colossians 3:3).
• You were buried (Romans 6:4).
• You were resurrected (Colossians 3:1).
• You were seated in heaven (Ephesians 2:6).
• Your life is hidden in God (Colossians 3:3).

Not one of those items is verifiable by experience—by this I mean that no one recalls being crucified or buried, for example—yet every one is affirmed and reaffirmed in Scripture. What is more, every statement in the list above forces the Christian into what philosophers would call an epistemological crisis: How do we *know* these things are true? Christianity becomes purely countercultural at this point, for the world is certain that no certainties exist in the realm of the spirit.

God intentionally forces the issue on us because every statement in the list above is a statement *about us*. God is not simply telling us about, for example, the beauties of heaven. Many a Christian is content to believe what God has said about the New Jerusalem or about the worship activities of angels or about the pearly gates. We are, after all, in no position to contradict any of it. We can only marvel.

When we are informed of realities about ourselves, however, we have firm opinions about what is true. Yet the texts above assure us that the most important and enduring realities about ourselves are matters that we know only because God chooses to tell us. It is here that Christians often wrestle with God, for these assertions leave us with a limited number of options when it comes to evaluating them. The statements are blatantly and obviously false to the evidence of my eyes and ears and memory. I certainly don't recall being crucified, and though my absentmindedness is pronounced, I think I would have remembered that. Nor do I have any recollection of dying and being buried, still less a consciousness of being seated with Christ in heavenly places.

These statements are, in fact, so obviously false to human experience that they leave us only two choices: (1) believe them on the grounds of our confidence in the nature of God and the truthfulness of His Word, or (2) dismiss them as high-sounding speculations told with good intentions (perhaps) by misguided people.

Why does God tell us things that contradict our senses? . . . Because they force us to confront His alternate spiritual reality head-on.

In other words, we simply have to take God's Word for what is true on the spiritual level or run in the other direction. After all, if He tells us things like these that are *not* true, He not only is telling us lies, but He is showing His contempt for us by insulting our intelligence; and it is hard to imagine behavior less consistent with the God of the Bible.

So, why does God tell us things that contradict our senses? We could say, "Because they're true," and that would be accurate enough. There is, however, more to it than that. In part, He tells us such things because they force us to confront His alternate spiritual reality head-on. If some aspect or part of me is seated in heaven, for example, I should want to know more about it. Then, too, I should want to learn how my connection with Christ illuminates these matters. After all, the assertions uniformly add a critical phrase:

- You were crucified *with Christ*.
- You died *with Christ*.
- You were buried *with Christ*.
- You were resurrected *with Christ*.
- You were seated *with Christ* in heaven.
- Your life is hidden *with Christ* in God.

Clearly God the Father identifies the believer so completely with His Son that the realities of the Cross, Resurrection, and enthronement are common to both. We are accepted in Christ, not on our own. God looks at us in a special way because of His Son.

WERE YOU THERE?

I can almost hear the gears inside the skeptic's mind: "How can someone be buried with Christ when he wasn't even alive when Christ was buried? Sounds like a logical impossibility to me." However, even those believers who were alive at the time weren't placed inside the tomb with Him, yet they were "buried with Christ," too. You were; I was. The statements are simply true on an entirely separate level of knowledge.

They are true in the mind of God, which is the level of ultimate reality. They are true on the same level that salvation is true. They are true on the same level that forgiven sins are true. I do not know my sins are forgiven because I feel forgiven. God has told me in His Word that the person who trusts in Jesus Christ will receive forgiveness of sins (Acts 10:43). That is a decision God makes. When it is true in His mind, it is finally and eternally true. I benefit psychologically from it only when I relax in the wholehearted confidence that God has dealt with my sins once and for all. We are told to *regard* or *reckon* them as true. Paul wrote, "Reckon yourselves to be dead indeed to sin, but alive to God in Christ Jesus our Lord" (Romans 6:11).

We can trust God's conceptions and His realities to be one and the same. What He proposes to do is as good as done. Pilgrims are supposed to build their lives around that reality.

During World War II, Murdo MacDonald was serving as a chaplain to American troops held in a German POW camp when the Allies landed in Europe on June 6, 1944. When a fellow prisoner who had been listening to a hidden radio informed him of the invasion, MacDonald relayed the information to his comrades. The result was a frenzied outbreak of rejoicing. Men were running to and fro, hugging one another, leaping for joy, even rolling on the ground. They were not foolish enough to ignore their confinement, but they knew—really *knew*—that deliverance was now certain.[3]

The gospel holds a parallel set of promises. The Lamb was slain from before the foundation of the earth. When God planned it, it was in the bank. When Christ died, pilgrim, you were as real to God as you are now. Were you there when they crucified my Lord? If you are a believer in Him, in the mind of God you were. Today He is asking you to honor that identification and to behave accordingly.

THE GUIDING PRINCIPLE OF THE PILGRIM

Here, then, is the guiding principle of the pilgrim way: *Accept the testimony of your intellect when it differs from the testimony of your senses.* This precept, unlike some irrational mysticism, constitutes the beginning of all real spiritual understanding.

The rule should not be unfamiliar to us. The ability to live by it lies at the foundation of almost all progress in relationships. When a toddler in a supermarket cart looks around and doesn't see his mother, he is likely to fly into a panic and begin screaming for her. Later, as he matures, he learns to overcome his hysteria, concluding that though she isn't visible at the moment she is probably nearby. He's learned to subordinate his senses—specifically the sense of sight—to his mind. That mind, trained through his brief experience and reinforced by repeated exhortations from his mother, finally begins to help him function. More importantly, as his mother continually vindicates the (at first) feeble faith he places in her, the relationship of trust in time becomes one of love.

Christian living proceeds along similar lines. Our minds are supposed to bring stability to our Christian experience as they counterbalance what is often an initially faulty reaction to the challenges our senses bring us.

I received a personal test of this principle not long ago while attending a wedding rehearsal dinner. The bride and groom were dear friends. My wife, son, and I were having a great time with them and with many other loved ones, and it was past eleven before there was a break in the festivities. I walked out of the building to get a breath of air, looked across the street to where I had parked on arriving, and discovered that my car was missing.

I remembered having parked behind my son Tim. His car was there, but behind it loomed a large Buick-shaped empty space. About that time, Tim walked out, saw the same vacancy, and said excitedly, "Dad, where's your car?"

My question exactly.

I began to use my mind; I concluded my car had been stolen. Next I was able to assess my emotions: I was pleased to discover in my own heart neither anger nor panic. Happily, I realized that the truths that I had often preached—that all our possessions belong to God, that we are merely stewards of them, and that God will provide for our needs—were things that I really believed. My mind had brought stability to my emotions. The disclosure proved a pleasant one even though the loss of the vehicle was not. Believe me when I tell you that there was a time when I would have reacted differently to having my car stolen.

Unfortunately, Christians don't come out of the box with a full-orbed consciousness of the living realities of God's kingdom. It is the business of spiritual pilgrims to learn God's ways and build their lives around those realities. That is why the apostle Paul said, "Set your mind on things above, not on things on the earth. For you died, and your life is hidden with Christ in God" (Colossians 3:2–3). The "things above" to which he referred do not change when the rent is overdue and it looks like you may lose your job soon and you seem to be catching a cold. If your real life is hidden with Christ in God, the world can only do so much damage to you, and even that will disappear in time.

The most profound realities of life are routinely believed on the testimony of credible witnesses.

Only those who can set their mind on such realities will know the calmness that such convictions can bring. We need to have utter confidence that what God tells us about our eternal worth to Him is not going to change regardless of what happens in the realm of what we see.

Someone might be thinking as he reads this, *Whoever heard of believing such important matters simply on the strength of someone else's testimony?* But the most important realities about any of us were first told to us by others. How do you know who your parents are? How do you know your own name? The answer: because people in whom you have confidence told you the answers to those questions. For most of us, that is all the assurance we need. We refuse to look back and call into question the truths that form the very foundation of human experience. The most profound realities of life are routinely believed on the testimony of credible witnesses.

Sometimes people do hesitate, of course. For example, it sometimes takes a parent many years to convince a child that the child is loved. Sometimes, in spite of a parent's sincere efforts, it never happens. Whether a child is persuaded of a parent's love or not, however, has no essential bearing on the reality of that love. Likewise, the believer died with Christ whether he *feels* that the assertion is true or not. He does not negate God's truths; he merely penalizes himself when he chooses to dismiss them.

TWO NATURES AT WAR

So why do believers sometimes ignore God's testimony about unseen realities and continue to engage in behavior that imitates the world system? Because during our earthly lives we possess two natures, one of which is utterly at home in the visible world. When confronted with temptation, our "old man," as the apostle Paul termed it, is powerfully drawn toward the pleasures of the visible world. Our other nature, what he called "the new man," will have no part with iniquity. (Sometimes the terms used vary slightly, but the ideas are consistent.) The Christian, upon conversion, finds a new dimension in his life, but a dimension that is far from unopposed.

The parallel existence of these two spiritual realities guarantees that the life of the Christian will resemble a war. Paul described it: "For the flesh lusts [sets its desires] against the Spirit, and the Spirit against the flesh; and these are contrary to one another, so that you do not do the things that you wish" (Galatians 5:17).

When some Christians discover the reality of this inner combat, they become discouraged. They somehow have concluded that when a person becomes a Christian he should no longer feel the power of sin's attractiveness. That notion, however, does not originate in Scripture. The inner war is, in fact, an evidence of life, not death. For the first time, the "real" person wants to do right.

That is where all the biblical talk about dying and being raised with Christ comes in; for when it comes to the Christian believer, the *real* person is the new man. Paul made this clear in the summary of spiritual living that he wrote to the Ephesian believers: "Put off, concerning your former conduct, the old man which grows corrupt according to the deceitful lusts, and be renewed in the spirit of your mind, and . . . put on the new man which was created according to God, in true righteousness and holiness" (Ephesians 4:22–24).

The old man is growing corrupt. He is like a dead body—putrefying and ugly. While he is present, he gives unmistakable evidence of the existence of an old life; but his days are numbered, and in time he will no longer exist.

The new man, by contrast, is perfect. God created him in Christ, and he possesses all the righteousness and holiness that God can confer. In fact, he can never possess any more righteousness than he has today. Additionally, the beauty of the new man is that he lives forever. When the old man has disappeared, the new man will still be there. Thus, the new man is the true you—the part of you that will live forever. Your real life is hidden with Christ in God. No spiritual enemy can touch it. Even if you behave in a way that denies it and dishonors Him who gave it to you, it remains unchanged, for it is eternal.

Do you think that none of this could have any bearing on moral behavior? Next time you are tempted to engage in a sinful activity, "see" yourself sitting in heaven next to Jesus Christ. You will discover that it does makes a difference—but only if you believe it is true.

THE VISION OF MOSES

The pilgrim way of seeing guided the giants of faith in the past. The writer to the Hebrews tells us that Moses "by faith . . . forsook Egypt, not fearing the wrath of the king; for he endured as seeing Him who is invisible" (Hebrews 11:27). Moses behaved as though God were personally present at his elbow—which He was. His spiritual vision, as the writer to the Hebrews noted, explains much about his accomplishments.

To call Moses a legend is to belittle him. His accomplishments depended, the biblical writer tells us, on his determination to see unseen realities. Pushing aside disappointment after disappointment, he endured. Only with God's help did he forge a group of slaves into a nation and became a mighty voice for his Master. Subjecting himself to abuse and rejection, hostility and misunderstanding, he did what most would have deemed impossible, and Scripture attributes it to his spiritual vision.

What did Moses' way of seeing mean in terms of the decisions he made? Hebrews 11 indicates he made four righteous choices that were possible because he saw the One who is unseen. We need to make the same choices, exercising a spiritual vision in our decision making.

First, Moses knew what to risk. He would risk the disapproval of people but never the disapproval of God. Like Moses, when you have a spiritual vision, you will see God's Word as present with you even when you don't have it open. "By faith Moses, when he was born, was hidden three months by his parents, because they saw he was a beautiful child; and they were not afraid of the king's command" (Hebrews 11:23).

> *[Be] willing to risk the hostility of a king.*

Even though Moses is the subject of this verse, the writer is telling us that the great emancipator did not become a man of faith in a vacuum. The vision that energized him first lived in his parents. They were willing to risk the hostility of a king—the pharaoh—though he held the power of life and death over them. They knew, however, that the God of heaven would not be pleased if they surrendered their son to be murdered.

The text tells us that Moses' parents were not afraid of the king's threat. It certainly would have occurred to them that they could be in danger by violating Pharaoh's instructions. Nonetheless, they decided that they would rather face the danger that they could see than to have God upset with them. Moses' parents knew what the king could do. Nevertheless, they feared God more profoundly and refused to put their son to death just because Pharaoh ordered it. The fear of God drove away their fear of man.

Second, Moses was willing to suffer. Seeing spiritually means choosing to suffer, but never by choosing to sin. "Moses, when he became of age, refused to be called the son of Pharaoh's daughter, choosing rather to suffer affliction with the people of God than to enjoy the passing pleasures of sin" (Hebrews 11:24–25). Moses' choice did not come because he possessed a misguided love of suffering. God did not invite him to experience pain for the fun of it. Moses simply preferred that people know him as a member of God's people than as a scion of the royal household of Egypt.

God had promised the spiritual children of Abraham a homeland and great honor. At the time Moses made his choice to identify himself with Israel, however, his people were enslaved. They gave no evidence of interest in becoming the nation that God had appointed them to be. Moses went against the evidence of his eyes and accepted the testimony of his intellect, because God had spoken of His plans to remove them from Egypt (see Genesis 15:13–14).

The alternative, according to the author of Hebrews, was dabbling in what the writer called the "passing pleasures of sin." The Scriptures, contrary to popular belief, do not deny that sin has its pleasures; they simply deny that those pleasures last. To insist on the contrary is not only unscriptural, it is poor strategy. Trying to tell people that sinning has no compensations doesn't work. Sin does have benefits—but they are benefits that run out suddenly and with terrible effects.

In many hymnals is a song that includes the words, "My Jesus, I love Thee; I know Thou art mine. For Thee all the follies of sin I resign." That is not, however, what the author originally wrote, which was, "For Thee all the pleasures of sin I resign." Some hymnal editor apparently felt that he had to protect the Christian public and changed "pleasures" to "follies" and subsequent generations of editors followed suit. Moses didn't renounce the sinful choice because it lacked pleasures, but because it contained no lasting pleasures. His vision made an enormous difference both for himself and his people.

Third, Moses looked toward a final, lasting reward. He visualized God's reward. Seeing spiritually means placing God's final reward near the front of your thinking and then moving in that direction. It means seeing God's generosity and judging it worth waiting for. Moses was "esteeming the reproach of Christ greater riches than the treasures in Egypt; for he [was looking] to the reward" (Hebrews 11:26). The writer tells us that Moses valued the "reproach of Christ." He did so by suffering a loss of reputation because he identified himself with Christ's people. Also, he chose a path that the Lord Jesus would choose much later—a direction that would cause Moses to lose his reputation in the pharaoh's palace but establish it before God.

What reward did Moses have in mind? Heaven?

No. Heaven is not a reward for faithfulness to God. Living with God forever doesn't come because we do anything for Him. He gives eternal life to everyone who is willing to receive it through faith in His Son. Moses had in mind pilgrim realities that go far beyond mere eternal survival (more on this in chapter 12).

Whatever the reward is, Moses had not received it yet: "All these, having obtained a good testimony through faith, did not receive [what was promised], God having provided something better for us, that they should not be made perfect apart from us" (Hebrews 11:39–40). Moses was looking forward to the day when God would be personally present on this earth and would call all His people together in celebration. He "saw" the rewards to come and kept the prospect before him at all times.

Fear of the unknown can destroy
Christian pilgrims faster than almost anything.

Fourth, Moses leaned on God alone. Seeing with spiritually focused eyes also means leaning on God for protection when the world issues its threats. "By faith [Moses] forsook Egypt, not fearing the wrath of the king; for he endured as seeing Him who is invisible" (Hebrews 11:27). This is a difficult verse, because it appears to describe Moses' original flight from Egypt, a departure apparently provoked by concern that the pharaoh would soon apprehend him. Moses left because the pharaoh issued an order for his arrest for murdering an Egyptian. The biblical account states that "Moses feared and said, 'Surely this thing is known!' When Pharaoh heard of this matter, he sought to kill Moses. But Moses fled from the face of Pharaoh and dwelt in the land of Midian" (Exodus 2:14–15). Since he clearly was afraid of Pharaoh at the time, the reference in Hebrews must not be to this incident, which came early in Moses' school of discipleship.

Rather, Hebrews 11:27 probably describes Moses' leading in the Exodus itself. The pharaoh initially granted Moses and the children of Israel an exodus from Egypt; he later reversed the decision, sending the army to annihilate the Israelites as they stood before the Red Sea. When the people saw the approaching army, they panicked; Moses, however, kept his calm, trusting in the One who was unseen to come to their aid. Through this trust, Moses was able to lead the people safely out of bondage (see Exodus 14:10–27).

Fear of the unknown can destroy Christian pilgrims faster than almost anything. If our spiritual vision is acute, however, we can look beyond the immediate threats to the place where Jesus Christ sits, at the right hand of the Father. No panic exists there at any time—only a High Priest, waiting to attend to the pleas of those who call on Him, as we will if we are walking the pilgrim way— as we must, if we are to make the hard choices that our homeland duly requires of us.

ON THE JOURNEY

1. What are the spiritual weapons you use in the inner combat between flesh and spirit? How effective is this spiritual armor against your fleshly weaknesses?

2. Give an example of how some event present to our senses is not the full picture of reality—especially based upon the spiritual truths that govern the event. How can we better see the whole picture?

5
THE ETHICS
OF A PILGRIM

All sober inquirers after truth, ancient and modern, pagan
and Christian, have declared that the happiness of man, as
well as his dignity, consists in virtue.

—JOHN ADAMS[1]

---

*I*n late 1997, the Evangelical Council for Financial Accountability announced that it was suspending from membership
the Gospel Rescue Mission of Washington, D.C., over its use of
deceptive fund-raising practices. It seems that the organization had
included in its annual Thanksgiving appeal letter the story of a
man named "Steve," whom the mission had helped out of his desperate situation. In a similar letter from a related Los Angeles mission, however, "Steve" was "Alex," and in other mission letters
in other cities he assumed still other names, though maintaining
the same life story—word for word. Quite a coincidence.

Though the appeal letter leads one to think that "Steve" was well-known by the author, in reality he wasn't. Steve doesn't live in Washington. The fund-raising letters were identical because they were all composed by the advertising agency that represents Gospel Rescue Mission (and many others).[2]

The elusive Steve was only part of the problem. The GRM letter bore a computer-generated signature—one that did not match the name below it. The letter's main purpose supposedly was for funds to help the mission "fill its pantry" for the Thanksgiving holiday. However, according to an investigation by *World* magazine, such appeal letters raise about $800,000 for GRM each year, and only $31,000 is actually spent for food (about $330,000 worth of food is donated annually).[3] That means that most of the funds collected go toward general expenses—a perfectly worthwhile cause, but not the basis upon which the money is raised. The mission excused itself with a fine-print disclaimer at the bottom of the letter, noting that surplus funds would be used throughout the year to "care for the hungry and homeless."

Technically and legally correct, perhaps; however, an ECFA official observed that it wasn't good enough: "A disclaimer doesn't get it done," said Paul Nelson, the organization's president. "They created a restriction that says this money will be used to buy food for the Thanksgiving season."[4] After an investigation, the ECFA suspended the mission until the ECFA could be satisfied that such practices would be discontinued. The mission announced that it was taking immediate steps to justify its readmission to ECFA.

We belong to an organization that the apostle Paul described as "the pillar and ground of the truth" (1 Timothy 3:15).

Many people were disturbed by the story, and not all for the same reasons. Some resented not the fund-raising tactic but the investigation, citing the mission's long history of worthwhile ministry. The advertising agency was irked that people would question the use of representative or composite stories, noting how cost-efficient they are. Others defended the deceptive letter because other ministries routinely did the same thing. Several letters to the editor of *World* magazine, which broke the story, criticized the periodical's snooping, noting that the Washington mission and others like it are doing a good job. And some suggested that recipients of the letter really didn't care whether Steve was a real person helped by the Washington mission. According to their logic, the organization was justified in sending out false information.

However, if it should be true that people don't care about the truthfulness of a fund-raising letter—and I, for one, don't believe that for a minute—it would say more about the readers than about those who sent the letter. Christian pilgrims are supposed to care about the truth. We belong to an organization that the apostle Paul described as "the pillar and ground of the truth" (1 Timothy 3:15).

Almost overlooked in the discussion was the man who brought the deception to the attention of the ECFA. Richard Shannon, an employee at Gospel Rescue Mission, decided that he could not with a clear conscience support the use of deceit even in a good cause. He took his concerns to the executive director of the mission. When his objections were dismissed, he went to its board. When they defended what he felt were misleading tactics, he resigned his position and took his information to the ECFA. In effect, he was unwilling to sell his integrity in exchange for a job.

Many people have since pointed out what is undoubtedly true: Gospel Rescue Mission has helped many real-life "Steves" over the years. Had they taken the time and spent the funds, they could have issued a letter describing an actual person helped by their ministry. (The advertising agency charges $1,500 extra to issue a customized, nonboilerplate letter.)

LESSONS LEARNED

Cost-efficiency, however, forms a poor basis for ethical decisions. Pilgrims are supposed to hold to standards that are absolute. Claiming to represent the God who fills eternity ought to make Christians lean hard on unseen resources. If we put integrity at the top of our value list, He will delight in underwriting the work we do. And if He doesn't, who can sustain what He has deemed unworthy of His support?

Parachurch agencies are not alone in the ethical malaise of Western Christianity. Much of the church has succumbed to the neopagan influences that dominate Western culture. One denomination recently decided to soften its teaching concerning premarital sex and men and women living together before marriage. Leaders claimed that since by the year 2000 about four out of five couples would be sleeping and living together prior to marriage, it is no longer healthy or productive to tell people to behave morally. That denomination and others now apparently regard morals as the product rather than the regulator of behavior.

Some church leaders act independently of their denominations. A pastor in Omaha solemnized the "marriage" of a lesbian couple not long ago, an action expressly forbidden by his denomination's documents governing pastoral behavior (to say nothing of God's opinion of the whole business). The church's official guidelines declare that "ceremonies that celebrate homosexual unions shall not be conducted by our ministers and shall not be conducted in our churches." Though the language seems clear enough, when his action was challenged, the pastor was acquitted by his local judicial council.[5] They claimed that the guidelines were only advisory. So much for advice.

Ecclesiastical leaders today speak unblushingly of "market-driven" churches. One British congregation recently took the idea to its logical conclusion. Recognizing people's inclinations to sleep late on Sundays, the church set its "worship services" on Tuesday evenings. Smoking and drinking are permitted at church meetings, which are held in a pub so as not to offend the tender sensibilities of modern parishioners, who might be put off by traditional church buildings. The service includes no hymns, no sermon, and no minister. It is not entirely clear how this remarkable "service" differs from what happens at other pubs on Tuesday nights.[6]

Every generation produces calls to "update" the church and to help it "get in step with the times." However, that which is timeless is always timely. I agree with the writer who said, "It can be exalting to belong to a church that is five hundred years behind the times and sublimely indifferent to fashion; it is mortifying to belong to a church that is five minutes behind the times, huffing and puffing to catch up."[7] As the Western church moves into the third millennium of Christian faith, its breathless condition is all too apparent.

So how is the Christian sojourner supposed to resist assimilation and be distinctive in the world? How are we to identify ourselves? The answer lies in the realm of integrity and biblical behavior. However, before answering the question, let's note how we are *not* to seek distinctiveness as pilgrims.

FALSE PATHS: WITHDRAWAL

One false path is to retreat from engagement with the world—in other words, to indulge in monasticism or one of its modern approximations. Withdrawal has its advantages, of course, which is why it is so often tried. It can help solve the problem of corruption of Christian morals. Christians can wall themselves off from the world and its temptations.

You need not enter a monastery to withdraw. Many Christian families have sought and moved into neighborhoods populated exclusively (or nearly so) by believers. Some real estate agents have even advertised new subdivisions as catering to Christian believers, and it no doubt provides a measure of comfort to know that your neighbors are people who share your values. Withdrawal creates other dangers, however, the chief of which is the loss of impact on the world.

Perhaps the ultimate caricature of withdrawal appeared some years ago in the form of a story entitled *The Gospel Blimp*, by Joe Bayly. In the book (and the clever film that followed), a group of Christians began discussing the spiritual condition of one of their neighbors. The man was a typically lost individual: amoral and given to some of the standard pleasures of the flesh. In their "concern" for this person, the believers in the film did not take the obvious measure of going next door and having a conversation with him. Instead, they decided to purchase a blimp from which they could bombard his home (and others) with gospel tracts dropped from the skies. What transpired shows the folly of avoiding simple engagement with people.

FALSE PATHS:
CULTURAL PRACTICES OR DRESS

Customs and appearance have sometimes been employed to make Christians appear distinctive in the world. Hudson Taylor discovered as much when he went to China. He and his fellow British missionaries were easily recognizable. To the Chinese they looked, well . . . odd. They wore top hats, morning coats, and conventional European dress. Taylor was wise enough to see, however, that the kind of distinctiveness they possessed reflected cultural rather than Christian values. Their clothing put the wrong kind of distance between them and the people they were trying to reach. They were sending the message that they expected the Chinese to become Europeans in order to become Christians.

After some struggle of soul, Taylor decided to abandon his cultural distinctiveness. He had his hair cut and dyed black and put into the customary Chinese pigtail. He put the morning coat in mothballs and donned the ordinary long robe of a Chinese man. His fellow missionaries were horrified and accused him of "going native." Taylor knew, however, that he hadn't come to China to import British culture, but to offer Christ to the people. God soon afterward began to bring people to Himself as a result of that decision.

THE PILGRIM PATH: PERSONAL INTEGRITY

Legitimate distinctiveness, by contrast to these substitutes, comes from two commitments on the part of the pilgrim.

The critical element in distinctiveness is personal integrity—making a commitment to do what pleases God in every area of life, no matter how "small" the issue. According to an old story, one minister, struggling with obedience to a local ordinance, once parked his car in a no-parking zone because he was short of time and couldn't find a space. He placed a note under the windshield wiper that read: "I have circled the block ten times. If I don't park here, I'll miss my appointment. 'Forgive us our trespasses.'"

When he returned, he found a citation from a police officer along with this response: "I've circled this block for ten years. If I don't give you a ticket, I'll lose my job. 'Lead us not into temptation.'"

Unfortunately, Christian ministers have led their flocks in far worse directions. Not long ago, a councilman in a southern city was arrested for speeding and driving under the influence of alcohol. When the arresting officer asked him to explain himself, the councilman issued what he considered to be an excuse: He was a part-time clergyman who was rushing to administer communion to a parishioner—at 3:00 A.M. I don't know what the police officer said, but he could be forgiven if he questioned the sincerity of these "extenuating circumstances." And even if the explanation was true, would any Christian who cared about the reputation of His Lord use it?

Integrity is *the* hallmark of the Christian pilgrim. Christians in the Western world have suffered the loss of much of their distinctiveness in the visible world because they have placed other values ahead of righteousness. We have sought to become distinctive on other fronts—but nothing can replace moral behavior. Our ethics must be consistent and unquestioned. Whoever sells his integrity for any price whatever has sold it too cheaply.

The individual Christian's integrity either gains or loses credibility for the gospel of Christ and the corporate witness of the whole church. When Nathan stood before a guilty David, the prophet rebuked him by saying, "By this deed you have given great occasion to the enemies of the Lord to blaspheme" (2 Samuel 12:14). David's sin affected the whole family of God.

Merriam-Webster's Collegiate Dictionary defines *integrity* as "firm adherence to a code of . . . values . . . an unimpaired condition . . . the quality or state of being complete or undivided." You see a related term in our English word *integer,* meaning, "a whole number." A person who sells his integrity discards the unifying principle of his life. He becomes a person in the process of dis*integr*ation.

Integrity often falls to the twin gods of fame and utility.

Some years ago, a professor at Vanderbilt University taught the importance of integrity even in the so-called "little things." Madison Sarratt, a teacher of mathematics, customarily gave a little speech before every exam. It went like this: "Today, I am giving two examinations; one in trigonometry and the other in honesty. I hope you will pass them both. If you must fail one, fail trigonometry. There are many good people in the world who can't pass trig, but there are no good people in the world who cannot pass honesty."[8] Every pilgrim faces such tests daily; and there are no "little things" when it comes to integrity.

True integrity requires that you do what is right when no one is looking—or even when everyone else is compromising. I heard a story not long ago about a bank employee who was in line for a good promotion. One day at lunch, the president of the bank, who happened to be standing behind the clerk in the cafeteria, saw him slip two pats of butter under his slice of bread so they wouldn't be seen by the cashier.

That little act of dishonesty cost him his advancement. The bank president reasoned that if an employee cannot be trusted in little things, he cannot be trusted at all. The employee had, in effect, sold his integrity and his usefulness for about twenty cents' worth of butter.

Integrity often falls to the twin gods of fame and utility. The results can be devastating to the individual and the community at large. Before the space shuttle *Challenger* flew its tragic final mission—exploding into a fireball seventy-three seconds after takeoff—several of the engineers assigned to the project warned their leaders that temperatures were too cold to risk launching the vehicle. But project leaders had a schedule to keep that chilly morning and downplayed the risk. They rolled the dice with seven lives and a billion-dollar project. In the process they lost more than their integrity.

The pollster George Gallup Jr. once told a group of fundraisers that 42 percent of people in America have serious doubts about the honesty of any given appeal for religious donations. This lack of credibility has been earned by the people the church has put forward as leaders through the public media.

It was not always so. Consider the well-known preacher of Victorian times, Charles Spurgeon. During England's Victorian period, people were deeply concerned about their reputations. As a result, extortion became a favorite vocation of the unscrupulous. Blackmailers once sent Spurgeon a letter warning that if he did not place a large amount of money in a certain place at a certain time, they would publish items in the newspapers that would defame him and ruin his public ministry.

Instead of remitting money, Spurgeon instead left at that station a letter. Later the blackmailers read this: "You and your like are requested to publish all you know about me across the heavens."

Spurgeon knew his life would hold up under the scrutiny of men. Integrity is the ultimate ticket to true freedom. The person who lacks it yields control of his life to anyone who can discover the dark secrets of his private life.

SIX MARKS OF INTEGRITY

If the church is an arrow, the point of it is the integrity of the individual Christian. The Psalms make much of this, and Psalm 26, as an example, unveils David's devotion to God. Six marks of integrity appear in the psalm. Have these marks and you will be a man or woman of integrity, truly ethical in your actions and distinctive to a waiting world. They are: (1) faith, (2) openness to reproof, (3) a commitment to Scripture, (4) moral independence, (5) open identification with spiritual realities, and (6) spiritual dependence.

First, a person of integrity demonstrates faith. David knew that integrity is impossible apart from the work of God inside the one who has it. He pleaded, "Vindicate me, O Lord, for I have walked in my integrity. I have also trusted in the Lord; I shall not slip" (Psalm 26:1). Integrity requires a moment-by-moment trust in the Lord. The person who stops trusting even for an instant, as David eventually did after he wrote this psalm, is a person who is on his way to slipping.

Second, a person of integrity is open to reproof. David knew that he had nothing to fear from a divine inspection of his interior. He invited such scrutiny by praying, "Examine me, O Lord, and prove me; try my mind and my heart" (Psalm 26:2). He was saying, "If there's something wrong with the way I am looking at life, I want to be aware of it." The statement is a recognition that our own assessment of our integrity can be at fault. We can be out of line when we think we are right. It is when we know we are wrong and choose not to notice that we are most at risk.

During his time as a rancher, Theodore Roosevelt and one of his cowpunchers lassoed a maverick steer, lit a fire, and prepared the branding irons. Gregor Lang, one of Roosevelt's neighbors, claimed the part of the range they were on. According to the cattlemen's rule, the steer therefore belonged to Lang. As his cowboy applied the brand, Roosevelt said, "Wait, it should be Lang's brand."

"That's all right, boss," said the cowboy.

"But you're putting on my brand," Roosevelt said.

"That's right," said the man.

"Drop that iron," Roosevelt demanded, "and get back to the ranch and get out. I don't need you anymore. A man who will steal for me will steal from me."[9] Roosevelt refused to compromise his integrity by claiming a single animal that didn't belong to him—or by letting an employee compromise it for him.

Third, a person of integrity is committed to Scripture. David wrote, "For Your lovingkindness is before my eyes, and I have walked in Your truth" (Psalm 26:3). The person of integrity reminds himself constantly of all that God has done for him. He commits himself to walking in the truth of God as found in His Word. He does not sacrifice integrity even in the name of compassion.

A woman who wanted to get into medical school found her own road full of ethical pitfalls. She wrote about it after the fact this way:

> In my early thirties it became clear to me that I would prefer a career in medicine, so I enrolled in a one-year premed program at a local college . . . to do the course work, prepare for the standardized exams and apply to medical schools. I was not on campus very long before I became aware . . . that my classmates were extremely dishonest: falsifying laboratory records, cheating on tests, and pressuring me to do likewise. . . . The pressure was no problem; I know how to resist pressure. But the professor in charge of the program is a man struggling with the twin demons of a mid-life crisis and a deplorable working environment. Under this intense pressure, his favorite phrase has become, "I don't want to know!" I could not bring myself to add to his burdens. Given a choice between intellectual integrity and compassion, I chose compassion. Bad choice. . . . In the end, I had no choice but to force him to face what he had to know.
>
> Things muddled along until March when some . . . were caught cheating on a take-home exam. . . . The culprits . . . defended themselves on the basis that they did not know that they were doing anything wrong. . . . The professor went before the disciplinary board and endorsed the students' behavior, thereby compromising his own integrity and that of the institution.
>
> At that point, I felt strongly that I had been silent too long. Too late, I protested . . . on the grounds that attempting to force the medical schools to accept fifteen highly unscrupulous people has devastating implications for society, as well as for the people who do such things. I cannot consider this a trivial incident. Dishonest students become dishonest professionals.[10]

The woman's disclosure was ignored. Noting her mediocre academic performance, the board told her she was "hopelessly incompetent and not worth knowing." To that charge, the woman answered: "I have character and that's more important than grades. Or medical school. Or money." Integrity stays in place whether adversity or prosperity comes.

Fourth, a person of integrity exhibits moral independence. David wrote in Psalm 26:4–5, "I have not sat with idolatrous mortals, nor will I go in with hypocrites. I have hated the assembly of evildoers, and will not sit with the wicked." By this, he didn't mean he looked down on them from a prideful position; rather, he simply recognized that if he went along with the crowd, he would certainly lose his uprightness. Therefore, he showed a healthy independence from society's shifting morals.

Indeed, we should seek moral independence. But what if we fail, giving in to pressures rather than remaining independent? It's true that Scripture holds no examples of great achievement after moral failure. Yet that truth does not diminish the reality of forgiveness. When believers confess their sins, God forgives totally (see 1 John 1:9).

Nonetheless, Proverbs 6:32–33 says, "Whoever commits adultery with a woman lacks understanding; he who does so destroys his own soul. Wounds and dishonor he will get, and his reproach will not be wiped away." The truth of this, of course, is seen in the fact that in spite of all David's accomplishments, he still is known to this day as a king who yielded to sexual temptation. His sins were wiped away before God, but the effects of those sins in the view of the public continued.

The lists of qualifications for church leaders found in both 1 Timothy 3:1–7 and Titus 1:5–9 have one term at the head of the list: "blameless." Not sinless, but above reproach. God forgives, but people remember; the lingering public memory of failure is what the Bible calls reproach.

Broken moral integrity means the spiritual leader forfeits the right to lead and invites divine discipline. Scripture insists that leaders are judged on a different scale: "My brethren, let not many of you become teachers, knowing that we shall receive a stricter judgment" (James 3:1). You will notice that in this warning James numbered himself among those who teach, but he urged caution upon those who would join him.

Moral independence requires that the person who discredits his ministry remove himself from his position of spiritual authority. He should not need an ecclesiastical body to call him to account. A pastor friend asked Chuck Swindoll in a letter what he thought about people who fell into sin in public ministry and then were restored to their ministries, sometimes right away. This is what Chuck wrote in reply:

> The forgiven sinner of today is often one who expects (dare I say demands?) more than he or she should. Scripture calls this "presumption." A broken and contrite heart is not presumptuous; it makes no demands, entertains no expectations. I've noticed that those recovering from a sexual scandal sometimes judge rather harshly others who are reluctant to allow them all the leadership they once exercised. I've often heard them refer to this as "shooting our wounded" when, in fact, those most wounded are the people who trusted when the fallen leader was living a lie.[11]

While consequences are (or should be) more severe for Christian leaders who fail morally, they also exist for the ordinary believer and for the truth he or she represents. Whether we like it or not, most peoples' opinion of the gospel of Christ is tied to their opinion of those who profess to believe it.

[As] pilgrims, [we] openly acknowledge
even an innocent mistake.

Fifth, a person of integrity will openly identify with spiritual realities. Christian pilgrims should make both their allegiance and their responsibility matters of public record. Our world is filled with people who are timid about their faith and reluctant to acknowledge their failures. David, however, said in Psalm 26:6–8, "I will go about Your altar, O Lord, that I may proclaim with the voice of thanksgiving, and tell of all Your wondrous works. Lord, I have loved the habitation of Your house, and the place where Your glory dwells." The person of integrity has gone on record. He knows that public worship requires accountability.

At the same time, integrity also demands that pilgrims take responsibility for their actions. When we have blundered, we own up to it. James wrote, "Confess your trespasses to one another, and pray for one another, that you may be healed" (James 5:16). The world isn't looking for perfect people, but it longs to see people with the courage to face their own faults.

Pilgrims ought to openly acknowledge even an innocent mistake. Doing so is so unusual that it attracts a lot of attention. The basketball coach at Rockdale County (Ga.) High School, not far from where I live, gained national attention not long ago when he called attention to one of his own. His team had just finished a glorious season which included 21 wins and a Georgia state title. After the season was over, someone told the coach that one player, a rarely used substitute, had been academically ineligible when he briefly played in an early tournament game.

Coach Cleveland Stroud promptly reported the blunder to the Georgia High School Athletic Association, which under the rules then deprived the team of its state championship trophy. "We didn't know he was ineligible at the time," the coach explained. "We didn't know it until a few weeks ago. Some people have said we should have just kept quiet about it, that it was just 45 seconds and the player wasn't an impact player. But you've got to do what's honest and right and what the rules say. I told my team that people forget the scores of basketball games; they don't ever forget what you're made of."[12] His young men were able to see in him a living example of taking responsibility for one's actions even when that responsibility produces pain.

I do not know whether Coach Stroud was a Christian. I do know his actions embody the attitudes and practices of integrity that every pilgrim should embrace.

Sixth, a person of integrity will display spiritual dependence. David was independent of the opinions of his peers, but dependent on the Lord. He pleaded, "As for me, I will walk in my integrity; redeem me and be merciful to me. My foot stands in an even place; in the congregations I will bless the Lord" (Psalm 26:11–12). The person of integrity is not perfect. He recognizes that he needs God's mercy. As long as he is dependent on the Lord, his foot stands in an even place. The moment he takes his eye off the Lord, he begins walking along the edge of a precipice.

Moses was a man whose heart beat close to God's. Nevertheless, even he was told that he could not enter the Promised Land because of his failure to obey. How many times did he fail? Once. That's all it takes—especially for a leader of the people of God.

A reputation for integrity takes years to build; it takes one lax, foolish moment to destroy.

A key concept ties Psalm 26 together. It is found twice: once at the beginning and once at the end. In verse one, David stated his confidence: "I shall not slip." Again, in verse twelve he proclaimed, "My foot stands in an even place." Why was David so concerned about "slipping"? Because he knew that a reputation for integrity takes years to build; it takes one lax, foolish moment to destroy. One false step ruins a hard-earned ability to speak for God. Many times that ability can never be regained, regardless of what tribunals and boards may say.

No matter how well we think through our priorities and goals, no matter how carefully we consider what God would have us do as His children, it all can be scuttled because one unthinking pilgrim, however briefly, betrays the Lord and loses his integrity. That is no accident. God has designed life so that it works that way. As a result, anyone who wants to speak for Him will have to walk close to Him every day.

THE PILGRIM PATH: BIBLICAL SUBMISSION

A second commitment for those who walk the pilgrim path is to cooperate with human authority. Peter wrote, "Therefore submit yourselves to every ordinance of man for the Lord's sake" (1 Peter 2:13). When we obey human authority, we are in the process of becoming obedient to God. When we obey human authority, we also are practicing humility, even as our Lord Jesus did. (See, for example, Matthew 11:29–30; Philippians 2:7–8.)

Just how far does this go? To what extent do we submit?

Peter said that we are to submit to "every human ordinance." The image of the Christian as a political or social revolutionary is totally lacking in the New Testament. Christians are to lead the way in cooperation with the authorities God has placed over them.

Submission has nothing to do with the appropriateness of the ordinance. If a believer lives in Saudi Arabia (as many westerners do today), and Islamic law insists that he not work on Friday, the Muslim holy day, then he ought not to work on Friday. Obedience to a law doesn't indicate one agrees with it. It simply says that he is not willing to have people question all he believes in for the sake of objecting to that law. Resistance properly comes only when the reverse situation prevails: The state compels the believer to reject the authority of the kingdom of God and to take steps to compromise his conscience.

Peter also talked about the purpose for which we submit. We are to do it "for the Lord's sake" (1 Peter 2:13). Christians win friends for Christ by being good citizens. We tend to think of this as not a particularly tough assignment, but that is because we live in a nation that was founded by Christians. Peter was writing to believers who lived in a society that was thoroughly pagan. That makes his words all the more forceful.

Every day, as Peter walked down the street in Antioch, he could look around and spot small altars on the city streets. Placed in front of these altars were images of Caesar Augustus ["the semi-divine"]. The local citizens would offer incense and animal sacrifices to Augustus every day, but they were offered on a voluntary basis. No Christian was compelled to offer sacrifice to Caesar (at least until later, when they did refuse). Peter did not say, "You believers need to rid your society of idolatry." He knew that submission to authority doesn't imply agreement with authority. He also knew that, in time, the force of the gospel would cause idolatry to decline, which in fact it did.

Christians are to make every effort to comply with what their leaders ask, and are not to refuse until the government invades the realm of their consciences by forcing them to reject God's authority for their own lives. So we pay federal taxes, even though part of the proceeds may fund agencies that counsel women to have abortions, a medical procedure that snatches the lives of unborn children. We pay state taxes, even though some of the revenue may pay for abortions performed at a county hospital. We can protest the procedures and lobby legislators to change the policies regarding the use of the monies for abortion. But we obey the laws as they exist, because God commands us to respect authority.

In addition, we can pray for wisdom and strength for our mayors, our representatives, and our president, even when their programs seem to ignore or violate biblical principles.

One other critical point: In nations with representative governments, the people ultimately rule. We elect our public officials, and we can hold them accountable—or vote to replace them. It is consistent with pilgrim living to participate in the political process. Let us vote, electing people who will allow us, as Paul wrote, to "lead a quiet and peaceable life in all godliness and reverence" (1 Timothy 2:2).

Peter also described the manner in which we submit. We are to do good. "For this is the will of God, that by doing good you may put to silence the ignorance of foolish men—as free, yet not using liberty as a cloak for vice, but as bondservants ["slaves"] of God" (1 Peter 2:15). When pilgrims do what is right, it places a gag in the mouth of foolish people. The will of God for us is to behave as God's slaves. Note the paradox: Only by becoming a slave of God and living for Him in the midst of a hostile society are we truly free.

Pilgrim living will mean obeying existing laws while challenging their continued existence. That may also mean being misunderstood or even criticized—but that's part of being distinctive pilgrims. As Charles Colson wrote:

> Orthodoxy often requires us to be hard precisely where the world is soft, and soft where the world is hard. It means condemning the homosexual life-style and being labeled bigots. It means caring for AIDS patients though many think us fools. It means respecting the rule of law though our culture is increasingly lawless. It means visiting the prisoners who offend that law though our culture would prefer to forget them. In every way that matters, Christianity is an affront to the world; it is countercultural. [13]

We become distinctive because God calls us to be like Him, and the world at large is moving in the opposite direction. We become distinctive because God calls us to be cooperative, and the world at large is rebelling and seeking to forcefully gain its own interests. Becoming Christlike will make anyone distinctive. It is behavior that gives evidence that we think of ourselves not as permanent residents here, but as resident aliens—those who are simply passing through.

ON THE JOURNEY

1. Complete integrity is a painful area for some of us. In what ways, large or small, have you compromised? Ask God to give you objectivity, to repent, and realize His grace will cause you to grow.

2. What are some examples of integrity clearly demonstrated to unbelievers, on either your part or the part of someone you know, that made a clear impact on their lives? How do acts of integrity go far beyond words?

6

THE ROAD MAP OF A PILGRIM

*The Bible is a window in this prison-world
through which we may look into eternity.*

—TIMOTHY DWIGHT[1]

*I*n a small village in north central India near the border of Nepal, a man walked into a small shop and bought three cigarettes. Buying a few cigarettes was not odd; people often bought odd quantities of goods in that region; you could buy a single carrot or a pencil or two sticks of gum. And because paper is expensive in India, shopkeepers typically would wrap a purchase from a supply of previously used paper.

When the villager returned home and unwrapped his cigarettes, the paper wrapper caught his eye, and he began to read. Quickly, he realized that he had never seen anything like this in his life. There was a problem, however; he had only half the original piece of paper. Part of the message was missing.

So the smoker, disregarding the summer heat, ran back to the shop and asked if he could have the other half of the paper. The shopkeeper replied, "You see those stacks over there? It might be in there and it might not. If you really want it, go ahead and look."

So for hours the smoker took each piece from the pile and examined it. Shoppers came in and looked at him, probably wondering what he was doing, and went out again. When he couldn't find the piece that matched his, he carefully reexamined the whole stack. Grieved at his lack of success, he started slowly home. On the way, he remembered that the paper referred to an address in a town about twelve miles away. So he borrowed a bicycle and began the long and uncomfortably hot ride.

He eventually found the address and knocked on the door. When a man answered, the cigarette smoker excitedly shouted at him, "Is this your address? Did you write this?" It took the man a few minutes to calm his guest so that he could explain. Yes, this was his address. No, he didn't write the words, but he did know them. He was a pastor; and he invited the smoker in to tell him more about the message that was on the paper, which turned out to be a gospel tract. Now the smoker, a new believer, cycles the twelve miles to the pastor's village each week to hear the Word of God—all because of one torn piece of a tract which contained a few words of Scripture.[2]

Having read this far, you can guess that the pilgrim's "road map" is the Bible. The challenge of living in two worlds requires the supernatural insight that only God's wisdom imported into this world can provide.

However, many, especially those living in the West, do not regard the Bible as inspired. They would look at the villager's high regard for those few words of Scripture as a waste of time. Indeed, if statistics can be believed, over half of the people who will read this book do not believe in the existence of absolute truth, and that makes a word of introduction to the road map imperative.

If you are a relativist, you need to know why I would advocate turning to Scripture as an absolute authority. If you're not, you need to understand how the relativism that dominates the visible world provides special challenges to living as a pilgrim.

Our era has been called "postmodern"—a period character-ized by the rejection of absolutes. The term *postmodernism* itself betrays the oxymoronic nature of recent man—we are even later than the latest it is possible to be, at a time when the most recent development of anything is by definition the most desirable one. Postmodernists are a lot like the puzzling Red Queen in *Alice Through the Looking Glass,* who can believe six impossible things before breakfast.[3]

THE POSTMODERNIST PROBLEM

The postmodernist denies the existence of absolute truth and elevates "tolerance" to the level of supreme virtue. Openness is the One Great Commandment inscribed on the tablets of today's Mount Sinai. It is not an exaggeration to call it the civil religion of the United States. Scholar Alan Bloom described the modern at-titude in his analysis of the mind-set of today's university stu-dent. He wrote, "The study of history and of culture teaches that all the world was mad in the past; men always thought they were right, and that led to wars, persecutions, slavery, xenophobia, racism, and chauvinism. The point is not to correct the mistakes and be right; rather, it is not to think you are right at all."[4]

For the first time in history, education has placed hostility to truth—in the guise of modesty—on its highest throne. For most of the last two millennia, Christians have claimed to possess the truth. It used to be that those who disagreed argued in a variety of ways in attempts to refute the claim. They claimed to know the truth, too, and in their minds Christianity wasn't it.

The postmodernist . . . [is] holding to one absolute: that there are no absolutes.

Nowadays, no refutation is necessary. Christians are wrong—not because their faith has been tested and found false, but mere-ly because they issue a claim of truth. "Your Christianity may be true for you," the postmodernist patronizingly observes, "but I like a smattering of many religions and worldviews. My views are just as true as yours. But don't talk to me about absolute truth; I know better."

Thus it is that we learn the depth of the postmodernist's convictions. He is absolutely convinced that his views are correct. It does not occur to him that the zeal with which he holds his position defeats it. If his postmodernism is true and all values are relative, then he is merely issuing a rival and inherently self-contradictory claim to the same absolute truth that he denies to everyone else. If, on the other hand, he cannot be sure of anything, then how can he be sure that absolute truth doesn't exist? The postmodernist finds himself in the strange situation of holding to one absolute: that there are no absolutes.

Today's university students seem unable to grasp this basic contradiction. Bloom notes that students hold to postmodernism so strongly because in their minds "the relativity of truth is not a theoretical insight but a moral postulate, the condition of a free society." The importance of this relativity "is revealed by the character of their response when challenged—a combination of disbelief and indignation: 'Are you an absolutist?' . . . uttered in the same tone as 'Are you a monarchist?' or 'Do you believe in witches?'"5

This strange—essentially unprecedented—twist in humanity's view of truth discourages some Christians because it seems to render irrelevant all attempts to defend or define the faith on the basis of reason and argument. However, we ought not to be so quick to abandon those defenses. For one thing, postmodernism is an intellectual fad. If God is merciful and allows humanity enough time, it will go the way of all philosophical flesh like many a movement before it. For another, if you scratch a postmodernist deeply enough, you will discover a vestige of moral absolutes lurking beneath his profession of indifference. Try as he might to avoid it, even the most postmodern of postmodernists responds intuitively when he experiences injustice himself. He doesn't like it when his wife is unfaithful or a coworker spreads gossip about him.

One bit of evidence supporting the continued existence of moral bedrock in the postmodern age is the enormous popularity of radio personality Laura Schlessinger, whose sometimes abrasive application of moral absolutes has catapulted "Dr. Laura" to the top of the talk-radio heap. If the modern world is as united against moral certainties as we are often told it is, there should be no one listening.

A still better support emerges from the apostolic observation: "When Gentiles, who do not have the law, by nature do the things in the law, these . . . are a law to themselves, who *show the work of the law written in their hearts,* their conscience also bearing witness, and between themselves their thoughts accusing or else excusing them" (Romans 2:14–15, italics added). The human heart, no matter how sophisticated, cannot obliterate the norms that God personally wrote upon it. It is only deep within the conscience, however, that this witness is given voice. Publicly, people are still free to proclaim as loudly as they please their freedom from absolute truth and its attendant moral restraints.

THE PILGRIM'S REGRESS

When we live consistently as biblical absolutists—accepting the Scriptures as absolute and true—we not only please God but emerge from the cultural swamp to become identifiable in our culture. While the world stumbles along in darkness from one level of depravity to another, Christian pilgrims can demonstrate the wonders of God's Word and God's ways by simply obeying Him and being faithful to His truth. Such pilgrims are part of God's powerful counterculture—sojourners on life's greatest journey.

The opposite approach, of course, is for Christians to adopt the postmodern view of truth. Many have; they have doubted and retreated from speaking God's revelation as found in Scripture.

At least two major reasons make such conformity seductive. For one thing, yielding to the culture is comfortable. No Christian likes to be told that he is wrong, and postmodernists will always insist that a Christian's opinions are awry. Why? Because he is asserting them *as* truth, and such is not permitted in a postmodern world.

For another, we don't enjoy the opposite necessity of declaring the errors of the culture. We don't like to have people look at us in astonishment as we suggest the existence of moral bedrock. It is easier to keep quiet on the grounds that, after all, our opinions ought not to be imposed on the world. We forget that declaring the truth is not imposing it on anyone. The postmodernist certainly feels no reluctance in asserting the inspiration of his own pronouncements on anyone within earshot; yet few accuse him of imposing anything.

In view of the potential unpleasantness involved in confrontation, we simply retreat from engagement and allow the postmodernist to squeeze us into his mold. After all, we want so much to be liked. When we elevate a desire for acceptance to the top of our priority list, however, we have strayed from the pilgrim road.

THE POWER OF THE ROAD MAP

If the church cannot assert the absolute truths of Scripture, we have nothing to say to our world. Before we can do that, we have to be convinced of the Bible's power and divine origin.

The apostle Paul wrote, "All Scripture is given by inspiration of God, and is profitable for doctrine, for reproof, for correction, for instruction in righteousness" (2 Timothy 3:16). English translators have always struggled with this verse, and understandably so. "Inspiration of God" represents a single Greek adjective *(theopneustos)* with no ready English equivalent. It might be rendered literally "God-breathed." Just as God breathed life into Adam's nostrils, so He exhaled His power and wisdom into the words of the text of Scripture. Several have noted that "expiration" might form a closer match to the original word, but it already has a completely different meaning.

So we use "inspiration" instead. We say that Scripture is "inspired by God." Of course "inspiration" has its own unfortunate associations. "Inspired" is the term people also use to describe the work of orators, composers, and artists. We read that Michelangelo was inspired when he carved his *David,* or speak of Beethoven's inspiration as he composed the Ninth Symphony.

Notice the downside of these word associations. First, if Scripture is inspired in the manner of great sculpture or music, that means that it issues merely from an elevated humanity. Its divine origins— the one point essential in the word itself—recede from view.

Second, "inspired" is a word that is generally associated with people, not products. When most people think of the inspiration of the Bible, they think of an elevated mental condition on the part of the writers, not the words themselves. The writers were, so it is thought, carried away into a supernormal state of mind. However, the word *theopneustos* specifically describes the Scriptures, not their human authors. God was especially and intimately interested in the product and only secondarily in the process. That is why you find biblical writers in almost every kind of psycho-

94

logical state as they do their work. The apostle John recorded visions seen in a trance (Revelation); Moses described what he saw and heard while trembling in God's presence on a mountain (Exodus); Luke penned the results of his historical research (Luke); Paul wrote a sober farewell letter from a prison cell (2 Timothy).

Inspiration means that God gave His personal authenticity and supernatural power to the truth of Scripture. It didn't even matter whether the human authors knew they were writing Scripture, though most did. What mattered was that the product was a gift of grace, a light in the darkness for believing pilgrims so that they might know the certainties of the homeland to which they were born anew. Pilgrims will err sometimes even when they try to use God's Word; but they will inevitably stumble if they ignore it.

The Christian church is growing most dramatically in just those places that revere the written Word of God.

The supernatural character of inspiration seems more evident to people in non-Western cultures today. Westerners dismiss this knowledge (if in fact they know it at all) as a symptom of backwardness; but it is surely no accident that the Christian church is growing most dramatically in just those places that revere the written Word of God.

God's road map showed its inspiration in the experience of Fyodor Dostoevsky. Though known today as a giant of world literature, Dostoevsky almost had his literary career—and life—ended abruptly. The series of events that saved him from death also gave him the Christian perspective from which he wrote so powerfully.

As a young man, Fyodor was a party lover who enjoyed drinking and gambling with his friends. As they played cards, they would often discuss political issues in Russia, which in those days nearly always involved the czar. When the czar received word through informers that this small group often met to discuss his mistakes, he decided that they were guilty of treason and dispatched the military to arrest them. Dostoevsky and his associates were tried, found guilty, and sentenced to death by firing squad.

Fyodor and his friends, dressed in burial gowns, were marched through the streets. The crowds hurled insults and debris. Finally, the convicts were blindfolded and tied to posts for their execution. The squad leader issued his orders: "Ready . . . aim . . ." but the order to fire didn't come. At the moment of truth, a messenger arrived with a (prearranged) message from the czar: In his imperial clemency, he had commuted their sentences to hard labor in Siberia. The "execution" had been a staged event to teach them a lesson.

In Dostoevsky's case, it produced the desired effect. He determined that he would never again treat his life, so nearly lost, as a lark to be spent in meaningless pursuits. He would use it well. As he boarded the train that would take him into years of hard labor, a Christian woman handed him the only book he would be allowed to have in prison: a New Testament. That Testament became his link with sanity and meaning during his ten years of affliction in Siberia. His daughter Aimee, writing later, reflected, "Throughout his life, he would never be without his old prison Testament, the faithful friend that had consoled him in the darkest hours of his life. He always took it with him on his travels and kept it in a drawer in his writing-table, within reach of his hand. He consulted it in the important moments of his life."[6]

He left prison a changed man, a Christian believer with a purpose in life—to allow his convictions to shine through in his fiction. Untold numbers of people have first met Christ or have at least been drawn to explore the faith because of Fyodor Dostoevsky's encounter with a stranger on a train bearing a small but priceless gift, a gift expressing God's absolutes.

THE FIRST PURPOSE OF THE ROAD MAP: DOCTRINE

After explaining the power of God's Word, Paul reminded Timothy of its value: "All Scripture . . . is profitable for *doctrine,* for *reproof,* for *correction,* for *instruction in righteousness,* that the man of God may be complete, thoroughly equipped for every good work" (2 Timothy 3:16–17, italics added). These four purposes constitute the aims God had in mind when He gave the world the Bible.

It is no accident that Paul placed doctrine at the top of the list of God's purposes. He could not have laid a greater challenge at the feet of postmodernism, which has no patience with prepositional truth.

Christian doctrine is a screaming affront to prevailing concepts of how human beings should be educated. Until the self-indulgent ramblings of Jean-Jacques Rousseau in France, the Western world assumed that older people knew more than children and thus ought to teach the latter the accumulated wisdom of the past. It advocated that parents in particular ought to teach their children what they had learned. From the Bible's own point of view, the Scriptures constituted the heart of a genuine liberal arts education.

Rousseau changed all that, insisting that everything that a child needs to know is already within. Education merely consists of bringing out what is already there. Help a child get in touch with his own innate goodness, and he will function beautifully in society . . . or so Rousseau believed.

The results of this approach are becoming increasingly evident in the Western world. I recently heard about how a Boston College philosophy professor, while teaching a unit on ethics, gave students a homework assignment. They were to write (anonymously) of some personal struggle they had endured involving a moral dilemma. They were to tell how they had struggled with right and wrong, good and evil. Several returned to class explaining that they found the assignment an impossible one, for one simple reason: They had never done anything wrong.

They were absolutely serious. People who are inclined to worry about terrorists and tornadoes might consider instead that revealing episode, which is *really* scary.

God's Word unabashedly insists that the root problem of humanity is ignorance. People live in darkness and are alienated from the life of God "because of the ignorance that is in them" (Ephesians 4:18). Peter urged his Christian readers to live distinctively, turning aside from their former ignorance: "[Don't conform] yourselves to the former lusts, as in your ignorance" (1 Peter 1:14). God's solution to the problem is regeneration followed by instruction in divine truth—to use the Bible's own term, *doctrine*. We need to know who God is, what His ways are, and what He expects of us. Such information is not lying around in unconnected ways inside of us, merely needing to be brought out by a skillful teacher. It originates outside of us and becomes ours through exposure to God's written Word and a careful observation of His created order.

THE SECOND PURPOSE: REPROOF

The Bible also issues reproofs, which may be defined as expressions of God's negative opinion of our wayward actions. The believer is reproved when he allows God, through His Word, to sit in judgment on his behavior. Such a notion is, to say the least, countercultural.

During the final fifteen years of the twentieth century, many people followed with interest the work of the so-called "Jesus Seminar." Labeled by many reporters as "distinguished biblical scholars," these men and women met periodically to analyze the New Testament records of the life and words of Jesus. Beginning in 1985, seminar fellows met twice a year to debate technical papers that had been circulated prior to the meetings. After each debate, participants voted on the degree of authenticity that should be accorded the words of Jesus as found in the passage under consideration. They did this by dropping colored beads into a box, indicating one of four conclusions:

- "Jesus undoubtedly said this or something very like it. The historical reliability of this information is virtually certain. It is supported by a preponderance of evidence" (a red bead).

- "Jesus probably said something like this. This information is probably reliable. It fits well with other evidence that is verifiable" (a pink bead).

- "Jesus did not say this, but the ideas contained in it are close to his own. This information is possible but unreliable. It lacks supporting evidence" (a gray bead).

- "Jesus did not say this; it represents the perspective or content of a later or different tradition. This information is improbable. It does not fit verifiable evidence; it is largely or entirely fictive" (a black bead).[7]

The seminar concluded that about 90 percent of the items attributed to Jesus in the New Testament are suspect. Most lack supporting evidence, or are largely or entirely fictive (distinguished biblical scholars almost never say "fictional"). For example, the group met in Atlanta in 1988 to decide whether Jesus uttered the Lord's Prayer. The conclusion of the group was that He did not, with one exception: They gave Him credit for the word "Father."

In the grand scheme of things, the Jesus Seminar wasn't terrifically important, nor was its work in any sense original. The conclusions it reached closely resembled the positions of nineteenth-century liberal theology. Given its participants and its presuppositions, any third-year seminary student could have predicted its "findings" before they were issued.

For unbridled arrogance, however, its deliberations may never find an equal. Seminar members were literally sitting in judgment on the Word of God. They didn't assemble to learn what it meant or how to apply it. They met to criticize it and decide what percentage of it could be dismissed as a not-always-clever forgery. In this respect, the Jesus Seminar exhibited what is precisely the opposite attitude to that of a pilgrim. The pilgrim respects God's inerrant and inspired Word, and he regrets such distortions of God's truth.

"Who is going to be the authority in my life?"
is a question that every person must answer.

If the Bible is designed to reprove, then reproof must lie at the heart of what God wants done in the pilgrim's experience. "Reproof" translates a Greek word that means "to use words to call a person to account for his actions." It carries with it the suggestion of creating shame for wrong behavior. It is usually translated "convict" in John 16:8, where Jesus describes the coming ministry of the Holy Spirit: "When He has come, He will convict the world of sin, and of righteousness, and of judgment."

"Who is going to be the authority in my life?" is a question that every person must answer. The obvious answer for the pilgrim is God and His inspired Word.

The pilgrim may be a citizen of two worlds, but only one throne exists in his life. Reproof is what results when I permit God to sit on my throne—to sit in judgment on my actions today. As such, it describes a reality that is badly needed in today's world, where shame is rapidly disappearing. The Bible takes the approach that when a person is ashamed of himself he has taken a pivotal step toward healing the problem. For pilgrims, biblical reproof is how God begins to separate us from the world.

THE THIRD PURPOSE: CORRECTION

The pilgrim's road map also engages in correction, which comes from a Greek word that is related to our medical term *orthopedic*. It means the practice of setting something straight or rebuilding it on a sound foundation, much as an orthopedic surgeon sets a bone so that it grows properly.

You can see that correction and reproof are closely related. The emphasis in "reproof" is negative. The Scripture is adequate to wound, and wounding is important to setting a person onto a healthy course: "Faithful are the wounds of a friend, but the kisses of an enemy are deceitful" (Proverbs 27:6). It is the friend who wounds by sharing needed but distasteful information. It is the enemy who deceives by telling the person he is wonderful when in fact he is not. God acts as our Friend when His Word points out our faults.

The emphasis in "correction" is positive. God's Word not only wounds, but it sets us in a new direction by helping us build good patterns to replace the old ones. God's Word constantly engages in this. Virtually every negative command in Scripture is accompanied by its corresponding positive. God is interested in building people, not tearing them down. Like a builder, however, He sometimes wants the property so that He can demolish the building and start His construction project from the ground up.

THE FOURTH PURPOSE:
INSTRUCTION IN RIGHTEOUSNESS

According to 2 Timothy 3:17, the Scriptures also provide instruction in righteousness. "Instruction" translates a Greek word that suggests the education of a child, in particular providing instruction in how to behave righteously. Pilgrims need to be taught right from wrong and how to put righteous principles into action in their lives.

Today's pilgrim especially needs instruction in righteousness, since in the world's view Christians are largely defined by what they *don't* do. The average person who knows little of biblical teaching refrains from investigating spiritual things in large measure because he thinks Christianity would rob him of all of life's enjoyments.

The Bible clearly teaches that God is not a cosmic killjoy, yet that is an image many people receive from watching Christians. Let's not forget that stereotypes do develop from real people.

Instruction in righteousness properly includes the fundamental biblical idea that Christians, above all people, are to be joyous. We are to do what is right in a manner that commends what is right. We are supposed to know that the world's lasting pleasures originate with Him: "You will show me the path of life; in Your presence is fullness of joy; at Your right hand are pleasures forevermore" (Psalm 16:11). It is in God's Word that we discover these. It is in God's world that we are to exhibit them. God's road map for pilgrims instructs us in these adornments to the doctrine we profess.

THE VIRTUES OF THE ROAD MAP

Psalm 19 unfolds God's authority to speak to His creation and to give His creatures their operating instructions. This psalm's opening section describes God's message as it is seen, universally, in the skies: "The heavens declare the glory of God; and the firmament shows His handiwork" (Psalm 19:1). God has left a testimony to Himself even in the things that we see in the physical world. In verse seven, however, the psalm shifts from describing God's message in the skies to the truth He has provided in the Scriptures. The psalmist explains how God's truth "is perfect, converting the soul; . . . is sure, making wise the simple; . . . [is] right, rejoicing the heart; . . . is pure, enlightening the eyes" (Psalm 19:7–8). According to the psalm, God's road map for pilgrims yields five fundamental—and decisive—benefits.

First, it prevents destructive behavior. The Scripture keeps pilgrims from engaging in behavior that is destructive to themselves or to others. The individual parts of the Scriptures are called "the judgments of the Lord" (v. 9). Why is this? Because the Bible only produces changes in your life if you allow it to sit in judgment on your life: "The judgments of the Lord are true and righteous altogether. . . . Moreover by them Your servant is warned" (Psalm 19:9, 11). For pilgrims who subject themselves to divine scrutiny, God's commands keep preventable disasters at a distance. By the Bible's truths, the psalmist says, we are warned.

Second, a biblical road map produces a richer life. Taking Scripture as an infallible guide for the pilgrim life makes that life a richer experience. That is conveyed by the words, "In keeping them there is great reward" (Psalms 19:11). These words echo the "correction" theme in 2 Timothy 3:16. Here we discover the positive side of godly behavior. God lifts us out of our sins to live on a higher plane of life. The New Testament says that godliness is profitable for all things, having a promise of life now and in the age to come (1 Timothy 4:8).

Third, a biblical road map approves confession. The Bible also keeps us in touch with its divine author. In Psalm 19:12, David asked, "Who can understand his errors? Cleanse me from secret faults." He was praying for cleansing, but for cleansing of a specific kind: cleansing from what he called "secret faults." Some who have read this seem to think that this is a prayer that God should keep David free from the guilt of those things he does in secret. That is, the secret sins are sins which are practiced in secret.

It's much more likely that David was appealing to be cleansed from sins that were secret even to himself. That idea is supported by the first part of the verse: "Who can understand his errors?" David knew himself well. He had grasped the fundamental teaching of Scripture that every child of God has two categories of sins: those that he is aware of and those that he isn't.

Not being aware of all one's sins at the time the pilgrim is reborn is a mark of God's great mercy. If on the one hand I care about God's opinion of me, and on the other hand the Holy Spirit had made me aware, on the day of my conversion, of everything that was wrong with my character, I shudder to think what might have happened. At that moment, I would have had to make a choice between my sanity and my concern to be right with God. I could not have borne the burden of knowing how far away I was from where God wanted me to be.

The Holy Spirit reveals our sins to us at strategic points in our lives, in a sensitive way, at just the moment that is most opportune for us to deal with them. So David asked for cleansing from secret sins. The apostle John tells us, in his first letter, that as we confess the sins we know about, God goes beyond that and forgives us and cleanses us from the ones we don't know about: "If we confess our sins, He is faithful and just to forgive us our sins and to cleanse us from *all* unrighteousness" (1 John 1:9, italics added).

C. S. Lewis properly applied the place of confession when he said,

No amount of falls will really undo us if we keep on picking ourselves up each time. We shall of course be very muddy and tattered children by the time we reach home. But the bathrooms are all ready, the towels put out, and the clean clothes in the airing cupboard. The only fatal thing is to lose one's temper and give it up. It is when we notice the dirt that God is most present in us; it is the very sign of His presence.[8]

Fourth, a biblical road map points out presumptuous sins. One of the Word's greatest benefits is how it makes us aware of the seductive pitfalls of presumptuous sins. "Keep back Your servant from presumptuous sins," David prayed (Psalms 19:13). He seemed to recognize that presumptuous acts form an especially lethal category of rebellion.

Presumptuous sins [can put] the Lord to the test. . . [and] can enslave a person.

A "presumptuous sin" is one committed intentionally in full knowledge that it is wrong. God made its character clear to Israel when He said, "You shall have one law for him who sins unintentionally, for him who is native-born among the children of Israel and for the stranger who dwells among them. But the person who does anything presumptuously, whether he is native-born or a stranger, that one brings reproach on the Lord, and he shall be cut off from among his people" (Numbers 15:29–30). In other words, people who sinned knowing what they were doing were to be summarily executed.

Presumptuous sins carry two special dangers. First of all, they are, in effect, a form of putting the Lord to the test. By raising our fist to heaven, we challenge God to do something about what we have chosen to do in defiance of Him. That He ordinarily does not take our lives on the spot testifies to His grace and mercy, not to the insignificance of what we have done.

Secondly, presumptuous sins can enslave a person. That is why David linked his appeal to be protected from presumption and its natural sequel: "Keep back Your servant also from presumptuous sins; *let them not have dominion over me*" (Psalm 19:13, italics added). Presumptuous sins can place a grip of iron around us and not let us go. In time, we find that, humanly speaking, they cannot be defeated. God has to give us special assistance—the same God whom we put to the test by engaging in them to begin with.

Sometimes, looking from the outside in, it appears that God is doing nothing when a believer sins. It is never safe to assume that, however. In reality, He is usually engaging in what might be called covert discipline—discipline that is invisible to the casual observer, but is going on nonetheless. Covert discipline sometimes takes the form of shame and depression. At other times, it involves enslavement to the sort of destructive sins or habits that David was so concerned about here. He prayed, "Lord, restrain me. I know that it is in me to shake my fist in Your face and try to do as I please. Please keep me from making a blunder like that. Don't turn me over to destructive habits that would enslave me."

Proverbs 22:14 provides an enlightening example of enslavement: "The mouth of an immoral woman is a deep pit; he who is abhorred by the Lord will fall there." When a person is tempted into an immoral relationship by enticing words, often people wonder (especially if the relationship continues over time) why God does not "intervene." Sometimes the truth is that the relationship itself is an intervention. A person is "abhorred by the Lord" only at the end of a long process during which the sinner refuses to acknowledge his guilt and turn away from it. We often cannot see such transactions going on, but God sees it all. When His gentle rebukes have been spurned long enough, He may choose to allow the person who rejects them to suffer in the form of a judicially imposed slavery.

Fifth, a biblical road map provides for meaningful worship. God's Word also helps us know how to properly approach Him in worship. That is the intent of the last verse of Psalm 19: "Let the words of my mouth and the meditation of my heart be acceptable in Your sight, O Lord, my strength and my Redeemer" (Psalm 19:14). When David prayed, he aspired to offer his prayer to God in an acceptable way. He wanted God to take him seriously, and that could not happen if he approached God with unresolved acts of disobedience in his life.

The area most sensitive in this regard, of course, is the tongue: "Let the words of my mouth . . . be acceptable." Even the finest pilgrims struggle with the perversities of the tongue. Isaiah, for example, was granted a glorious vision of God at a strategic moment of his life (in Isaiah 6:1–10). Though a pious man, his first reaction upon seeing the Lord exalted in heaven was regret for a wayward mouth. He cried out, "Woe is me, for I am undone! Because I am a man of unclean lips, and I dwell in the midst of a people of unclean lips; for my eyes have seen the King, the Lord of hosts" (Isaiah 6:5).

The words of our mouths are frequently unacceptable when juxtaposed with a vision of the holiness of God. The Scriptures reveal God's holiness and thus make us want to worship Him. That is why it is so important not only to be acquainted with God's road map, but to make it a part of our inner being. Thus it was that David appealed to God, "May . . . the meditation of my heart be acceptable in Your sight, O Lord" (Psalm 19:14).

Meditation is the biblically recommended method of assimilating the Word of God. As I have written elsewhere,[9] meditation is the personalizing of the Word of God in the believer's life. David devoted the longest chapter in the Bible, Psalm 119, to a prayer expressing his zeal to know God's truth and make it his personal possession. Christians are never to be satisfied merely to read the Word, as important as that is; we are to ponder it "day and night" (Psalm 1:2). We are to delight in God's road map for our lives. It is to be our preoccupation. Pilgrims are not supposed to be obsessive people, as a rule; but if we are properly obsessive about anything, it ought to be the Scriptures. Then we will worship Him. Then we will honor and obey Him.

The Bible ought to belong to us, and we to its precepts—with all their absolutes. There and there alone will we find the direction we so clearly need in a world that specializes in misdirection and distractions; for the Scriptures speak repeatedly and attractively of the beauties of our true King.

ON THE JOURNEY

1. Review in this chapter all of the ways that Scripture should be used by the pilgrim. What are the usual ways you utilize Scripture? Which do you not practice?

2. We focus on our personal testimony or living the Christian life by example but often fail to testify to the validity of Scripture. How can you better promote God's Word to those who are ignorant or skeptical?

7

THE WORK
OF A PILGRIM

---

*In nothing has the Church so lost her hold on reality as
in her failure to understand and respect the secular vocation.
She has allowed work and religion to become separate
departments, and is astonished to find that, as a result,
the secular work of the world is turned to purely selfish
and destructive ends, and that the greater part of the world's
intelligent workers have become irreligious, or at least,
uninterested in religion. But is it astonishing?
How can anyone remain interested in a religion
which seems to have no concern
with nine-tenths of his life?*

—DOROTHY SAYERS[1]

An American businessman took time out during a venture in
Mexico to visit a small village on the seacoast. He enjoyed a
sport fishing expedition and upon his return noticed a small boat
nearing the dock. In the approaching vessel, he could see several
large yellowfin tuna along with the boat's Mexican owner. When
the successful fisherman stepped out, the American compliment-
ed him and asked how long it had taken to boat such a fine catch.

"Only a little while, señor," was the reply.

"Why don't you stay out longer and catch more fish?"

"Oh, señor, I have plenty to provide for my family and to sell
a little besides."

"But what do you do with the rest of your time?"

"Well . . . I sleep late, fish a little, play with my children, take siesta with my wife, Maria, stroll into the village each evening where I sip wine and play guitar with my amigos; I have a full and busy life, señor."

The American said, "I am a Harvard MBA and I think I can help you. You should spend more time fishing and use the proceeds of your larger catch to buy a bigger boat; then in time you could buy several boats; eventually you could have a fleet of fishing boats. Instead of selling your catch to a middleman, you could sell directly to the processor, eventually opening your own cannery. You could control the product, both in processing and distribution. You would need to leave this small coastal fishing village and move to Mexico City, then Los Angeles, and eventually to New York City where you will run your expanding enterprise."

The fisherman asked, "But señor, how long will this all take?"

"Oh, about fifteen or twenty years."

"But what then, señor?"

"That's the best part. When the time is right, you announce an initial public offering and sell your company stock to the public and become very rich. You would make millions."

"Millions, señor? Then what?"

"Then you would retire. You could move to a small coastal fishing village where you can sleep late, fish a little, maybe play with your kids, take siesta with your wife . . . you could stroll to the village in the evenings where you could sip wine and . . . uh . . . play guitar with your amigos. Well . . . it was just an idea."[2]

Many turn to their work in the hopes of finding a transcendent satisfaction. In the Western world, people spend prodigious amounts of time working, often without asking what they hope to gain by their efforts. American culture believes strongly in hard work without being entirely sure what that work is supposed to accomplish for the worker beyond a paycheck. Still, even though ultimate satisfaction may not come through our occupations, our work does possess great significance because of the dignity given to it by God.

Almost the first thing God did after creating man was to give him something useful to do. He planted a garden and gave it to Adam to till and keep (Genesis 2:15). As our wise Creator, He knew that mankind is made to work in the same way that we are made for Him. We are not truly functional as human beings until we engage in useful labor, no matter how humble it is.

Strangely, many people consider work a part of the curse in spite of the fact that God gave man work to do *before* the Fall. Work was part of a divinely made paradise. The subsequent rebellion and God's cursing of the ground may have made labor more difficult, but they did not make it part of God's sentence against rebellion. Jesus described Himself by saying, "My Father has been working until now, and I have been working" (John 5:17). Clearly, work is part of God's will for mankind.

In spite of this, large numbers of Christians do not find their work either engaging or fulfilling. I caught part of a radio interview not long ago that included the comments of a church leader concerning Christians and their performance in the workplace. He noted that in his experience, few believers are genuinely happy in what they do. Even more disturbing, he said, was the realization that Christians often perform poorly on the job and in some cases cannot be trusted to handle money or property with integrity.

"I owe, I owe, so off to work I go." That bumper-sticker philosophy can be found in the minds of believers and nonbelievers alike. Indeed, for much of the Christian workforce, "that's the best reason they can muster for going to the job each day. According to one poll, only 43 percent of American office workers are satisfied with their jobs."[3] This dissatisfaction often comes from a suspicion that what they do really isn't important in the long run.

Many recent books and articles on work have described how even people who make good salaries are unhappy in their jobs. It is not uncommon to see an executive leave to take a position with a lower salary to find stimulation in the workplace. During World War II, inmates in a German-run concentration camp were driven insane by doing meaningless work. Problems began when guards commanded inmates to move a huge pile of sand from one end of the camp to the other. The next day, they were told to move the sand back to its original position. On succeeding days, the process was repeated. After several days of this, one older man began crying uncontrollably and was taken away. Another began screaming. Then a young man who had survived three years of camp life ran away from the group and took hold of the electrified fence, killing himself.

Reviewing the prisoners' responses, Charles Colson wrote,

"The gruesome lesson is plain. Men will cling to life with dogged resolve while working meaningfully, even if that work supports their hated captors. But purposeless labor snaps the mind."[4]

A HOLY DISTINCTIVENESS
IN THE WORKPLACE

Christian workers want their labor not only to matter to themselves, but to God—and most of them don't think it does. That's a problem, because most of us are defined in significant ways by the work we do. It stands to reason that in something so central to human experience, Christian pilgrims need to express by their attitudes a holy distinctiveness in the workplace.

It is possible to do so, as demonstrated by the experience of Daniel the prophet. That remarkable man consistently exhibited pilgrim virtues in his occupation. He was forced, through no fault of his own, to live at a distance from his homeland, yet became a treasured worker in Babylon as well as a capable ambassador for God's enduring City.

Daniel's testimony began when he was a teenager and continued until he was past eighty years of age. Even though he sought no honors for himself, his excellence in the workplace brought them to him. He became a consultant to mighty kings, fearlessly speaking the truth while other royal servants cowered in fear. His influence outlived him by many centuries, being seen not only in the biblical book that bears his name, but also in historical events.

When Daniel was taken by Nebuchadnezzar into Babylon in 606 B.C., he was among a talented group of captives. The Babylonian military had raided Judah's choicest young people to find talented as well as attractive people for the king's court. The captives were to be "gifted in all wisdom, possessing knowledge and quick to understand, who had ability to serve in the king's palace, and whom they might teach the language and literature of the Chaldeans" (Daniel 1:4). Daniel's behavior once in Babylon makes it clear that he fit the description. And though his countrymen had clung to their idolatry, Daniel was different—which made all the more painful the fact that he was forcibly taken from his home and made to serve in the court of a pagan king. Instead of becoming bitter, however, he chose to exhibit the character of a pilgrim.

OUR CHARACTER AS
PILGRIM WORKERS: TACTFUL

As pilgrims, our character at work should exhibit at least four traits: We are to be tactful, loving, faithful, and respectful of authority. Those traits typified Daniel.

The first test of character for Daniel and his friends came when they were prescribed a diet that was incompatible with a believing lifestyle. The exact nature of the defiling food is not specified. Most likely, it included items that would have been placed off limits by God's law. Some have suggested that the food may have been offered to the idols of Babylon, constituting another attempt to "Babylonize" Daniel and his friends.[5]

However, even though the apostle Paul wrote centuries later, Daniel understood the principle of Colossians 3:23: "Whatever you do, do it heartily, as to the Lord and not to men." Daniel behaved "as to the Lord"; he worked and made choices as though God were at his elbow—which He was. He knew that there are no small choices in life because each one is an opportunity either to represent or repudiate the kingdom of God. Daniel determined to maintain his allegiance to the Lord even in the matter of his diet.

Nonetheless, Daniel also looked at things from the perspective of his employer and used gentleness and forbearance in his speech. At one point, the man in charge of Daniel's training expressed anxiety about his physical condition should he maintain the modest and spare diet of his homeland. Daniel was sensitive to his employer; he tactfully suggested a test.

"Please test your servants for ten days, and let them give us vegetables to eat and water to drink. Then let our appearance be examined before you, and the appearance of the young men who eat the portion of the king's delicacies; and as you see fit, so deal with your servants" (Daniel 1:12–13). The chief officer discovered that nothing would be lost by allowing Daniel his proposed diet, and as a result Daniel's tact allowed him to maintain a testimony for God.

OUR CHARACTER AS PILGRIM WORKERS: LOVING

Once past his apprenticeship in Nebuchadnezzar's court, however, Daniel encountered a severe trial of his pilgrim faith. The performance of the court magicians apparently had been subpar for some time. The king experienced a dream one night and decided to put the magicians' guild to a test. He demanded that they not only *interpret* his dream but that they *describe* the dream itself— without any hints from him.

When the magicians were unable to meet the royal demands, Nebuchadnezzar issued an edict that the entire guild be executed and their property destroyed. Since Daniel was a member of the group, he stood to lose his life through no fault of his own. He decided to appeal to the king for time so that he might ask God for the dream's description and interpretation. His prayers were answered. Significantly, Daniel then interceded for the lives of the magicians: "Daniel went to Arioch, whom the king had appointed to destroy the wise men of Babylon. He went and said thus to him: 'Do not destroy the wise men of Babylon; take me before the king, and I will tell the king the interpretation'" (Daniel 2:24).

When he lived up to his promise, Daniel not only became a famous man, he also was recognized as the savior of the people in the magicians' guild. It would have been understandable if he had resented anything Babylonian and allowed the king's pagan advisors to take what was coming to them. Instead, he acted in love toward people who themselves were the victims of spiritual deception. Pilgrim workers should always display love.

Nebuchadnezzar rewarded Daniel by reversing the decision to do away with the magicians. Instead, he made Daniel the head of the entire organization: "The king promoted Daniel and gave him many great gifts; and he made him ruler over the whole province of Babylon, and chief administrator over all the wise men of Babylon" (Daniel 2:48).

It would have been out of character for Daniel to simply let things rest at that point. As determined as he was to represent the true God in his confinement, Daniel would undoubtedly have attempted to bring a knowledge of God to the magicians. It ought not to surprise us that, given Daniel's credibility as their rescuer from death, at least some of them would have turned in faith to the God of Daniel. Many of them would have resisted, too; but it is likely that a segment of the magicians' guild would have considered themselves to be Daniel's disciples.

Have you ever wondered how the Magi from the East recognized the baby Jesus as the future King? Indeed, they came to Bethlehem to worship the infant Jesus. The story seems to leap out of a historical vacuum. How did the Magi know to associate celestial phenomena with Jesus? It is entirely plausible that the Magi were believers themselves, spiritual descendants of Daniel.

> *Those Magi who appeared in Bethlehem bearing gifts for the Christ Child could have been the spiritual descendants of Daniel. . . . living testimonials to how well Daniel allowed his pilgrim status to shine.*

This servant of God received the most important vision of his career during the years of Medo-Persian control of Babylon. The prophecy of Daniel's Seventy Weeks predicted the time of the death of Jesus Christ (Daniel 9:24–27).[6] You can imagine that the worshipers of Yahweh among the Babylonian magicians' guild would have passed that information down from one generation to the next. Since the descendants of these men would have been able to predict from Daniel's prophecy the time of Messiah's death, they could easily have approximated His birth within a decade or so. When an unusual star appeared in their night sky, they apparently took this as confirmation that their great patron's prophecy was being fulfilled, so they mounted an expedition to Judea.

Thus those Magi who appeared in Bethlehem bearing gifts for the Christ Child could have been the spiritual descendants of Daniel. More specifically, they could be considered living testimonials to how well Daniel allowed his pilgrim status to shine through while he did his work in Babylon.

This is not provable, of course. We do know, however, that Daniel distinguished himself in so many ways during his years of service to the crowns of Babylon and Medo-Persia that it is likely that his name was held in reverence for many centuries after his death. It would be surprising if the descendants of those men whose lives he saved—physically and spiritually—did not continue to revere his name for many generations. As worshipers of the true God, they, too, would have needed to learn how to live as pilgrims in Babylon.

OUR CHARACTER AS PILGRIM WORKERS: FAITHFUL

Daniel also became an example of faithfulness on the job. Everyone who has attended Sunday school is familiar with the story of Daniel and the lion's den. Far fewer, however, know why Daniel was sent there. It was because he did his job so well.

Confused? I don't blame you. Even after the Babylonians were overthrown by the Medo-Persians, Daniel's work performance was so outstanding that King Darius "gave thought to setting him over the whole realm" (Daniel 6:3). The prospect of a foreigner and a worshiper of a foreign God leading the Medo-Persian state was so repulsive to some of his colleagues that they sought to discredit him. In the process, they added an unwilling testimony to Daniel's effectiveness. One hundred twenty-two government leaders met in caucus. One hundred twenty-two people put their heads together to try to find fault with Daniel's job performance, with this result: "They could find no charge or fault, because he was faithful; nor was there any error or fault found in him" (Daniel 6:4). That is the evaluation of Daniel's *enemies*.

These jealous government officials were nothing if not creative, however. They manipulated the king into issuing a decree against his own interests and against Daniel's. Their tactics began with an appeal to the royal ego. They urged him to sign a ridiculous proclamation: "Whoever petitions any god or man for thirty days, except you, O king, shall be cast into the den of lions" (Daniel 6:7).

The officials were crafty and manipulative. They knew that the human heart is susceptible to flattery, and so concocted a form of flattery on a grand scale in their attempts to discredit Daniel. They were persuaded that Daniel would violate the edict by continuing to pray to the God of Israel, and they were not disappointed.

Sometimes I get the impression that people dismiss the impact of a man like Daniel because they think he didn't have to cope with the pressures of today; but Daniel's environment was anything but conducive to godly living.

For one thing, he worked for a pagan. Daniel 6:16 makes this clear: "So the king gave the command, and they brought Daniel and cast him into the den of lions. But the king spoke, saying to Daniel, 'Your God, whom you serve continually, He will deliver you.'" He is Daniel's God, not the god of Darius.

Daniel . . . was a man in the midst of a hostile workplace filled with crafty, manipulative, jealous people.

Daniel also worked alongside pagan officials. Daniel 6:5 explains that those coworkers recognized the difference between their worldview and Daniel's own: "Then these men said, 'We shall not find any charge against this Daniel unless we find it against him concerning the law of his God.'"

His colleagues' paganism sometimes produced dishonesty. For example, they reported to the king, "All the governors of the kingdom, the administrators and satraps, the counselors and advisors, have consulted together to establish [this] royal statute" (Daniel 6:7). Their report was blatantly untrue; Daniel certainly did not participate in the consultation. His coworkers also lied later when the outcome of their chicanery became evident: "They answered and said before the king, 'That Daniel, who is one of the captives from Judah, does not show due regard for you, O king, or for the decree that you have signed, but makes his petition three times a day'" (Daniel 6:13). That wasn't true, either. Daniel was not praying to show disregard for the king, but to show regard for a higher King.

So when we look at Daniel's work environment, we need to be realistic. He was not working in an ideal setting for godly behavior. He was a man in the midst of a hostile workplace filled with crafty, manipulative, jealous people. Sound familiar?

In the face of the fateful decree, Daniel continued to pray toward Jerusalem three times daily, just as he had always done. It ought not to be passed over too quickly that this remarkable man, who served in a pagan environment for seventy years, decided that *time spent with God was more important than life itself.* I wonder how many Christian employees would be willing to say that today. Having a pagan government pass a law that turned a devotional time into a capital offense was not about to deflect Daniel from meeting with God.

Ultimately, it was just such integrity that set Daniel apart. He was the same man in private that he was in public. His relationship with God was the core of his life, both public and private—that is what made him such a great worker. Even pagans long to have people of integrity working for them. His rescue from the den of lions and his accusers' fate merely added more luster to the record of this man, who became an example of living the pilgrim way on the job.

His value as an employee is openly stated in the biblical text: "The king, when he heard these words, was greatly displeased with himself [he realized that he had been a dope], and set his heart on Daniel to deliver him; and he labored till the going down of the sun to deliver him" (Daniel 6:14). He considered what losing Daniel might mean to him and his administration, and his thoughts were unhappy ones: "Now the king went to his palace and spent the night fasting; and no musicians were brought before him. Also his sleep went from him" (Daniel 6:18).

This was very unroyal behavior. Remember, the king was an Oriental potentate. Pleasure was his life. Why was the king so distressed that Daniel was in danger? Because he was the most valuable employee he had.

OUR CHARACTER AS PILGRIM WORKERS: RESPECTFUL OF AUTHORITY

Daniel demonstrated a pilgrim attitude by being respectful. When the morning came and the king inquired about his safety, "Daniel said to the king, 'O king, live forever! My God sent His angel and shut the lions' mouths, so that they have not hurt me, because I was found innocent before Him; and also, O king, I have done no wrong before you'" (Daniel 6:21–22). Even though the king was an unbeliever, Daniel didn't speak down to him. He greeted him with the standard greeting of royalty. He treated him with honor and respect, even though he was an idol worshiper, because Daniel knew something critical—in the workplace, the truth of God gets only the hearing that the child of God can win for it.

Daniel practiced the pilgrim principle articulated in Ephesians 6:5, "Bondservants, be obedient to those who are your masters according to the flesh, with fear and trembling." So should we. Paul's phrase "fear and trembling" doesn't mean that we should tremble because we are afraid we might be fired. He means that we should be afraid to show disrespect to our employer, because that would reflect on our heavenly Boss, who asks us to be willing servants.

Paul said that we should serve "in sincerity of heart" (Ephesians 6:5). That means that you shouldn't take an employer's money and then criticize him behind his back or speak ill of his business. If you can't speak respectfully of him, get another job.

When my children entered the workforce for the first time, I took each of them aside and tried to convey the importance of faithfulness at work. "All you have to do," I explained, "to be an outstanding employee on your job is to do what you say you will do. Show up when you are supposed to. Do your job without complaining. Try to be helpful and cooperative. Your boss will sing your praises." All three found the advice to be true. It has never been easier to maintain a pilgrim testimony in the workplace. All you have to do is be a person of character—a character built, as Daniel's was, on time spent with God.

Daniel taught by example what the New Testament makes explicit. The apostle Paul set forth four principles in Ephesians 6:5–8 that deserve to be shouted from the rooftops. The workplace is the largest arena in existence to express a pilgrim distinctiveness. Here are four marketplace values that will make you a valued employee and an effective pilgrim.

MARKET VALUE #1: WORK AS CALLING

First, view your job as your calling. Paul's expression of this principle is illuminating: "Bondservants, be obedient to those who are your masters according to the flesh, with fear and trembling, in sincerity of heart, as to Christ; not with eyeservice, as menpleasers, but as bondservants of Christ, doing the will of God from the heart" (Ephesians 6:5–6). Every pilgrim has two bosses: his employer and his Creator.

This exhortation was not written to modern industrial employees working a forty-hour week. It was written to slaves, and that makes the underlying truth all the more applicable to those of us who can choose our occupation. If the slaves of Ephesus could view their work as a calling, so can we.

Some of the people Paul addressed were born slaves; others were captured in the many military actions on the fringes of the empire. Slaves made the wheels of the Roman Empire go around. One writer explained: "Rome was the mistress of the world, and therefore it was beneath the dignity of a Roman citizen to work. Practically all work was done by slaves. Even doctors and teachers, even the closest [associates] of the Emperors, their secretaries who dealt with letters and appeals and finance, were slaves."[7]

Legally, the slave was not a person but a thing. Aristotle called a slave a "living tool." He said that a freeman would no more think of having a slave for a friend than he would think of having a hammer for a friend. The law made it clear that a master had the absolute power of life and death over a slave. Caesar Augustus had a slave crucified because he killed a pet quail. Slaves who had grown old and were no longer capable of work were commonly expelled from the household to starve, or sent to the arena to serve as lion's food and entertainment for the public.

Obey your master as you would if Jesus Christ Himself were giving you orders, Paul wrote. Pilgrim theology insists that even the cruelest and most unreasonable owner (or boss) is not a free agent. Pilgrims are to live under the conviction that people with authority over them move only inside fences constructed by heaven: "The king's heart is in the hand of the Lord, like the rivers of water; He turns it wherever He wishes" (Proverbs 21:1). The Nebuchadnezzars and Dariuses of the world, though appearing to be independent agents, draw each breath as the gift of a God whose existence they may deny.

Christian pilgrims express confidence in the unseen God of heaven by approaching their work as His calling. Many churches (mine included) display missionary maps complete with pins and pictures detailing where their missionaries serve. Without taking anything away from those worthy servants of God, His missionaries include not only the "vocationally Christian" but also every believer across the board. That's a foreign concept to us, because most people have an odd and unscriptural view of the will of God. We think of it like a target with a bull's-eye. Preachers, evangelists, and missionaries are in the center. The Christian businessman is one or two circles off. His primary responsibility is to work hard and support the people who do the work of God. Others are still farther out.

From God's perspective, it is just as sacred to change a tire as it is to preach a sermon.

But this characterization is based on a faulty division between the sacred and the secular. The theological name for this false division is Docetism—the view that God only cares for spiritual things. According to the Docetists, the material world itself is unimportant and illusory. God only likes that part of His creation that is involved in overtly religious service. (Docetism held, as a result, that the crucifixion and the resurrection of Christ were mere illusions, since only what is spiritual is important.)

But from God's perspective, it is just as sacred to change a tire as it is to preach a sermon. It is just as holy to work hard at school as it is to be a missionary. The refutation of Docetism is found in the New Testament teaching on the human body. In 1 Corinthians 15, the apostle Paul insisted that there is just as much hope for the believer's body as there is for his spirit. God made man as a combination of body and spirit, for both realms issue from God.

Harry Ironside was for years the pastor of Moody Memorial Church in Chicago. He wrote dozens of books, including commentaries on most of Scripture, and had a ministry of great significance. He was, among other things, one of the hardest-working men in the ministry. He seemed to have a boundless energy when it came to the work God had given him. Part of his zeal derived from an episode that took place when he was a teenager. In an effort to assist his widowed mother, he worked during nonschool hours for a Scottish shoemaker named Dan MacKay.

Dan was a devout Christian believer, who delighted in sharing his faith in a winsome way, and who sought to validate his message by the way he did business. It was not unusual for people to return to the shop after having repairs made—not to do business but instead to discuss the tracts that the cobbler would routinely distribute with his wares. To many a person, that shoe repair shop became their entry point into the family of God.

Harry's work in the shop was both mundane and monotonous. His responsibility was to pound out pieces of leather to be used in shoe soles. Taking a piece of cowhide cut to size and soaked in water, he would spend hours pounding the soles until they were hard and dry. The work was hard, but it was the tedium that put Harry to the test, especially since he knew that only a block down the street another shopkeeper, one of Dan MacKay's competitors, had eliminated the monotonous pounding. The owner, a coarse man who often proved a bad influence on neighborhood youngsters, seemed to thrive in spite of his godlessness. Harry noticed that the unscrupulous competitor took shoe soles directly from the water and nailed them on in their dampened condition:

> One day I ventured inside, something I had been warned never to do. Timidly, I said, "I notice you put the soles on while still wet. Are they just as good as if they were pounded?" He gave me a wicked leer as he answered, "They come back all the quicker this way, my boy!"
>
> Feeling I had learned something, I related the instance to my boss and suggested that I was perhaps wasting time in drying out the leather so carefully. Mr. MacKay stopped his work and opened his Bible to the passage that reads, "Whatsoever ye do, do all to the glory of God."
>
> "Harry," he said, "I do not cobble shoes just for the [money] I get from my customers. I am doing this for the glory of God. I expect to see every shoe I have ever repaired in a big pile at the judgment seat of Christ, and I do not want the Lord to say to me in that day, 'Dan, this was a poor job. You did not do your best here.' I want Him to be able to say, 'Well done, good and faithful servant.'"
>
> Then he went on to explain that just as some men are called to preach, so he was called to fix shoes, and that only as he did this well would his testimony count for God. It was a lesson I have never been able to forget. Often when I have been tempted to carelessness, and to slipshod effort, I have thought of dear, devoted Dan MacKay, and it has stirred me up to seek to do all as for Him who died to redeem me.[8]

VALUE #2: OFFERING WORK TO CHRIST

Second, offer your job to Christ. If you are a pilgrim, what you do on the job ought to be done as service to Jesus Christ Himself. Paul insisted that believers work "not with eyeservice, as men-pleasers, but as bondservants of Christ, doing the will of God from the heart" (Ephesians 6:6). As far as God is concerned, all of life is under His command. Some of us have the suspicion that in a perfect world, a world in which everybody was in a state of per-petual obedience to God, that all of humanity would be preach-ers. (That's a scary thought.) We know from Scripture, however, that when God set up His own state in ancient Israel, only about one-twelfth of the people attended to the sanctuary. The rest of the nation was engaged in all the so-called secular pursuits.

"Eyeservice" (Ephesians 6:6) is a term apparently coined by Paul. It appears only in the New Testament at this point in the development of Greek literature. Eyeservice is service rendered be-fore the eyes of the master. It is exhibited when the student does what is necessary to get the grade, but doesn't care about the qual-ity of the work. It appears when the contract is met, but there is no pride in the product.

At the carpenter shop of Joseph and Son in Nazareth, you can be sure that there was plenty of religious activity. But you can also be sure that they produced good furniture. If you are a carpenter, do all the things that Christian pilgrims are supposed to do, but (literally) for heaven's sake, produce good merchandise. If you are a salesman, go to church regularly, but put your faith to work by turning in truthful reports. If you are a contractor, do all the "spiritual" things that believers are supposed to do, and provide the service you agreed to provide in a quality manner.

When Paul commanded, "Whatever you do, do it heartily, as to the Lord and not to men" (Colossians 3:23), his "whatever" was instructive. It is not the form of labor that matters; it is the at-titude the pilgrim brings to the work. Martin Luther showed that he understood this when he wrote, "The maid who sweeps her kitchen is doing the will of God just as much as the monk who prays—not because she may sing a Christian hymn as she sweeps but because God loves clean floors. The Christian shoemaker does his Christian duty not by putting little crosses on the shoes, but by making good shoes, because God is interested in good crafts-manship."[9]

Some think that the only reason God wants us to do well on the job is so that we will be able to evangelize the non-Christian world. That is emphatically not true. In fact, to share your faith on the job—if it detracts from your performance or the performance of others—may be in itself unethical and unchristian. It is far better to share the faith at some time when work performance is not in jeopardy. Doing our jobs as to the Lord is virtuous and valuable in its own right. Think about the people Daniel influenced—and still is influencing centuries later.

VALUE #3: BEING RESPECTFUL AND EAGER

Third, serve respectfully and eagerly. The two are related. We discussed being respectful of authority as the final character quality of the pilgrim worker. Paul explained that as bondservants of Christ, we are to "be obedient to those who are your masters according to the flesh" (Ephesians 6:5). We serve an employer respectfully.

As we work respectfully, we also work eagerly. The boss who has a Christian employee should not need to motivate him to produce. The apostle explained that we are to do "the will of God from the heart, with goodwill doing service" (vv. 6–7). This means serving with gladness and eagerness, primarily because our service is to be "to the Lord, and not to men [alone]" (v. 7).

"Exhort servants to be obedient to their own masters, to be well pleasing in all things, not answering back, not pilfering," wrote Paul. Instead, God's servants should exhibit "all good fidelity, that they may adorn the doctrine of God our Savior in all things" (Titus 2:9–10). The words "not pilfering" ought to make employers pay attention. Each year employees steal away forty billion dollars in cash and goods in the United States, according to the U.S. Chamber of Commerce. That is more than the gross national product of many of the countries of the world. Why is right behavior at work to be a concern? Why serve eagerly? Because such conduct "adorn[s] the doctrine of God our Savior." It sets forth Christian teaching in an attractive fashion.

VALUE #4: REMEMBERING THE REWARD

Fourth, remember the reward, even when present loss comes. The biblical theology of work does not require forgetting oneself totally, for God always builds rewards into human experience. What you will receive back—both now and in eternity—for your work will come from Christ: "knowing that whatever good anyone does, he will receive the same from the Lord, whether he is a slave or free" (Ephesians 6:8).

Really living these principles, however, might put your job in jeopardy in certain cases. Not long ago, I heard the report of how a businessman in Dallas was told to hire a secretary for his supervisor. "Be sure and make her understand," the boss explained, "that there is some traveling required on the weekends. I like to take my secretary with me to be my roommate when I go out of town."

The Christian businessman balked, saying, "I can't do that."

The boss said, "You will do that, or you are going to be fired."

When a friend asked the Christian employee if he couldn't appeal this demand over his boss's head, the believer replied that his boss's supervisor was doing the same thing. He determined not to participate in his boss's travel practices—and lost his job.

In the Roman world, Christians were attacked on many fronts. They were called atheists because they did not worship the Roman state gods. They were called disloyal because they didn't offer sacrifice to the god-emperor. They were called immoral because they met around the Lord's table, which they called "love-feasts." Because of these attacks, there arose a group of people in the early second century who came to be called "apologists"[10] because of their defense of Christianity. These writers used an unanswerable defense—one which overpowered the ancient world and gave the Christian faith wonderful credibility.

They did not say, "Come to church and hear our preachers. They are wonderful speakers, and they will explain it all to you." They did not say, "Read our doctrinal statements. They are the brilliant products of great scholarship."

They did say, "Look at the lives of the Christians around you. They are your best workers. They are the really capable and conscientious people in this empire. Where would you be without them?"

That is the kind of authenticity that the alien is supposed to have. Believers are supposed to make their behavior on the job an adornment, a decoration of the doctrine of Jesus Christ. At the same time, a pilgrim attitude recognizes that ultimate satisfaction is not to be found in professional accomplishments. The pilgrim works with an eye on eternity.

ON THE JOURNEY

1. Review Paul's definition of "eyeservice" and ask yourself about your motives. Do you perform mainly for external approval or internal quality of the work you do?

2. All of us need rewards or we lose motivation. What are the heavenly rewards in Scripture that will keep you doing things God's way, even if earthly rewards are not forthcoming?

8

THE POLITICS
OF A PILGRIM

Psalm 146 warns, "Put not your trust in princes."
Even when they are your princes and you think you
put them on their little thrones. Especially when they
are your princes, because that is when the temptation
arises to invest your soul and your highest allegiance
in their rule. No politics can liberate us from the limits
of a fallen creation. We can probe and press at the limits,
but the politics for which we were made . . .
the politics of the Sermon on the Mount, will,
short of the Kingdom, always elude us.

—RICHARD JOHN NEUHAUS[1]

*P*erhaps the believers in Rome scratched their heads in wonder upon reading Paul's assertion that government is "God's minister to you [Christians] for [your] good" (Romans 13:4). To them, the pagan rulers and governments didn't always seem to be God's instruments toward Christian pilgrims. Even today, such governments' leaders often lead the parade when it comes to persecuting believers and encroaching on their liberties.

The apostle Paul, however, was not writing as an armchair theorist, still less from the protection of a distant democracy. He, too, was subject to Roman authority, and at the time he wrote his epistle, the ivory throne of the empire was occupied by one Nero Caesar, a man whose character hardly commended the submission of his citizens. Nero attained his office at the age of seventeen by trickery and the connivance of his mother, whose death he ordered after gaining the emperor's crown. The emperor entertained himself during the early years of his rule by going into the streets of Rome at night, finding young like-minded friends, and committing muggings and burglaries with them.

As emperor, he had several longtime friends and capable counselors executed because of his wrath, and he killed his second wife by kicking her in the stomach when she was in an advanced state of pregnancy. After the burning of Rome (probably started when some of his imperial slaves lost control of a small fire), he decided to placate the populace—suspicious of their emperor because of past monstrosities—by blaming the deed on Rome's Christians.

According to the Roman historian Tacitus, at that point Nero arrested believers in large numbers and put them to death for the amusement of the locals. Some he crucified; others he had torn to pieces in the arena by wild dogs. He even had many covered with pitch and set ablaze in the imperial gardens. In the midst of his fun, he declared Christianity to be an illicit religion, removing the recourse of law from believers. As a result, if the children of Christians were killed or their wives were assaulted, they could not appeal to the authorities for redress.

This was clearly a horrendous time for Christians in Rome— and it began shortly after Paul's letter. Still, Paul would not have altered his counsel to the Roman believers, since it was based on eternal principles. The apostle urged upon the Roman Christians (and through them upon us) submission to governmental authority as a fundamental of pilgrim living. Submission is not approval, of course. Paul knew as well as anyone the potential that lay in the abuse of power, but he also knew that the king's heart is like channels of water in God's hands (Proverbs 21:1). God may turn those channels in what appear to be strange directions, but the apparent strangeness is a product of our limitations, not His.

Throughout history, most of the spread of the Christian faith has taken place not with the support of governments, but in spite of their opposition. No greater example exists than what has happened in the last half century in China. When the communists rose to power in 1949, they ordered all Christian missionaries expelled. The Chinese church was tiny—about 700,000 believers—and apparently powerless, and the expectation of learned minds in the West was that it would be expunged by the inevitable persecutions to come.

The church in China contains upwards of 70 million adherents . . . [even though] they are subject to severe persecution, including imprisonment and torture.

Instead, the Chinese church has undergone one of the greatest expansions in the history of the Christian faith. Today, the church in China contains upwards of 70 million adherents, making it a nation with one of the world's largest Christian populations; and few of those resemble the casual Christians of the Western world. They can't afford to be uncommitted, since they are subject to severe persecution, including imprisonment and torture.

During the cultural revolution in China in the late '60s and early '70s, historians record that about 30 million people were killed who were regarded by Mao Tse-tung as enemies of the state. Among these were tens of thousands of Christians, with pastors among the early targets. Author and Chinese authority Carl Lawrence noted how one pastor was beaten and tortured in an effort to get him to renounce his faith in Christ. Nothing worked. Finally, the communist officials brought a coffin and made him lie in it. They told him, "We want you to make a final decision. Either deny Jesus Christ, or we will bury you alive."

His reply: "I will never deny my Lord." They nailed the lid on his coffin. They waited to see if he would cry out. There was no sound. They buried him.[2]

A SHORT COURSE ON CHRISTIAN/GOVERNMENT ALLIANCES

Since the state has often shown cruelty and hatred to believers, perhaps it is not surprising that Christians periodically long to occupy ruling positions themselves. We have had our chances, beginning with Constantine. The military leader supposedly saw a vision of a cross in the sky with the words "By this sign conquer!" and from that decided to become a Christian. He went on to victory at the battle of the Milvian Bridge in A.D. 312, became the new emperor, and issued the Edict of Milan, making Christianity the official religion of Rome.

The edict changed everything. One day believers were at best tolerated and at worst slaughtered. The next day it was illegal *not* to be a Christian. That is when troubles of a different sort began to emerge. Romans were about to find out that Christians in power could be a mixed bag. Christians, in turn, were about to discover the validity of Cal Thomas's observation: "The kingdom of this world, which regularly demands compromise, cannot be reconciled to a kingdom not of this world that allows for no compromise."3

Unfortunately, compromises were plentiful in those years when the church tried to carve out a hybrid existence as the leader of both the political and religious realms. Among other things, the state insisted in mediating theological and ecclesiastical disputes.

Only a few years after the edict, the city of Milan became the scene for the first great church-state confrontation. It seems that a certain charioteer in Thessalonica was accused of homosexual practices and arrested by the governor. The citizens of Milan were great fans of the charioteer, who was scheduled to participate in an important upcoming race. When racing fans heard of the arrest, they rioted and demanded their hero's release. The governor refused, whereupon the populace marched on the palace, murdered the governor, and freed their idol. The Milanese took their chariot racing seriously.

As it happened, the Roman Emperor Theodosius was in Milan at the time. The emperor took exception to the city's treatment of a duly appointed imperial magistrate and decided that Milan's people needed to be taught a lesson. As the next chariot race was in progress, Theodosius ordered his soldiers to shut the gates of the hippodrome. He then sent in troops with orders to slaughter those inside. After three bloody hours of violence, some seven thousand people had perished at the emperor's command.

Ambrose, the bishop of Milan, publicly challenged the emperor's harshness, demanding that he submit to public humiliation. He then gave instructions that the emperor be excluded from communion until he had undergone Ambrose's prescribed punishment. The emperor yielded, setting the precedent for many centuries that civic rulers would be subject to punishment by ecclesiastical leaders.[4]

Pope Gregory VII declared that the emperor was excommunicated. . . . Henry [IV] crossed the Alps in midwinter to . . . ask for forgiveness and restoration.

Ecclesiastical dominance reached its acme in the eleventh century. At the time, Henry IV, the Holy Roman Emperor, was the most powerful ruler on earth. The sovereign of most of Europe, he possessed enormous wealth and great military power. However, Henry made the mistake of challenging the pope over an ecclesiastical issue. As a result, Pope Gregory VII declared that the emperor was excommunicated—which was, in the pope's view, the equivalent of consigning him to hell—and that as a result of his misbehavior, all of his subjects were henceforward released from all obligations to him. They would owe him neither obedience nor taxes.

The resolution of the dispute took place a year later, when Henry crossed the Alps in midwinter to seek out the pope in his castle at Canossa to ask for forgiveness and restoration. He knocked on the door and was told to wait. According to some accounts, he tarried outside the papal castle barefoot in the snow for three days while waiting for an audience. The pope eventually acceded to his request and rescinded the order of excommunication, but the whole episode had the effect of increasing the political power of the church and of humiliating political rulers.

Unfortunately, the church's possession of political power didn't do the cause of Christ or the world the good one might have hoped. In fact, the period of time when the church held its greatest measure of political power is known as the Dark Ages. Western culture has been struggling ever since to define the relationship between the two kingdoms.

POLITICAL OPTIONS

A great deal of ink has been spilt in the past few generations in attempts to declare exactly how Christian believers are supposed to relate to the political process. Nothing I will say in this chapter is likely to settle the issue. It is precisely because citizens belong to an unseen kingdom that the tension exists. When it comes to determining the degree of believers' involvement in the government of the country in which they live, however, Christians generally fall into one of four camps. These correspond to the four options that Richard Niebuhr outlined in his book *Christ and Culture*.[5]

First, some Christians choose politics over Christ. Regarding politics as a higher calling than that of Christ, the politics-over-Christ approach generally constitutes the outlook of liberal theology. According to this viewpoint, Christianity must always adapt to the pressures of modern culture. For many years, the National Council of Churches expressed this perspective as their motto: "The world sets the agenda for the church."

Few evangelicals are comfortable with this option. It jettisons the Word of God at the point where believing pilgrims need its wisdom the most.

Second, others choose Christ against politics. This camp opts for a withdrawal from politics entirely. Such a retreat mentality solves certain kinds of problems for believers, but causes others. Its most serious difficulty comes because it voices no competition for the hearts and minds of people who are victims of the world system. Those who would hold this viewpoint would discourage Christians from running for office, for example, on the grounds that politics, as part of a decaying world system, is intrinsically evil and therefore to be shunned.

It also vanishes from the fray when difficult questions arise, as inevitably they must. For example: Should public schools be required to teach evolution only as an option with regard to origins? If so, should creationism be taught as the other option? If so, who will teach it? I, for one, have misgivings about children being instructed in creationism by teachers who consider it a position beneath contempt. Better not to have heard it at all than to

THE POLITICS OF A PILGRIM

hear it from the lips of those who—even through nonverbal com-
munication—do not present it fairly. Such questions are left for
others to settle in the Christ-against-politics camp.

Third, still others choose Christ over politics. They advocate
the domination of politics by Christians. This has actually been
tried, and not just in the Middle Ages by the Roman Catholic
Church. John Calvin, for example, attempted to create a Protestant Christian state in Geneva in the mid-sixteenth century. His
city government proved to be rather intrusive—and downright
lethal. Between 1541 and 1546, at least 134 people were either
executed or exiled for various breaches of Christian doctrine or
conduct. The Genevans did not take unmixed delight in their government.

The city's unhappy experience confirms the wisdom of Martin Luther's observation. He warned, "It is out of the question that
there should be a Christian government even over one land . . .
since the wicked always outnumber the good. Hence a man who
would venture to govern . . . with the gospel would be like a shepherd who should place in one fold wolves, lions, eagles and sheep
together and let them freely mingle."[6]

Nonetheless, a small but able number of people advocate res-
urrecting the effort. Dominion Theology or Christian Reconstructionism, as it is sometimes called, insists, "Every jot and tittle
of the Law of Moses, with the exception of the ceremonial code,
is binding upon mankind today."[7] Reconstructionism thus includes the belief that Old Testament civil laws were intended to be
a blueprint not just for ancient Israel but for all countries at all
times. Reconstructionists, or theonomists (advocates are comfortable with either label), insist that we must prepare the earth to
be a fit place for the return of Christ and advocate the peaceful
overthrow of democracy as a system of government. Dominion
theology says that Christians not only should make it a primary
motive to *influence* the government, but that they must eventually *be* the government. Reconstructionism's father, Rousas Rushdoony, asserted that "the saints must prepare to take over the
world's government and its courts."[8] This change will not be ef-
fected in one generation or two, proponents say; when it happens,
it will happen because society in general has become convinced
of its wisdom.

Reconstructionism takes Calvin further and advocates, among

other things, a return of the institution of slavery and the execution of incorrigible children, homosexuals, adulterers, Sabbath breakers, astrologers, and false teachers. Some in the Christ-over-politics camp have suggested the forming of a separate political party that would be exclusively Christian. At first blush, that might seem plausible, but many have foreseen the limitations. The Christian apologist and scholar C. S. Lewis noted:

> [Such a party] will have no authority to speak for Christianity; it will have no more power than the political skill of its members gives it. . . . But there will be a real, and most disastrous novelty. It will be not simply a *part* of Christendom, but *a part claiming to be the whole.* By the mere act of calling itself the Christian Party it implicitly accuses all Christians who do not join it of apostasy and public betrayal. It will be exposed, in an aggravated degree, to . . . the temptation of claiming for our favorite opinions that kind and degree of certainty and authority which really belongs only to our Faith.[9] (Italics in the original.)

At least it is safe to say that implementing the Christ-over-politics approach is a minefield that most Christians are reluctant to probe.

Fourth, there are those who choose Christ and politics in paradox. They advocate exercising the options that the culture gives us to influence our world politically while still maintaining a primary loyalty to our heavenly citizenship. According to Gene Edward Veith, this perspective recognizes the validity of both earthly and heavenly kingdoms under God: "The church is the company of those called by the gospel for eternal life, ruled by his Word. Just as God rules his natural creation by the laws of nature, he rules human cultures by his power, his providence, and the moral law that he wrote upon the hearts even of Gentiles. God works through human institutions—families, governments, laws, economic structures—even of unbelievers."

Christian pilgrims function in both realms, and respect the rules of both, Veith argued. "A prisoner converting to Christianity is forgiven and becomes a citizen of God's eternal Kingdom, but must still pay the penalty for his—or her—crimes against the earthly kingdom."[10]

Of the four options, the last seems to struggle with the fewest problems from the biblical and practical point of view. Implementing the view—and holding to it consistently—is where the complications and disagreements come. The apostle Paul placed the paradox of the Christian pilgrim in bold relief when he wrote the Philippians, "Our citizenship is in heaven, from which we also eagerly wait for the Savior, the Lord Jesus Christ" (Philippians 3:20). The alien mentality meant earthly politics were secondary to the heavenly cause.

Paul's statement here is especially significant in historical context. Of all the churches he dealt with, the Philippian church was Paul's favorite. Among other things, it was about the only church he served that didn't require some sort of rescue or rebuke. The church was healthy, though not large, and Paul regarded them highly.

> *The Philippians felt great pride in being Romans. . .[but] the Philippian believers had only one true claim to importance. . . . their heavenly citizenship.*

Philippi had been founded by and named for Philip of Macedon, father of Alexander the Great. Philip established the city because of its military usefulness—it commanded the only road in the region which linked Europe to Asia. The highway had already proven important when one of the great battles of history was fought near it—when Marc Antony and Octavian defeated Brutus and Cassius, and in the process determined that Rome thereafter would be an empire instead of a republic.

Philippi was a Roman colony, governed by Roman laws and completely subject to Roman rule. It was a "little Rome" in the midst of Greek culture. Such colonies were initially populated by veteran soldiers who had finished their enlistments and who had, as a result, been granted Roman citizenship. By salting the empire with such colonies, Rome always had veteran troops available in case trouble broke out in the region. As a colony, the Philippians felt great pride in being Romans. That pride is almost palpable in the accusation made against Paul and Silas in Philippi: "These men, being Jews, exceedingly trouble our city;

and they teach customs which are not lawful for us, being Romans, to receive or observe" (Acts 16:20–21).

Notice, however, that the apostle Paul noted that the Philippian believers had only one true claim to importance. Their worth was found in their heavenly citizenship: "Our citizenship is in heaven, from which we also eagerly wait for the Savior, the Lord Jesus Christ" (Philippians 3:20). The believers of Philippi now formed an outpost of the kingdom of God. Like those who originated their hometown on behalf of Rome, they were to become a center for bringing their true homeland's values into their pagan society.

Paul's words included a reminder that today pilgrims are to "eagerly wait for the Savior, the Lord Jesus Christ." In my experience, Western pilgrims don't wait particularly well. As the anticipation of the Second Coming has receded in modern thought until it is more a curiosity than a hope, we have become correspondingly concerned about what politics can bring us today. We are attracted by the trappings and potential of political power.

WEAPONRY FOR A GREATER CAUSE

Yet Christian pilgrims possess far greater weapons than politics to gain heavenly objectives. Paul explained to the Corinthian Christians, "For though we walk in the flesh, we do not war according to the flesh. For the weapons of our warfare are not [fleshly] but mighty in God for pulling down strongholds" (2 Corinthians 10:3–4). The strongholds in question are those satanic spiritual realities that undermine the purposes of the kingdom of God. When Satan showed Jesus all the kingdoms of the earth, he said, "All this authority I will give You, and their glory; for this has been delivered to me, and I give it to whomever I wish. Therefore, if You will worship before me, all will be Yours" (Luke 4:6–7).

Today, Satan possesses control of the governments of the earth. The battle is primarily spiritual, not political, and the solution is largely spiritual. How can Christians expect to engage in battle in the spiritual realm by using less than spiritual weapons?

A caution here: Paul's description of his tools that were "mighty in God for pulling down strongholds" does not form an argument for Christian pilgrims abstaining from political involvement. Far from it. His words do, however, suggest that believers must recognize that their political efforts can only take them so far unless they are wielded alongside the spiritual weapons that are the true tools of His kingdom.

And what are those tools? Paul gave a beautiful summary of them earlier in the same letter:

> We give no offense in anything, that our ministry may not be blamed. But in all things we commend ourselves as ministers of God: in much patience, in tribulations, in needs, in distresses, in stripes, in imprisonments, in tumults, in labors, in sleeplessness, in fastings; by purity, by knowledge, by longsuffering, by kindness, by the Holy Spirit, by sincere love, by the word of truth, by the power of God, by the armor of righteousness on the right hand and on the left, by honor and dishonor, by evil report and good report; as deceivers, and yet true; as unknown, and yet well known; as dying, and behold we live; as chastened, and yet not killed; as sorrowful, yet always rejoicing; as poor, yet making many rich; as having nothing, and yet possessing all things. (2 Corinthians 6:3–10)

Patience and tribulations rank low on the pecking order of getting things done in the minds of many Christians. Sleeplessness and fastings don't make it onto many priority lists, either. Yet they were foundational to Paul's ministry—and they ought to be to ours. The reason for God's honoring such unobtrusive and despised methods is not hard to discern. He does not place His pilgrims in the world to affirm and extol human brilliance. We are here for His glory, not our own. Apart from Him, we can do nothing. God delights in getting things done through people who are impressed with Him rather than with their own abilities.

ACTION POINT ONE:
USE THOSE FREEDOMS WE HAVE

So what can pilgrims do to influence governments for the good? Let me suggest three action points.

The first is to use the freedoms we now possess. For centuries, Christians had few rights they could use. We have some now. It is true that governments in the democracies are encroaching on Christian freedoms, yet many go unused.

Interestingly, the apostle Paul, Roman citizen that he was, showed how Christian pilgrims should not hesitate in using political options that are available to them. When he was flogged without trial, a violation of Roman law, he held the magistrates of Philippi accountable. When the city leaders tried to send Paul away quietly the next day, he refused to go, explaining: "They have beaten us openly, uncondemned Romans, and have thrown us into prison. And now do they put us out secretly? No indeed! Let them come themselves and get us out." The officers then relayed those words to the magistrates, who were surprised and afraid upon hearing that the prisoners were Romans. Then the magistrates "came and pleaded with them and brought them out, and asked them to depart from the city" (Acts 16:37, 39). Paul was leaving a fledgling church behind him in Philippi, and undoubtedly acted as much for their sake as for his own.

Two out of three evangelicals didn't vote during the American elections of November 1998.

Later, when the apostle discerned a plot that threatened his life, he chose to exercise a right available to every Roman citizen. He explained to the Roman procurator Festus:

> "If I am an offender, or have committed anything deserving of death, I do not object to dying; but if there is nothing in these things of which these men accuse me, no one can deliver me to them. I appeal to Caesar." Then Festus, when he had conferred with the council, answered, "You have appealed to Caesar? To Caesar you shall go!" (Acts 25:11–12)

Again, many Christian pilgrims today don't use the political and social rights they have. For one thing, we can vote—yet two out of three evangelicals didn't vote during the American elections of November 1998.

Voting means more than merely placing in office candidates who will be sympathetic with Christian political concerns. It means providing a voice for the defenseless in the public square. It means refusing to hide God's light by withdrawing.

Voluntarily forfeiting our right to vote seems especially foolish in light of how other rights of Christians are being eroded at an alarming pace. For example, the American judiciary appears determined to silence Christian expression in the public square. In 1995, Judge Samuel Kent of the U.S. District Court for the southern district of Texas heard the case of whether a short prayer could be spoken at an upcoming high school graduation in his jurisdiction. A student was going to lead in an invocation, and that made some parents and students nervous. What if that student said— horror of horrors—"In Jesus' name"? So, the parents went to court to prevent it. Judge Kent finally decided that any student mentioning the name of Jesus in a graduation prayer would face up to a six-month jail term. These are his words:

> Make no mistake, the court is going to have a United States marshal in attendance at the graduation. If any student offends this court, that student will be summarily arrested and will face up to six months incarceration in the Galveston County Jail for contempt of court. Anyone who thinks I'm kidding about this order . . . [or] expressing any weakness or lack of resolve . . . had better think again. Anyone who violates these orders, no kidding, is going to wish that he or she had died as a child when this court gets through with it.[11]

The First Amendment, which assures individuals the right of free speech and expression of opinion, apparently applies to all citizens of the United States except Christians. Tim Crater, Special Representative of the National Association of Evangelicals, wrote of such absurd judicial decisions, "The majority should not lose their speech rights because their voluntary desire to speak *to* God (in prayer) makes the minority uncomfortable but does not coerce them to participate, any more than a minority speaking blasphemously *about* God should lose their free-speech rights because it makes the majority uncomfortable. . . . The disbelieving minority must practice the same respectful toleration it ceaselessly and unctuously enjoins upon the believing majority."[12] (Italics in the original.)

Yet Western (particularly American) society and institutions seem determined to push Christians not only out of the corridors of influence, but as far away from the center of public life as possible. This tendency (which of course the institutions themselves would deny) grows from the soil of moral relativism. If objective truth does not exist, then the transcendent values of Christian faith cannot be permitted to intrude into the public square, where they will be "divisive." Instead, the state should adopt a stance of neutrality in all things moral. The rationale is a little elusive: "The prevailing notion is that the state should be neutral as to religion, and furthermore, that the best way to be neutral about it is to avoid all mention of it. By this sort of logic, nudism is the best compromise among different styles of dress."[13]

The state's intrusive tendencies showed through with great force in a case involving Georgetown University, a Catholic university in Washington, D.C. A group calling themselves the Gay People of Georgetown University demanded recognition and financial support from the school to promote homosexual education and to fund gay social events. The school refused, citing the inappropriateness of having a Catholic university fund a cause opposed to the church's moral standards. The student group sued.

Initially, the university won. The case went to appeal, however, and the appellate court reversed the decision. The court decided that the guaranteeing of homosexual rights is so critical to government's role in public life that it overrode the right of religious organizations to distribute funds according to their own religious standards. Georgetown University, at the dictates of the government, was told that they must not only tolerate a homosexual organization, but fund it.

Fortunately, the cause of religious freedom had a friend in the legislature. Senator Bill Armstrong of Colorado managed to have two amendments passed by the Senate to counteract the damage. One ordered the District of Columbia council to change the law so that it specifically exempted religious institutions. When that was overturned by another appellate court, the senator sought relief through the Congress's right under the Constitution to alter directly the District of Columbia's statutes. Georgetown University as a result does not have to fund the social events of homosexuals on its campus. However, the trend toward ever-increasing intrusion by the government into church-related affairs is apparent to any thinking Christian.

God has given pilgrims a job to do. We are supposed to be pursuing the goal of getting His truth to the ends of the earth. We need to have our hands untied to do that. The signs are increasingly dark that the government feels it can invade the sanctuary and tell us what we can and can't do. But we should exercise the freedoms we do have. Voting is one way we can elect legislators like Senator Armstrong, who are sensitive to true religious freedom, and remind lawmakers of issues important to the pilgrim mind.

ACTION POINT TWO:
CHANGE SOCIETY BY RESCUING INDIVIDUALS

Pilgrims can certainly recruit new pilgrims one by one. Change in any society ultimately happens at the grass roots; it occurs when God changes individuals. Disciple building, not legislation, is the long-term solution to the ills of the human race. Paradoxically, that is one of the strongest arguments for a Christian presence in the public square, for the absence of it virtually guarantees that freedom to proclaim our message will diminish. Even now, forces that wish believers ill are doing everything in their power to paint Christianity with a terrible brush, and they are succeeding. In many circles today, for example, parental discipline is regarded as indistinguishable from child abuse. Another example: People who defend the existence of moral absolutes today are regarded as engaging in a form of hate speech.

Still another example: At a conference I attended, Johnny Miller, then president of Columbia International University, referred to a 1997 newspaper survey identifying evangelical Christians as the most feared group in America, ranking just ahead of Arab terrorists. Somehow, at least part of the public has subscribed to the notion that the perverse individual who shoots an abortion doctor or bombs his clinic is a representative of evangelical Christianity. Some of that is due to journalistic stereotyping, but it is at least fair to say that our message is not coming through clearly.

The heart disease that plagues humanity—sin—does not yield to minor surgery; a transplant is the only option. People are changed one at a time as they respond to the gospel message. When enough individuals respond, the social effects can be widespread, even if they arrive slowly.

At the height of Billy Sunday's fame, journalist Bruce Barton received an assignment to write a series of articles exposing what some suspected was the evangelist's fraudulent lifestyle. Barton visited three towns where Sunday had preached and interviewed people who had seen the effects of his ministry. He wrote, "I talked to the merchants and they told me that during the meetings and afterward people walked up to the counter and paid bills which were so old that they had long since been written off the books." In one town, visited three years before by Sunday, the president of the local chamber of commerce declared, "I am not a member of any church. I never attend but I'll tell you one thing. If it was proposed now to bring Billy Sunday to this town, and if we knew as much about the results of his work in advance as we do now, and if the churches would not raise the necessary funds to bring him, I could raise the money in half a day from men who never go to church. . . . A circus comes here . . . and leaves nothing. He left a different moral atmosphere."[14]

As Billy Graham has gone about offering Christ to communities, results of his work are not hard to find. One Louisiana observer noted that liquor sales in Shreveport dropped by 40 percent after a local crusade, while the sale of Bibles increased 300 percent. During one Seattle crusade, a number of impending divorce actions were cancelled. In Greensboro, North Carolina, one report concluded that the entire social structure of the city had been affected because so many had been converted.[15]

In smaller communities the effects of spiritual change are even more noticeable. Many people have read *Mutiny on the Bounty* or seen one of the movie versions of the tale. Fewer are aware that the book and its two sequels are based on actual events. In 1790, nine mutineers from the *Bounty,* together with six Tahitian men and twelve Tahitian women, put ashore on Pitcairn Island. One sailor soon began distilling alcohol, and the little colony was plunged into debauchery and vice.

Ten years later, surrounded by native women and a few children, only one man, a sailor named Alexander Smith, survived. In an old chest from the *Bounty,* Smith one day found a Bible. He began to read it, took its message to heart, and then began to teach it to the others. The result was that his own life and ultimately the lives of all those in the colony were changed. When the American ship *Topaz* discovered the group in 1808, Pitcairn had become a prosperous community with no jail, no crime, and a lot of contented people.

ACTION POINT THREE:
RESIST THE PRIVATIZATION OF BELIEF

Earth's visible kingdoms want to suppress religious expression; that should not surprise pilgrims. The Chinese government, for example, is wise enough to know that if the church's growth in that country continues, it may compromise the government's ability to oppress the population. In the West, however, Christian pilgrims ought to take advantage of their admittedly eroding freedoms and resist the push toward privatization of faith. At the moment, Christianity is where homosexuality was a few years ago: It will be tolerated, but only between consenting adults behind closed doors.

Early in the 1984 U.S. presidential race, candidate Mario Cuomo, former governor of New York, was asked about his views on abortion. The governor explained that as a Roman Catholic he subscribed to his church's views on the issue. However, as an officeholder he could submerge those views for the sake of his constituents and endorse proabortion legislation. Cuomo lost in his bid to become the Democratic nominee, but other Catholics and Protestants have followed in his steps, removing their moral beliefs on abortion and other issues from any public decision making.

Christian pilgrims need to exhibit the courage of their convictions in the public square. We do the world little good by behaving as though we are ashamed of them. And we need to stop worrying whether or not our views make us popular or admired— or even "successful" in the world's eyes. When we do, the effort nearly always explodes in our faces. Cal Thomas thinks the low point of this tendency was reached in the mid-1970s at the National Religious Broadcasters annual convention in Washington, D.C. The NRB invited two notables to address it. One was Eldridge Cleaver, the ex-Black Panther who had professed conversion some time before. The other was Larry Flynt, the pornography kingpin who had reputedly been brought to Christ through the ministry of Jimmy Carter's sister-evangelist, Ruth Carter Stapleton. Thomas observed:

> Neither Flynt nor Cleaver lived up to his advance billing, but the scene was instructive. Delegates needed to feel accepted by the world. They hungered for significance, and they wanted validation by the same people who grant "significance" to celebrities. . . . Sadly, but not unpredictably, parading these two "converts" around the convention turned out to be another embarrassing fiasco. It was the last time Flynt would ever appear in public at a religious gathering. He quickly returned to publishing his dirty magazine. As for Cleaver . . . he flirted with the Mormons and the Unification Church . . . [and] died in 1998.[16]

When Christians crave the approval of the world, they bring shame on themselves and disrepute on their message. In effect, they deny that they are pilgrims.

Above all, Christian pilgrims ought to turn away from presenting a face in the public square characterized by anger and hostility. According to author Warren Wiersbe, the gentle weapons of the Savior ought to be our hallmark:

> What we need today is not anger but anguish, the kind of anguish that Moses displayed when he broke the two tablets of the law and then climbed the mountain to intercede for his people, or that Jesus displayed when He cleansed the temple and then wept over the city. The difference between anger and anguish is a broken heart. It's easy to get angry, especially at somebody else's sins; but it's not easy to look at sin, our own included, and weep over it.[17]

We also need the courage of our convictions. Do we believe God's kingdom is a living reality or not? If so, we ought to proceed without fear and with full confidence in our King. In this connection, Cal Thomas told the story of an encounter with Madalyn Murray O'Hair, the noted (and perhaps late) atheist. Years ago, while working as a reporter for a Houston television station, Thomas interviewed O'Hair, who took credit for getting prayer and Bible reading eliminated from America's public schools. He asked her why so many people were afraid of her. "I'll tell you, Mr. Thomas, why some Christians are afraid of me. They're not sure what they believe is really true. If they were sure, I wouldn't be a threat to them at all."[18]

For once, Madalyn Murray O'Hair was right. It is the people who know their God who have nothing to fear from outside attacks. But first they must know Him. They cannot become at home in this world. They cannot claim to know Him on the basis of His reputation. To settle down and be at home in this dark world constitutes disloyalty and self-destruction. Søren Kierkegaard saw the dangers: "As soon as Christ's kingdom comes to terms with the world, Christianity is abolished."[19] On the other hand, when we stand firm for God's truth we become radiant lights on a hill—as Christ urged us to be (see Matthew 5:14, 16).

ON THE JOURNEY

1. Give a couple of examples of how Christians can get overly involved in politics, to the detriment of the kingdom of God. What about those who refuse to get involved?

2. How would you demonstrate the need to be assertive in politics and our religious freedoms without being intolerant or aggressive? What should our perspective be when we lose a battle?

THE WEALTH
OF A PILGRIM

You can't take it with you,
but you can send it on ahead.

—CHURCH BULLETIN BOARD

*F*or some years now, I've noticed how anxious banks are to lend me money. About twice a month I receive an appeal from some financial agency inviting me to apply for their gold card or platinum card or some other great benefit, for which I can gain the privilege of paying them about 20 percent interest per year. I found out not long ago, however, that I should be grateful for these solicitations. At least I'm alive.

Once someone in my church told me how a man faced such recruitment *after* his death. In fact, Richard Williams (not his real name) died nearly twenty years ago, but his wife "Arlene" continued to receive credit card solicitations addressed to him, including three from one company in a recent year.

She finally decided to answer one of the latter in a way calculated to get her late husband off that mailing list for good. She returned the application unsigned after filling in enough obviously false information to make sure that anyone reading it wouldn't take it seriously. For example, in the space for Social Security number, she filled in all zeroes. Next to the slot for "date of birth" she inserted "date of death" instead and filled in the appropriate numbers. Under "employer" she wrote "God."

When a personal letter from the company arrived, Arlene expected it to be an apology. Instead, they were requesting a signature so that they could process the application. Making one final try, Arlene filled in the signature space by *typing* "no pens in heaven" and returned the application. Three weeks later, she received a Gold Card in the name of her late husband.

In the mystical world of Western economies, those who want us to spend money are running neck and neck with those who want us to borrow it, and death is no deterrent to either. Keeping any kind of sane attitude about finances can be difficult. We need an eternal perspective.

A person who had one was the late J. Vernon McGee, a particular hero of mine. His *Through the Bible* radio program nurtured my Christian growth at a strategic stage in my life, and I have always regarded his zeal for God's truth as especially infectious. Even now I listen to his taped broadcasts when I can. One missions executive told me that in parts of India, Dr. McGee's ministry supplies the essential—sometimes the only—spiritual food for Christians in many remote villages. The headman will crank up the community's one generator just in time to tune in to *Through the Bible,* and nearly the whole village will gather around the radio.

When I first heard Dr. McGee in person, he had recently been diagnosed with lung cancer and had been given (mistakenly, as it turned out) only a few months to live. He confessed, "Certain things have changed since my doctors gave me the news. Probably the most noteworthy is how I view my bank account. It doesn't seem nearly as important now."

During life's greatest journey, unseen yet eternal realities ought to drive the pilgrim's attitude about money. Nowhere, in fact, should a pilgrim exhibit more distinctiveness from the world than in the area of finances.

In my experience, most of what preachers have to say about money concerns giving. Since giving forms a legitimate and substantial subject in the Scriptures, and since I am going to have some things to say about it later in this chapter, I won't take issue with that. However, God's Word addresses far more than just how we divide up the money that comes our way. It also hammers on how we think about financial matters across the board.

Being conscious of belonging to the kingdom of God adds an important dimension to financial issues. The pilgrim's resources are not limited to what he sees. God is able to take care of our needs, so He issues a challenge to pilgrims: "Let your conduct be without covetousness; be content with such things as you have. For He Himself has said, 'I will never leave you nor forsake you'" (Hebrews 13:5).

CONTENTMENT IN MONEY AND IN LIFE

Just as integrity is the mark of the pilgrim in the realm of morals, contentment is the supreme hallmark of the pilgrim when it comes to money. A believer's contentment should not rest on a stoic submerging of desire, but on the promises of Jesus Christ. "I will never leave you nor forsake you" is a statement to build your life on if you are a believer in Him. He also said, "I am with you always, even to the end of the age" (Matthew 28:20). Still more examples could be given, but how often does God have to say it to convince us?

Such promises have sustained believers through many a dark valley. David Livingstone is a case in point. Livingstone's name has come down to most in the Western world primarily as a result of Henry Stanley's famous statement, "Dr. Livingstone, I presume?" He was one of only a handful of missionaries to Africa in the mid-nineteenth century. By the time Stanley found him, he had long been in the remotest part of that continent. Though the work cost him dearly, he never wavered in his devotion to the task, for Livingstone found the Lord Jesus' presence all he needed.

His journal provides an excellent example of the Christian who can take Christ at His Word and rely on His faithfulness. In his seventeenth year of work as a missionary in Africa, Livingstone found himself surrounded by hostile and infuriated tribes, and was strongly tempted to flee his mission station. Right before an anticipated attack, he wrote in his journal:

> January 14, 1856. Evening. Felt much turmoil of spirit in prospect of having all my plans for the welfare of this great region and this teeming population knocked on the head by savages tomorrow. But I read that Jesus said: All power is given unto Me in heaven and earth. Go ye therefore, and teach all nations, and lo, I am with you always, even unto the end of the world. It is the word of a gentleman of the most strict and sacred honour, so there's an end of it! I will not cross furtively tonight as I intended. Should such a man as I flee? Nay, verily, I shall take observations for latitude and longitude tonight, though they may be the last. I feel quite calm now, thank God![1]

The explorer's pilgrim mentality can be seen clearly in his evaluation of the promise of Christ: "It is the word of a gentleman of the most strict and sacred honour, so there's an end of it!" For most of us, that is anything but the end of it. We doubt and waver and vacillate in the most illogical ways. We are willing to trust Jesus Christ with our eternal souls, but not for money to pay next month's power bill. We do not possess that glorious pilgrim quality of contentment.

DEFINING TRUE CONTENTMENT

Contentment as it is taught in Scripture is quite different from how it is generally viewed in the world. At the time of the New Testament, stoic philosophers had set forth contentment as a virtue in Greek culture. The stoics believed that contentment was reached when you had come to the point of total indifference, when you had rid yourself of desire.

In other words, you talked yourself into an "I don't care" attitude. The philosopher Epictetus said,

> Begin with a cup or a household utensil; if it breaks, say, "I don't care." Go on to a horse or a pet dog; if anything happens to it say, "I don't care." Go on to yourself; if you're hurt or injured in any way say, "I don't care." And if you go on long enough and if you try hard enough you'll come to a state when you can watch your nearest and dearest suffer and die and say, "I don't care."[2]

That is the Stoic contentment of indifference, the contentment that holds emotions in contempt. As another writer noted, "The Stoics made of the heart a desert and called it peace."[3] That is not what the Bible is talking about when it advocates contentment. The Scriptures do not advocate a passionless indifference based on a kind of self-hypnosis to crush one's desires. God's commands to be content say, in effect, "If you have enough, thank God because you have enough. If you don't have enough, rest assured that God has not forgotten you. If you know Him, you have lots of reasons to be calm and confident that He will take care of you. If you have an abundance, be generous and ready to share." Stoic contentment was based on self-sufficiency. Biblical contentment is built on Christ-sufficiency. Indeed, we can say that true contentment is being satisfied and calm based on Christ's provision for us.

Still, Christian pilgrims persist in believing that their problems could be solved if they only possessed a little more money. The feebleness of that position was impressed on me several years ago when I read about the prizewinner in a McDonald's "Monopoly" contest. A North Carolina woman won a million dollars when she stopped at a local McDonald's in Durham for lunch. She had stopped to pick up a Big Mac and a Coke on her way home—from a round of chemotherapy for kidney and breast cancer. She was pleased, but she told the press that she was hoping she would live to collect it.

THE PLEASURE OF A CONTENTED HEART

Usually we can't do anything about what happens to us. What we can do is use what we have and learn the grace of contentment to reflect credit on a gracious God. In this world, that kind of behavior stands out. I noticed an article in a national publication some time ago describing the severance package given to the terminated chief executive officer of the American Express Company. It included $1.1 million in severance pay, $750,000 per year in retirement benefits, a luxury office, a secretary paid for by the company for the rest of his life, plus a special bonus of $3.2 million at the end of three years—if he did not go into competition with American Express or try to recruit former employees.

The article pointed out that the terminated executive was unhappy with the deal. Think of that: a ten-million-dollar settlement . . . and he was unhappy.

Contentment is not exactly common in Western society. If you have it, you'll be distinct in our cash-mad world.

Contentment can be a priceless advantage. If you ask any person how much money he would need to be extremely well-off, chances are he will give you a figure that is about 80 percent higher than he is making now in annual salary. However, if you had asked him ten years ago for the figure that would make him prosperous, he would have given you an amount close to what he is making now.

Contentment can save you thousands of dollars every year—because you won't feel the compulsion to have the latest and the best of everything. You can make a three-year-old car last a fourth year. You can still be a functional person without a stereo VCR or a microwave with the latest bells and whistles.

In the third part of *King Henry the Sixth,* Shakespeare described the king wandering alone in the countryside. He encountered two men who recognized him as the monarch. One asked, "But, if thou be a king, where is thy crown?" His majesty gave a great answer:

> My crown is in my heart, not on my head;
> Not deck'd with diamonds and Indian stones,
> Nor to be seen; my crown is call'd content;
> A crown it is that seldom kings enjoy.[4]

Some of us commoners find it pretty elusive, too. Pilgrims must do battle with the propaganda that surrounds us. The entire fabric of retail sales in the United States is built on one carefully managed goal—the creation of discontent. After all, if you're contented, you are not going to be inclined to buy lots of new gadgets in an effort to become happy. If you have the essentials, you will be content. We may run the risk of tanking the economy by being content, but it is a risk worth taking. Contentment is an unmistakable mark of the Christian sojourner.

By contrast, Satan is the winner of our discontent. When you are not content with what God provides, you will be inclined to do foolish things. Consider, for instance, the person who has to have a $20,000 new car instead of a used one at half the cost. The purchaser may enjoy the ride, but he places himself under indebtedness, higher insurance costs, higher taxes, and the anxiety associated with not wanting to have one's automobile scratched.

*Belonging to inanimate objects is
beneath the dignity of God's pilgrims.*

The contented person loses little sleep over his less expensive vehicle; he is glad he isn't walking. Albert Schweitzer is reputed to have said: "If you have something you can't live without, you don't own it; it owns you." Belonging to inanimate objects is beneath the dignity of God's pilgrims.

One of the great sections of Scripture on the subject of contentment is found in chapter four of Paul's letter to the Philippian believers. The apostle Paul was in prison awaiting trial, unjustly accused by his enemies. Yet he wrote the Philippians, "I rejoiced in the Lord greatly" (4:10). Paul was free to exult in unpleasant surroundings because his heart was contented. Contentment is the wellspring from which joy comes.

The Philippians had been part of Paul's support team for many years. They had been faithful in sending him money so that he could extend the gospel throughout the Roman world. Yet for a while he had not received anything from them. It may be that they had no one trustworthy enough to send to Rome with the gift. They finally connected with Epaphroditus, however (Philippians 4:18), and the money arrived; so Paul wrote to congratulate them on their gift. Yet, with or without money, the apostle felt contentment.

The apostle would have agreed with the illustration of the writer of Proverbs, who explained, "All the days of the afflicted are evil, but he who is of a merry heart has a continual feast" (Proverbs 15:15). Our natural tendency is to think: "If I have enough to eat, it will produce a merry heart. I will be happy if I have enough." God says, "If your heart is right, you will be joyful. What you bring *to* the table is far more important than what is *on* the table."

An ancient legend tells of a king who was suffering from a mysterious malady and was advised by one of his court consultants that he would be cured if the shirt of a contented man was brought for him to wear. People went out to all parts of the kingdom looking for such a person, and after a long search they found a man who was really contented. Unfortunately for the king, the man did not even possess a shirt.

THE PROTECTION OF A CONTENTED HEART

Why is contentment so important? Because, among other reasons, it protects us. The wise person knows that there is calmness in contentment, a calmness that rejoices in the vast resources of God. One way to foster contentment is to transfer ownership of your possessions to God. Then if something happens to them, you haven't lost anything, He has; and He can replace it easily enough.

I remember when I first decided to do this many years ago. I had been thinking a lot about how it was only right to stop thinking about possessions as *my* things and regard them instead as the Lord's. I got a chance to put my convictions to the test in a strange way.

Many of my friends regard me as the world's most absentminded individual, and not without justification. Some people, at least, call it absentminded. I prefer to think that I have great powers of concentration. When I have something on my mind, I don't notice little distractions such as what I am supposed to bring to the office or home from it, or whether I am supposed to shave before coming to church. When my wife wants me to bring something home, she calls my secretary and asks her to put it in my car. She learned long ago that it works better that way. I even remember receiving a call after coming home from services on a particular Sunday. The caller called my attention to the fact that I had left one of my children at church. Don't laugh; a busy pastor can't be expected to remember everything.

On a certain Saturday, I was in the office early to get some things done. There was a church softball game that day, and as a member of the team, I took my uniform with me to the office so I could change later for the game. About noon, I donned my uniform and took my street clothes and shoes out to the car. I tucked the hanger inside the back door of the car. I had placed my shoes on the roof of the car, and in my haste forgot to put them inside.

So I drove off with my shoes on the roof of the car. I had just gotten on the freeway when—you guessed it—I heard a "clonk" and looked in my rearview mirror just in time to see those shoes go tumbling beneath the tires of an eighteen-wheeler. The first thought that popped into my mind was, "Look at that—the Lord's shoes bouncing down the freeway." I found it a refreshing perspective.

---

*Contentment . . . can be among
the most priceless assets you have.*

Some serious spiritual dangers issue from discontentment. Paul exhorted Timothy, "Those who desire to be rich fall into temptation and a snare, and into many foolish and harmful lusts which drown men in destruction and perdition. For the love of money is a root of all kinds of evil, for which some have strayed from the faith in their greediness, and pierced themselves through with many sorrows" (1 Timothy 6:9–10). Note the spiritual dangers he listed: temptation, snares, foolish and harmful lusts, straying from the faith (he clearly was thinking of Christians in this verse), and many sorrows.

Contentment is the best way to escape from these dangers. It can be among the most priceless assets you have because it helps soothe the itch of acquisitiveness. The writer of Proverbs offered God an illuminating prayer. Out of everything he could ask for, two requests were particularly important to him. He wrote, "Two things I request of You [deprive me not before I die]: remove falsehood and lies far from me; give me neither poverty nor riches—feed me with the food allotted to me; lest I be full and deny You, and say, 'Who is the Lord?' Or lest I be poor and steal, and profane the name of my God" (Proverbs 30:7–8).

That is a wise prayer indeed. Many people pray to be kept from poverty. The writer of Proverbs saw equally clearly the spiritual dangers of riches. If I am too poor, he said, I am likely to steal, and God's reputation will be harmed. If I am too rich, I will probably kid myself into thinking that I don't need God. Either way, God's purpose is hindered in me.

HOW TO HAVE A CONTENTED HEART

So how is that glorious financial asset of contentment to be acquired? Painfully, in most cases, for it has to be *learned*. Paul was contented because he had learned how to be contented. He wrote, "I have learned in whatever state I am, to be content" (Philippians 4:11). No one comes packaged as a contented individual. The word here translated "learned" means to learn not by study but by experience.

Like the writer of Proverbs, Paul knew that both poverty and wealth contain spiritual chuckholes: "I know how to be abased, and I know how to abound. Everywhere and in all things I have learned both to be full and to be hungry, both to abound and to suffer need" (Philippians 4:12). Lots of people have learned contentment in poverty. Learning it in abundance is far less common. Below are a few ideas.

First, be alert to the tiniest indication of greed in your life. Nothing can blind a pilgrim to the beauties of his homeland like a longing to accumulate. You will not learn contentment in a week, or even in a year. You probably could learn it in a year were it not for the fact that our entire economy conspires to push you in the other direction.

In Western culture, greed often sprouts in response to advertising. Advertisers insist that no one could, or ought to be content without their product.

If you believe what advertising tells you, when you travel, your entire survival depends on having the proper brand of traveler's checks. If you believe advertising, you will be convinced that one particular vintner sells no wine before its time—and isn't it lucky for us that they happen to have about 100,000 bottles sitting around whose time has come? If you believe advertising, then you will be convinced that acquiring a perfect figure and wavy blonde hair is all a matter of choosing the proper diet drink. If you believe advertising, you would be of the opinion that stockbrokers work for the fun of it. If they didn't, they would take their own advice and retire in their early twenties. If you believe advertising, you would hold to the notion that an anxiety problem does not need to be dealt with through counseling; all you have to do is switch to the proper brand of decaffeinated coffee. You must be alert to that sort of blatant propaganda if you are going to fight it.

Second, resist yielding to the siren call of every new product. Before you sign your credit card voucher, ask yourself, "How is it that I have survived these years without having this item?" Then ask yourself, "Am I willing to be enslaved for the next five years to the company that sells such products?"

Then consider alternative uses of the money you are about to spend. How could you invest it in more eternally profitable channels? I don't mean simply writing checks to the Lord's work, although that would be useful, to be sure. Could it be better spent on taking some time off to spend with the family? Visualize the consequences of yielding. Every financial choice you make is a rejection of something else.

Try this interesting exercise: If you have an attic or basement where you store little-used items, go there. Walk over to some box at random. Open it up. Look inside. Chances are you will find something that at one time seemed quite important to you. You were sure that if you had that item you would be happy. Then ask yourself, "Have I even missed this?" The experience can be illuminating.

Third, don't forget the source of all deep contentment: Jesus. Philippians 4:13 concludes Paul's instruction in how to be content. It's one of those verses that people get excited about: "I can do all things through Christ who strengthens me." The beauty of the verse, however, is only matched by the tendency of those who love to divorce it from its context.

When Paul penned this line, was he thinking about performing great miracles? Was he seeking an understanding of great mysteries? Neither. He was considering the possibility of victories even more significant—of overcoming his own inclination toward greediness. What he was saying is simply this: "Through the inner ability Christ gives me, I can keep myself from postponing the enjoyment of life until I have one more possession."

Remember the real power for contented living. The Lord Jesus can make His pilgrims contented people, and that is a supernatural victory. If you can learn contentment, you can do virtually anything.

USING FINANCIAL RESOURCES

When a preacher starts talking about money, people start building mental walls. In a survey of unchurched people, hundreds were asked why they didn't attend church regularly. An overwhelming number of respondents said that their absence was due to the fact that all the church ever did was talk about money. I'm sure that in many cases, the respondents were kidding themselves; but the complaint is heard too persistently to be utterly without a basis.

The pastor of a Methodist church in Atlanta decided that he would publicly post the annual contributions of his church members. (He also planned to be in Europe for the two months following the posting.) On the bulletin board and in the church newsletter was listed the name of every church member and the amount contributed over the last year.

Many people became angry, and some left the church. But, the pastor pointed out, it was only those who did not give who walked away. Those who were faithful in giving were not ashamed or threatened. The rest simply did not want everyone knowing just how stingy they really were. "It was embarrassing," he said, "for people to discover that a secretary gave more than her wealthy boss, that the man who rode around in an expensive automobile gave less than the widow who was sending her son through college on a pension." Isn't it fascinating, though, that Christians are dreadfully embarrassed to have people discover what God already knows?

Striking a balance while talking about giving in a local church can be terribly difficult. When I helped plant the church I have been serving for nearly thirty years, we faced the question of how much emphasis to place on giving. We who were church leaders decided to demonstrate that we could trust God for the financial health of the church by not passing offering plates. Instead, we placed offering boxes [and continue to do so] at the exits to the auditorium. People told us that it would never work, that the church would suffer. For three decades, however, we have been able to pay our bills on time, construct decent church facilities, support global missions, and pay our staff adequately. I have attempted over that time to preach on giving in approximate proportion to how often the issue appears in Scripture.

Of course, the approach we adopted isn't trouble free. We have attracted people to the church who simply don't want to be faced with a weekly reminder in the shape of offering plates. And we have blurred the connection between giving and worship that is simplified by passing plates.

Let's not forget that the wealth of pilgrims is returned to God as tithes and offerings that form worship. As far as God is concerned, giving is the essence of worship. God told His people in Exodus 23:15, "None shall appear before Me empty." In Exodus 22:29, God had already said, "You shall not delay to offer the first of your ripe produce . . . to Me." In Exodus 34:20, He again warned, "None shall appear before Me empty-handed."

Every person's checkbook is the loudest possible testimony to what he really loves.

What profound statements! Why would God say such things? Because He knows how He made us. He constructed us in such a way that we come to love that in which we invest ourselves. Every person's checkbook is the loudest possible testimony to what he really loves. It is there that we find our genuine value system—not in what we profess to love, but in what we really do.

The converse is true, as well. What is easily available for no cost can easily become valueless to us. When the people of Israel were wandering in the wilderness, God provided manna for them every day. All they had to do was pick it up. That was okay for a while, but after a few years, it became tiresome. They began to despise it. When people refuse to let their faith cost them anything— when they do not share the firstfruits of their income with God, after a while it becomes a demoted aspect of their lives.

King David knew the danger of this. When he was offered a piece of property at no cost on which to build the temple, he refused to accept it. He said, "[I will not] offer . . . to the Lord my God with that which costs me nothing" (2 Samuel 24:24). God builds into life what might be called a contentment cycle: (1) giving results in receiving; (2) receiving results in contentment and worship; and (3) worship results in more giving. The cycle goes on indefinitely unless the pilgrim chooses to break it by hoarding his goods. Giving God a significant portion of one's income forms a clear declaration that you really believe there is an unseen world in addition to the visible one.

ON THE JOURNEY

1. Are you truly content with your material status in life or do you find happiness in purchasing more things? What does this tell you about your spiritual state?

2. What is your philosophy of giving to God from your financial resources? How do you make decisions about what to give, and what does this tell you about your view of material possessions?

THE TEMPTATIONS
OF A PILGRIM

*There are several good protections against temptation,
but the surest is cowardice.*

—MARK TWAIN[1]

*I*recently read the story of a pastor who had graduated from a seminary I had attended. After receiving his degree, the graduate enjoyed useful ministries in a couple of good evangelical churches. In the second, along with a fine pulpit ministry, he demonstrated a strong evangelistic gift. Many of the people in the church are Christians today because of his clear and powerful elucidation of the gospel. Unfortunately, he is no longer there to help disciple them. Instead, he sits languishing in a Texas prison, serving a ten-to-twenty year term for attempted rape—a crime to which he eventually confessed.

He had also sustained a fine ministry of discipleship in his second church. So many lives were changed through him that when his crime was discovered and he had admitted his guilt, the people in the church raised over $20,000 for his legal defense. In one horrible moment of yielding to temptation, he lost his reputation, his ministry, and his family, and left behind a vivid scar on the testimony of Christ in that Texas community.

You can't encounter a story like that without sadness. The account reminds us, however, that no one is immune to moral failure. It also suggests that temptation is nothing to be trifled with. In the heart of every pilgrim who takes life's greatest journey lies the potential to become a monster.

Robert Louis Stevenson wrote about the possibilities in his classic *The Strange Case of Dr. Jekyll and Mr. Hyde*. Dr. Jekyll was a pillar of the community, a highly respected professional man. However, he dabbled in several vices, practices that he kept carefully hidden from public view. Wanting to indulge in these depravities without restraint and without endangering his standing in the community, he concocted an exotic potion that would allow him to transform his physical features at will. In theory, he would then be free to move about the city and practice his sins without anyone knowing who he was.

Unfortunately, the beast hidden within him began dominating his life and wreaking terror in the community. He became guilty, under the influence of his potion, of a series of beatings and murders that terrorized his neighbors. Such destructive evil could not be kept in check for long, and the consequences of the battle within Dr. Jekyll ended in great tragedy. Stevenson's point was that each of us can have a battle going on inside that the rest of the world cannot see. Yielding can produce tragic results, for people are not only punished for their sins, but by them.

Why is this so? How is it that a man like that imprisoned pastor, or someone like Dr. Jekyll, can yield to such destructive temptations? How can pilgrims remain distinctive amid a world system that seems hungry to destroy them?

These questions find answers in the temptation experience of Jesus. No greater model exists for learning how to deal with the ongoing temptations every pilgrim will face.

The scene of Jesus' testing was one of great desolation. It is called in the New Testament "the wilderness" (Matthew 4:1;

Mark 1:12; Luke 4:1), an area of about four hundred square miles between Jerusalem and the Dead Sea. The Old Testament called it *Jeshimon,* which means "the devastation."

I have traveled through this desolate area a number of times, always with a lump in my throat when I think of what happened there. Almost nothing grows in that lonely place. The innumerable sharp-edged rocks are light gray or off-white, and on bright days the glare hurts the visitor's eyes. The hills are steep and irregular and occasionally terraced by the trails of the goats that find a little pasture there in the spring. The few showers that fall race down stony gullies to form flash floods on the way to the Dead Sea. In summer, the temperature sometimes reaches 120 degrees. In Jesus' day, foxes and bears prowled the hills, always looking for prey.

---

*[Jesus] gave Satan all the advantages—
and still He won, for He is the true Pilgrim.*

No one living other than the Lord Jesus Christ was present to record the event of the Temptation. The fact that we have the story means that the Lord probably told it to His disciples personally. He deemed it important enough to merit preservation in the sacred record.

There were three attractions in the Temptation. The first was for a hungry Jesus to turn stones into bread; the second, to throw Himself down from the pinnacle of the temple; the third, to accept rule of the earth. The Temptation is the first item on His agenda because He was about to undertake a public ministry, and no one should engage in such work with unproven character. Therefore, Jesus met the devil on his turf. After forty days of fasting, He was tempted in a devastation, surrounded by hostile predators (see Mark 1:13). He gave Satan all the advantages—and still He won, for He is the true Pilgrim. His eye is always on the other world. He is always in touch with the Father: "The Son can do nothing of Himself, but what He sees the Father do; for whatever He does, the Son also does in like manner" (John 5:19).

CHARACTER COUNTS

As the Lord Jesus faced His testing, He was, to give the literal rendering of the Greek text in Luke 4:1, "full of the Spirit." The adjective is used often in Scripture to describe people with a proven record of spiritual accomplishment. For example, this was the same requirement that the apostles set forth for what was arguably the first formally recognized group of deacons in the Jerusalem church. They had to be "full of the Holy Spirit and wisdom" (Acts 6:3). The expression describes a settled condition of character rather than simply a right relationship to God at the moment.[2]

The principle that emerges from the expression is this: The character you bring to your temptation generally determines whether you will resist and the force of that resistance. That is why there is no such thing as an unimportant confrontation with sin. Every sin you commit weakens your character for the next temptation.

It works the other way, too. Every sin you walk away from strengthens you for the next encounter—and there always is a next encounter.

Our capacities for
rationalization seem bottomless.

No person becomes so spiritual that he rises above the possibility of temptation. If Jesus can be tempted, you and I can be tempted. When God was about to bring Israel into the Promised Land, He explained how they would overcome their enemies: "I will not drive them out from before you in one year, lest the land become desolate and the beasts of the field become too numerous for you. *Little by little I will drive them out* from before you, until you have increased, and you inherit the land" (Exodus 23:29–30, italics added). That is the way God generally works in overcoming sins—little by little. You never outgrow your vulnerability to temptation, although each age seems to outdo the previous one in finding rationalizations for sinning.

The fashionable justification for yielding to temptation is the postmodern era's appeal to desire. God gives us desires, we are told; therefore, it is normal to satisfy those God-given longings however we can. Our King, however, did not approach His own needs that way, even though the Father placed within the Lord Jesus Christ a personal need for food: "In those days He ate nothing, and afterward, when they had ended, He was hungry" (Luke 4:2). God gave the need, but because it was God given was no reason to use it as a rationalization for wrongdoing.

Clarence Macartney once wrote:

Satan knows all the appetites of our nature and tempts us accordingly. These appetites have their proper and natural uses; but it is Satan's sophistry to say, as so many are saying today, that it is never a sin to indulge an appetite, because God has implanted it in us. . . . That in substance is what every man who yields to the temptation of the flesh says, either before his transgression or after it. "God put this appetite in me and I will satisfy it." But that is not what the great souls said; not what Joseph said when he was tempted; not what Daniel or John the Baptist and other great souls said. They did not say, "A man must live, therefore I will do this wrong"; but rather, "The soul must live, even if the body should perish."[3]

Our capacities for rationalization seem bottomless. An associate told me the story about an overweight businessman who decided it was time to shed some excess pounds. He took his new diet seriously, even changing his driving route to and from work to avoid his favorite bakery. One morning, however, he arrived at work late carrying a delectable—and gigantic—coffee cake. People in the office chided him, but he remained unruffled.

"This is very spiritual coffee cake," he explained, ignoring his coworkers' skeptical looks. "I accidentally drove by the bakery this morning and there in the window were a host of wonderful pastries. I felt this was no accident, so I prayed, 'Lord, if you want me to have one of these delicious coffee cakes, let me have a parking place directly in front of the bakery.' And sure enough," he continued, "the eighth time around the block, there it was!"

THE THREE TEMPTATIONS OF JESUS

In the first temptation, Satan said to the Lord Jesus, "Command this stone to become bread" (Luke 4:3). Satan presented a perfectly good end: food. The Father did not send the Son into the world to conveniently invoke divine privileges whenever problems arose. Man as such can routinely claim no such prerogative. To invoke it would be to step outside the Father's will. The price for such a lunch is too high; and the problem with many a pilgrim is that they have a price at all.

But we do. Instead, we must resist, and we can—but only when we ask for help. A ship's captain was in port in Miami when he was approached by some shady-looking types who offered him $10,000 to bring in a load of cocaine from Colombia. He turned them down. Two days later, they approached him again, this time offering $50,000. He refused again. The next day they came back and promised $150,000. He stalled them and called in drug agents. When he told them the story, they asked why he called them so late in the process instead of at the first offer. He said, "Well, they were getting pretty close to my price, and I was scared."[4]

Temptation constitutes one of those places where fear is a good thing. Any Christian ought to be frightened when he thinks about the possibility of yielding to temptation. At the same time, the presence of temptation is not by itself sin. You can't prevent wrong thoughts from springing into your head. That does not constitute sin. Sin happens when, instead of asking God for deliverance, you begin to enjoy the thoughts and eventually you yield to them. Martin Luther is reported to have said: "You cannot prevent birds from flying around your head, but you can keep them from building a nest in your hair." In all temptation, let us ask God for help.

So Satan first tempted Jesus with something good—food—but for the wrong reason—to declare His independence by escaping hardship. Satan then approached Jesus with the temptation of power gained wrongly: "All this authority I will give You, and their glory; for this has been delivered to me, and I give it to whomever I wish. Therefore, if You will worship before me, all will be Yours" (Luke 4:6–7). The very privileges Satan was offering would belong to the Lord Jesus one day anyway. God and Satan were offering the Lord Jesus the same prospect: rule of the world. So what was wrong with His taking it from Satan? The answer is simple: Jesus would be acting independently of the Father's timing and will. Similarly, the pilgrim behaves with a full consciousness of the reality of God's presence. He is willing to trust God's plan and timetable.

Finally, the devil brought Jesus to Jerusalem, where he set Him on the pinnacle of the temple. Then the Evil One announced and said to Him, "If You are the Son of God, throw Yourself down from here. For it is written: 'He shall give His angels charge over You, to keep You,' and, 'In their hands they shall bear You up, lest You dash Your foot against a stone'" (Luke 4:9–11). The pinnacle of the temple was on the southeastern corner of the temple platform, some two hundred feet over the Kidron Valley at the time. To leap from it in the ordinary course of things meant a sudden and violent death.

Satan appeals to one of the supreme values of the world system: fame and admiration.

The tempter's approach is utilitarian: "Think of it, Jesus! How many people will be impressed with you! How rapidly your reputation will be built up in the land! Let me cut through all the difficulties and give you a real boost to your ministry—just toss yourself off this high spot here!" Satan appeals to one of the supreme values of the world system: fame and admiration. Who doesn't want to be admired? After all, what is wrong with fame? That is a temptation we will face—to receive admiration, to put the focus on ourselves and our accomplishments instead of honoring God our Creator. Sometimes we may desire fame, thinking it will increase our ministry on behalf of God.

Watch out! Temptation generally comes clothed in righteous garments. The serpent was more subtle than any beast of the field. One such subtlety comes in the guise of an enhanced ministry. A Christian may be encouraged to say, "I'm going to involve myself in this activity which I know is wrong because if I don't I won't be able to have a ministry with those friends of mine who are indulging themselves in it." That is a form of kidding oneself. It also requires forgetting one critical fact: The Lord Jesus had a perfect ministry with sinners without engaging in sin Himself.

FACING TEMPTATION WITH
A KNOWLEDGE OF SCRIPTURE

Three times in the temptation account Satan posed a temptation. Three times Jesus rebuffed the temptation by saying, "It is written . . ." He brought His personal knowledge of the Father's truth to bear on each test. His awareness of God's truth helped make Him continually conscious of the Father's will, and that was crucial. The trouble with temptation is not that we openly rebel against God. Instead, we simply forget that God is present.

We fall into the pit described by Dietrich Bonhoeffer. Bonhoeffer was a German Lutheran theologian and pastor who was hanged by the Nazi SS in April 1945 at the age of thirty-nine. Bonhoeffer had achieved distinction as a scholar and had won the respect of Christian people all over the world. He described what happens at the moment we yield to temptation: "At this moment God is quite unreal to us, He loses all reality, and only desire for the creature is real; the only reality is the devil. Satan does not here fill us with hatred of God, but with forgetfulness of God."[5]

There has to be something inside of us which is able to counteract this forgetfulness—to call back before our eyes the danger we are in. Memorized Scripture does this. If you find yourself yielding to temptation, you can do yourself no greater favor than to memorize passages of Scripture which address that area.

You might want to start with 1 Corinthians 10:13, which declares, "No temptation has overtaken you except such as is common to man; but God is faithful, who will not allow you to be tempted beyond what you are able, but with the temptation will also make the way of escape, that you may be able to bear it."

FACING TEMPTATION WITH PRAYER

No pilgrim graduates from the school of temptation: "Now when the devil had ended every temptation, he departed from Him *until an opportune time*" (Luke 4:13, italics added). Vigilance in prayer is essential. Someone has said that opportunity knocks only once but temptation hammers on your door for years. Jesus knew the power of temptation over the human soul. Listen as He instructed His disciples on the night of His betrayal: "He went, as He was accustomed, to the Mount of Olives and His disciples also followed Him. When He came to the place, He said to them, 'Pray that you may not enter into temptation'" (Luke 22:39–40). Notice that linkage—prayer and temptation.

What follows is a description of Jesus' final battle with the tempter. It is here that He prayed, "Father, if it is Your will, take this cup away from Me" (Luke 22:42). The description of His struggle in Luke's gospel indicates that His prayer was no mere formality—"His sweat became like great drops of blood falling down to the ground" (Luke 22:44). He knew what it was to battle temptation. His humanity was engaged in a great contest with His divinely appointed task.

We must not toy with sin—trying it "just a little." We also must recognize every temptation as an entry point to spiritual battle.

Many years ago, a large fishing boat sprang a leak. Bringing it in for repairs, the owners discovered a hammer that had been left in the bottom of the boat years before by the builders. The constant motion of the ship had caused the hammer to beat against the insides of the boat until it had worn away the wood and the metal and caused the leak that nearly sank the ship. Sin has a tendency to destroy from within—one inch at a time. Therefore we must not toy with sin—trying it "just a little." We also must recognize every temptation as an entry point to spiritual battle. We must be wary and we must pray.

We also must be practical, not intentionally placing ourselves in harm's way. The best way to gain victory over temptation is to avoid the temptation entirely. A pastor warned his handsome new single assistant about the dangers of immorality in the ministry. The assistant said that he always did his socializing in a group setting. He said, "My motto is that 'there is safety in numbers.'"

The wise pastor replied, "Yes, that is so; but there is more safety in exodus!"

Prayer that God will keep you out of the problem area is always in order; but you have to be flexible. God may answer prayer in a way that you least expect. It may not be according to your timetable, or it may not be handled exactly according to the preferences of your heart; but God is faithful in answering prayer. The mother of Augustine prayed her son would not fall into temptation; she asked for divine protection for him. Yet he decided to leave their home in North Africa and travel to Rome. Though Monica pleaded with him not to go and asked God to keep her son from Rome with all its temptations, Augustine determined that he would go anyway. He attempted to deceive his mother by professing to board the ship only to wish his friends goodbye. Monica was so disturbed that all that night she prayed that God would interfere with his departure—and to no apparent avail. During the night, the ship left Carthage harbor and set sail for Italy.

Though Monica feared that God had dismissed her appeals, He was simply granting her long-term desires in a way she could not have predicted. While in Italy, Augustine came under the influence of Ambrose, the famous Milanese preacher. Ambrose was a remarkable man, competent in several fields, having risen through the tiers of the Roman legal system to become governor of Milan.

When he began his ministry, Ambrose brought to his work a warm and practical approach to things that attracted the wayward Augustine. He said, "At first I did not care a fig for the preaching of Ambrose, but his love could not be ignored." In time, Augustine came to faith in Christ and wrote of his mother's prayers: "You in Your wisdom, granted the substance of her desire, yet refused the thing she prayed for. She longed to keep me with her as mothers wish, yet she knew not what joy You were preparing for her out of my desertion."[6]

Ultimately, God has to do something inside us to enable us to defeat temptations. That is what happened to Augustine. When he came back to Africa from Rome, shortly after he got off the boat, he was accosted by one of his old girlfriends—one with whom he had had a long history of immoral experiences. He was with some friends and as he walked through the city, she stopped him, turned him around, and said, "Augustine—it is I."

He looked at her and said, "Yes—but it is not I." By the grace of God, he had become a true pilgrim.

FOOLISH ATTEMPTS TO EXCUSE SIN

If you think about it, and look at what the Bible says about sin for any length of time, you can come to only one conclusion: In addition to being wrong, sin on the part of the believer is insanity. When we decide to do wrong in the face of the reasons we have to do right, we simply are not thinking clearly. The tempter attempts to place us in a privileged position just as he tried to put the hungry Son of God in a privileged position. We boast of our special status against God.

What happens next takes a variety of forms and usually involves either inventing a cover-up or making some sort of excuse. Of course, we learn from the previous generation how to do this. Someone handed me a list recently of some of the actual excuses parents had written to teachers on behalf of their children. In this amazing list, we see parents showing their children creative—and misleading—excuses for skipping school.

For example: "Dear School: Please excuse John being absent on Jan. 28, 29, 30, 31, 32, and also 33." Or this one: "Please excuse my son's tardiness. I forgot to wake him up and I did not find him till I started making the beds." Another parent wrote, "Stanley had to miss some school. He had an attack of whooping cranes in his chest." (Many of us were under the impression that the disease was extinct.) A prophetic parent wrote, "Sally won't be in school a week from Friday. We have to attend a funeral."

So we learn the fine art of the excuse from reliable sources—as if, in fact, we needed any instruction. When it comes to King David, we can trace his steps from one level of sin-induced insanity to the next. He began as a king who had achieved a lot in a relatively short time. God had blessed him richly. He ended up involved in adultery, deception, and murder.

THE SAD STORY OF A FALL INTO SIN

David got into trouble through a clearly discernible series of steps, a sequence many have followed before and since. Study David's fall into the sins of adultery and murder, and you will see how sin results from certain wrong choices we make. David's first and major step into the abyss, the one upon which all the rest depended, involved something he *wasn't* doing.

First, David failed to be about the right things. Scripture strongly implies this at the beginning of the narrative of David's failure. The author of 2 Samuel implied David was not doing the right thing: "It happened in the spring of the year, at the time when kings go out to battle, that David sent Joab and his servants with him, and all Israel; and they destroyed the people of Ammon and besieged Rabbah. But David remained at Jerusalem" (11:1). Notice that the text says, "at the time when kings go out to battle," not "when armies go out to battle."

David should have been campaigning. The borders of Israel were insecure, and the Ammonites posed great danger to the people of God. David stayed behind and let others do the fighting. Why? We don't know. It doesn't matter; he did.

He should have been concerned for his people's welfare. The land that God promised to Abraham was still not in his offspring's hands at the time of this incident. God had sternly warned Israel not to compromise with any of the peoples who were occupying that property, but to drive them out. This work still remained to be done. David should have buckled on his sword and gone out to battle.

Mark it well: The episode with Bathsheba never would have happened if David had simply been applying himself to the work that God gave him to do. He strayed from the task at hand and gave the devil just the leverage he needed to entice him into failure.

This is the most important part when it comes to understanding temptation and staying away from it. If you will simply be about God's business in your own life, if you will occupy yourself with the healthy activities that we all need to engage in, major on the majors and not coddle yourself, you will find that you will have fewer opportunities to be faced with the destructive temptations that David was confronted with here. But there was a second step, too.

Second, David became curious about the wrong things. "Then it happened one evening that David arose from his bed and walked on the roof of the king's house. And from the roof he saw a woman bathing, and the woman was very beautiful to behold. So David sent and inquired about the woman" (2 Samuel 11:2–3). Since he had failed to keep busy with the right things, he now was confronted with a sight he ordinarily would have missed.

At the point he saw Bathsheba, the monster was lurking, but he still had several options open to him. For example, he could have left the roof. First Corinthians says to believers, "Flee sexual immorality" (1 Corinthians 6:18). It is not cowardice to run away from this situation; it is wisdom. Failure to do so is foolhardy. David stayed put to enjoy the view, misjudging the strength of his own evil impulses.

Alexander Graham Bell, in his younger days before he invented the telephone, used to entertain people by getting a piano to play a note without striking the keyboard. He would open the lid of the piano, hold down the pedal, and sing middle C. The string that represented that note would begin to vibrate and produce its own middle C in response to the frequency of his voice. There were properties in the string which responded to movement outside itself. That is what makes temptation so powerful. Temptation is outside the believer, but when it sends out its call, it finds an answering chord within us. The wise course is to flee. To entertain those wrong thoughts or linger upon unhealthy sights is foolish.

David could have turned his head. That would be a less acceptable method of dealing with temptation, however, because he could always turn it back. He would be staying within range of the temptation, and that is never a wise approach. Or he could have left his interest there, walking back into his palace and doing nothing. There was nothing in this encounter with temptation which forced David to pursue an interest in Bathsheba. At this point, his experience with temptation was strictly on a mental level. He could have, and should have, dealt with it there. Apparently he had already forgotten the lesson from his own experience with Goliath. Years before, when he was just a shepherd boy, he proved that when you deal with an enemy by attacking him in the head, even giants are vulnerable. You never want to get into a wrestling match with a Goliath. Regrettably, that is exactly what he now proceeded to do: "So David sent and inquired about the woman" (2 Samuel 11:3).

[David] was behaving foolishly . . .
he was behaving dangerously . . .
[and] he was behaving irresponsibly. . . .
[Soon] he would behave wickedly.

Then he took *the third step into the abyss: He chose to find an opportunity.* The writer of 2 Samuel noted: "Then David sent messengers, and took her; and she came to him" (2 Samuel 11:4).

Now the temptation had been brought within reach. Now rebellion could get its clammy fingers around David's throat. He had intentionally and insanely made himself vulnerable. Now he had the opportunity to indulge.

It has surprised some people that this narrative says nothing about Bathsheba's guilt in the matter. Didn't she sin, too? How is it that all the condemnation of the Scriptures falls on the shoulders of King David? The answer is that she indeed was guilty. She should not have participated. She was wrong to be unfaithful to the Lord and to her husband.

However, nothing in the text suggests she knew why David called for her to come to his home. David was her king. She owed him the courtesy of coming to him, and in any case he had the power to force her compliance. So the Scriptures are silent about the nature of her participation in this. We don't know her attitude about David at this point.

But above all, it was David who is guilty because he ought to have known better. He knew God's heart well, and he knew how the Lord would feel about his actions. He was a leader and an example in Israel, and the responsibility for honoring God rested squarely on his strong shoulders. He was behaving foolishly when he stayed home from his military campaigns. He was behaving dangerously when he started asking questions about Bathsheba. He was behaving irresponsibly by having her brought to him. In the fourth step, he would behave wickedly.

The fourth wrong choice David made was to actually participate in sin. "He lay with her" (2 Samuel 11:4). The deed was done; temptation had won.

David was now about to discover the truth of James 1:14–15, "Each one is tempted when he is drawn away by his own desires and enticed. Then, when desire has conceived, it gives birth to sin; and sin, when it is full-grown, brings forth death." He had been drawn away by desire. He had been enticed. Desire had conceived. Now it gave birth to sin. Unfortunately, sin now had a life of its own within David's life, and it would mature rapidly and produce, in short order, death.

James's warning that sin produces death would refer not to Uriah's death, but David's. For all who sin, the pain is most inflicted upon ourselves. A pilgrim acts self-destructively when he pushes ahead with sin in the face of knowing better.

Let's not forget that the pleasures of sin that attracted David had a price tag attached. Not only was death stalking him as the natural product of his actions, in Israel his actions were worthy of capital punishment, for that is the legal end result of adultery. Any two members of his staff who knew what had happened—and you can bet there were more than two—had the option of bringing charges before the high priest, and David could have been tried and executed.

That explains in part *the fifth and worst step into the abyss: the choice to conceal.* I believe concealment is the worst step, because it leads to more sin, and worse sin. Instead of a simple opponent, David was facing a Hydra—the monster from Greek mythology with its many serpent heads that seemed a never-ending nightmare. Every time the warrior cut off one head, two grew in its place. That was what David soon discovered. The proper choice is to confess and return to the heavenly Father, but often we, like David, try to cover it up.

The concealment began with deception. He summoned Bathsheba's husband, Uriah, to the palace. Second Samuel 11:7 says, "When Uriah had come to him, David asked how Joab was doing, and how the people were doing, and how the war prospered." David had suddenly become interested in the military campaign. You remember, that campaign he chose to stay home from. He was painting a picture of himself as the concerned commander here that is less than sincere. "And David said to Uriah, 'Go down to your house and wash your feet.' So Uriah departed from the king's house, and a gift of food from the king followed him" (2 Samuel 11:8). He wanted to make Uriah's home environment the essence of comfort. Come winter, he wanted Uriah's wife to have a baby that Uriah would think was his. The deception is a foot thick and furry all over; but it was only the beginning.

The concealment was complicated by David's disregard of Uriah's noble character.

> So when they told David, saying, "Uriah did not go down to his house," David said to Uriah, "Did you not come from a journey? Why did you not go down to your house?" And Uriah said to David, "The ark and Israel and Judah are dwelling in tents, and my lord Joab and the servants of my lord are encamped in the open fields. Shall I then go to my house to eat and drink, and to lie with my wife?

As you live, and as your soul lives, I will not do this thing." (2 Samuel 11:10–11)

David was thinking like a lowlife. Uriah was the one who was thinking like a king. He was the one concerned for the welfare of his soldiers, not David. Scripture holds few examples better than this one to show that sin blinds and deceives. You don't find people of the quality of a Uriah every day. He was a person of character. Not only that, he was a man of great military prowess, an accomplished soldier. Later in 2 Samuel, a list appears of some of the warriors who made David's kingdom possible, a sort of military Hall of Fame. There are thirty-seven members of David's hall, and one of them is Uriah the Hittite (2 Samuel 23:39). Yet David was trying to pull this noble warrior away from duty. The king was engaging in deception here, and he was deceiving himself in the process.

David also managed to engage Uriah in temptation. He urged Uriah to stay in Jerusalem, and "he made him drunk" (see 2 Samuel 11:12–13). He offered the noble warrior food and drink to soften him up and again made possible a night with his wife. Uriah resisted. David was running out of options to rid himself of personal responsibility. He soon learned that Uriah thought more clearly when he was drunk than David did when he was sober.

No more easy methods were available, so the king resorted to murder. "David wrote a letter to Joab and sent it by the hand of Uriah. And he wrote in the letter, saying, 'Set Uriah in the forefront of the hottest battle, and retreat from him, that he may be struck down and die'" (2 Samuel 11:14–15). He used the enemy to do his dirty work. "Sin, when it is full-grown, brings forth death" (James 1:15). What an incredible irony that Uriah was considered so trustworthy by David that he could put the letter in his hands that contained his own death warrant! Failure to be about the right things . . . curiosity about the wrong things . . . opportunity . . . execution . . . concealment. Those are the five steps into the abyss.

THE BEST PLACE TO STOP

The best place to deal with temptation is as far back in the process as you can get. Begin at the beginning: Don't be curious about the wrong things. Instead, apply yourself to the right things. If you do, you will limit the opportunities you have for being tempted. Little in life is as dangerous as having time on your hands. If, once you find yourself tempted, you will not follow up your curiosity, you will keep yourself from serious danger again.

God is gracious, and if most of us are honest with ourselves, we have to admit that the times we have given in to temptation have been in the face of plenty of opportunities to withdraw from it. The best place for a pilgrim to win over temptation is when it is in the distance.

ON THE JOURNEY

1. As you look at the five steps in the temptation process, at what place are you weakest and most vulnerable? What are your best weapons to counteract this weakness when you reach this step?

2. Do you ever move through the temptation process because you think you can bail out anytime? How can you better learn to bail out at step one?

THE SUFFERING
OF A PILGRIM

*For I consider that the sufferings of this present time
are not worthy to be compared with the glory
which shall be revealed in us.*

—ROMANS 8:18

*A*doniram Judson, born in 1788 to a Congregationalist pastor in Massachusetts, became the first overseas missionary from the United States. Settling in Burma, Judson began evangelistic work and Bible translation. When war broke out between England and Burma, however, he was arrested as a spy (although he was an American) and placed in prison to await execution.

His ankles were bound in irons during his time in the rat-infested prison. At night, guards would hoist his ankle fetters to a pole suspended from the ceiling so that only his head and shoulders rested on the ground.

His wife, left alone during his imprisonment, gave birth to a daughter while they were separated. Both mother and daughter fell ill and nearly died. After eighteen months, Judson was released. "One of the most pitiful and pathetic pages in the history of Christian missions is the page that describes the subsequent return of Mr. Judson to his stricken home. He was scarred, maimed, and emaciated by long suffering."[1]

His wife Nancy and their daughter Maria also were weak and ill. Shortly afterward, both died while on a trip to the United States.

Judson's theme and undergirding support while enduring such horrors was to turn his spiritual eyes onto the love of Christ. "'Think much on the love of Christ,' he used to say to all his converts and inquirers, 'think much on the love of Christ!'"[2] To think on the love of Christ while enduring unbelievable suffering is hardly a natural reaction. Then again, pilgrims are supposed to live with their eyes steadily focused on their supernatural homeland. Only by so doing can they exhibit a biblical attitude toward their pains.

THE PILGRIM'S ATTITUDE

The way we think about suffering doesn't remove it, but our attitude can temper it. Peter opened what is arguably the most profound discussion of suffering in the New Testament by identifying his readers as pilgrims: "Peter . . . to the pilgrims of the Dispersion in Pontus, Galatia, Cappadocia, Asia, and Bithynia" (1 Peter 1:1). For centuries, the word "Dispersion" had been used to refer to Jews from Palestine living among the Gentiles in places far from their birth. Peter put a new twist on the word. Peter's readers themselves were Gentiles,[3] but since becoming believers they knew the hardships of bearing witness to their eternal homeland. Now they were facing the strange experience of being outsiders in the place where they were born and even among their own families.

The going wasn't easy. They were facing stiff opposition, even slander, and that is why Peter was writing his letter.

We may never be asked to suffer to the degree Adoniram Judson did. Yet we may encounter suffering, including undeserved suffering. There is no more effective way for us to demonstrate our distinctiveness from the present age than when we exhibit a biblical attitude toward suffering—particularly the undeserved variety.

The Word of God speaks to the issue in some depth, but it does not give every answer we long for. It ultimately points us to the Ruler of the universe and challenges us to trust His goodness. The Scriptures teach us four ways we should view sufferings as we continue on life's greatest journey:

1. Suffering is inevitable in a fallen world.
2. Suffering is indispensable in a fallen world.
3. Suffering is irreplaceable in an uncertain world.
4. Suffering is invaluable in a curious world.

First, the Scriptures tell us that *suffering is inevitable* in the fallen world we inhabit. Suffering didn't exist until sin entered human existence. People now make choices not in an idyllic garden but in a dangerous environment. If we blunder, those choices can cost us dearly. What is more, the Bible speaks both of deserved and undeserved suffering. For example, Peter wrote, "For this is commendable, if because of conscience toward God one endures grief, suffering wrongfully [that is, undeservedly]. For what credit is it if, when you are beaten for your faults [that is, deservedly], you take it patiently? But when you do good and suffer, if you take it patiently, this is commendable before God" (1 Peter 2:19–20).

The Scriptures offer many examples of both varieties of suffering. First Corinthians 11:29–30 tells us that there were Christians in Corinth who were weak, sick, or even dead because they had been guilty of drunkenness and gluttony at the Lord's Table. That is deserved suffering. Peter insisted that no credit comes from such experiences.

When it comes to undeserved suffering, we think of the Lord Jesus Himself, who did everything right and nothing wrong, yet suffered both emotional and physical pain to the extreme. Yet it is such undeserved suffering that usually causes us internal struggles. We can understand the criminal receiving his just desserts for his actions. But what about those who haven't done anything to bring suffering on themselves?

What we also sometimes forget is that the world is a confusing place from the point of view of suffering. We often do wrong and *don't* suffer for it. That bothers us very little. It is rare to hear someone say, "Something happened yesterday that really disturbed me. I drove eighty miles an hour down the freeway and no one stopped me." But let us be pulled over when we are below the speed limit and we are incensed at the injustice of life.

Whether the suffering seems just or unjust, however, we must realize that suffering is inevitable, for pilgrims reside in a fallen world littered with the debris of sin. Furthermore, *suffering is indispensable,* allowing us to express our love for God. The Scriptures show that suffering is bound together with love There can be no *real* love in a world in which righteousness always yields rewards and wickedness always results in punishment. People would "love" God only because of the immediate consequences. To do right simply because it is right would be impossible if every such act was instantly rewarded and every choice an inexpensive one.

If a person were programmed to say, "I love you, God," surely the Creator would not regard that as worthwhile. But when Adoniram Judson could say from his scarred body, "Think much on the love of Christ," the statement is significant. When Job could sit in the ashes of his destroyed life and say, "Though He slay me, yet will I trust Him" (Job 13:15), that is significant. God places such a premium on freely given love that (humanly speaking) He placed His entire creation at risk in order to have it demonstrated.

What other kind of world than the one we have would permit freely given love to be displayed? One cannot have it both ways. Either people are truly free to love God, and there is the risk of rebellion (and the suffering that flows from it) because they are free not to love Him; or there is no risk because man is a machine.

Adam exhibited how wrong but meaningful choices result in suffering. Jesus Christ, on the other hand, demonstrated that real love for God is possible even in a world darkened by rebellion.

Before suffering . . . pilgrims must possess unsoiled character. . . . During suffering, pilgrims should show calmness.

People often speak of the example of Jesus, but rarely in the context that Scripture itself discusses His suffering. Peter said: "For to this you were called, because Christ also suffered for us, leaving us an example, that you should follow His steps" (1 Peter 2:21). Christ suffered in innocence—the only acceptable kind of suffering for pilgrims. Peter revealed three aspects of innocent suffering in this portion of his first letter.

Before suffering takes place, pilgrims must possess unsoiled character, as Jesus did: "[He] committed no sin, nor was deceit found in His mouth" (1 Peter 2:22). Two people can have exactly the same circumstances of suffering, but they will react differently because of the character that they bring to the experience.

During suffering, pilgrims should show calmness. "When He was reviled, [He] did not revile in return" (1 Peter 2:23). Christ took verbal abuse without returning any threats of retaliation. Someone told me the story of a pastor who was confronted by an angry church member. Upset over something the pastor had said, the parishioner met him outside church, clipped him with a solid right cross, and laid him out. One of the pastor's friends, hearing of the event, asked the victim, "So what did you do?"

The pastor answered, "Well, I remembered what Jesus said about turning the other cheek, so I got up and did so."

"Then what happened?"

"He hit me again."

"So what did you do?"

"I figured that the Scripture had been fulfilled, so I got up and let him have it."

That isn't exactly what Peter had in mind in his discussion of innocent suffering, but pain does commonly lead pilgrims to lose their heads. Instead of calmly appraising their situation, some have resorted to sulking or bitterness toward God. They think, *The Lord is the one who put me in this mess. I have Him to thank for it.* People pout and write off their relationship with God. Many people have gone through what they assess as one bad experience with the Lord, and have concluded that they can never trust Him again.

Another approach when rattled by suffering is to indulge in self-pity. People conclude that no one should be asked to endure what they are going through, and they bemoan their fate.

None of these reactions is acceptable to God. Instead, we are to be calm, recognizing that nothing passes our way which hasn't been approved at God's throne first. Again, we find help when we "see" the things that are invisible.

The supreme applicability of the example of Jesus, however, is found in His complete commitment to the Father during suffering. He "committed Himself to Him who judges righteously" (1 Peter 2:23). In other words, He looked outside the limitations of this world. He trusted the Father's good intentions for His life and waited patiently for the Father to vindicate Him.

Third, the Scriptures teach that *suffering is irreplaceable in an uncertain world.* Suffering usually must be involved if we are to grow spiritually. We all have impurities mixed with our faith, and most of the time we don't know how critically they affect us. Suffering brings that unwanted dross to the surface where we can't miss it.

Suffering more than anything else will make us truer reflections of the Savior.

I remember hearing about a Sunday school teacher who was teaching a unit on Malachi 3:3, "He will sit as a refiner and a purifier of silver; He will purify the sons of Levi, and purge them as gold and silver, that they may offer to the Lord an offering in righteousness." Since she knew little about precious metallurgy, she went to a jeweler and asked for a layman's introduction to the process of refining silver. The craftsman obliged, beginning with a small pot full of silver ore. He ignited a gas flame beneath it and waited for the ore to liquefy. Then he sat near the pot and waited for the impurities to float to the top of the bubbling mixture. When they did, he patiently scraped them off, exercising great care not to remove the silver itself. After watching for a while, the teacher thanked her instructor and made as if to go; but the craftsman stopped her.

"Wait," he said, "don't you want to know how I know when the process is over?"

"Certainly," she said.

"I know the silver is ready when I can bend over the pot and see my face reflected on its surface."

Suffering more than anything else will make us truer reflections of the Savior. Those who would escape the heat cheat themselves of being made like Him; yet we invariably want to get away from the pain. It's part of human nature, though God has gone to great lengths in taking away at least some of our options.

In his classic, *Where Is God When It Hurts?*, Philip Yancey described a medical experiment aimed at helping lepers. The physician in charge had concluded that leprosy is primarily a disease of the nervous system. People who have it lose fingers and toes simply because they have no pain warning system. So the doctor and his team spent five years trying to invent an artificial pain system for the hand. It consisted of a battery pack and a set of sensors. They invented an artificial nerve that could be placed on the fingertip like a glove. It would send an electric shock to the body when too much pressure was being applied.

They finally abandoned the effort. Why? Partly because the pain network in the body is incredibly complex and difficult to duplicate. But there was another reason, too. The doctor explained: "We also found out that the signal had to be out of the patient's reach. For even intelligent people, if they wished to do something which they were afraid would activate the shock, would switch off the signal, do what they had in mind to do, and then switch it on again when there was no danger of receiving an unpleasant signal. I remember thinking how wise God had been in putting pain out of reach."[4]

When suffering comes our way, we can't always turn it off—and it is good for us that we can't. We find out what is real in our faith, and what is not. Suffering teaches us about ourselves in ways that nothing else can. It is a unique, irreplaceable teaching tool that we should accept.

Fourth, the Scriptures pronounce *suffering is invaluable in a curious world*. Peter emphasized that Christ's suffering benefited others. Those outside the faith are drawn to Christ when they see godly suffering. Peter wrote, "Who is he who will harm you if you become followers of what is good? . . . Sanctify the Lord God in your hearts, and always be ready to give a defense to everyone who asks you a reason for the hope that is in you, with meekness and fear" (1 Peter 3:13–15).

People will look at you closely if you suffer in a godly way, and they will ask, "How can you handle what you are going through?" They're curious, and usually they're impressed. Don't think that they won't consider what you have to say. Righteous suffering will give you a wonderful basis for sharing unseen realities.

Your courageous suffering also can encourage other pilgrims to endure. Paul said in 2 Timothy 2:10, "I endure all things for the sake of the elect, that they also may obtain the salvation which is in Christ Jesus with eternal glory." Paul sometimes enumerated a long list of experiences of how he had suffered for the kingdom of God. People saw him and said, "If he can do it, so can we."

When he was released from death row in Burma after a year and a half of unspeakable suffering, Judson pleaded, upon his release, for permission to enter another province with the gospel. The ruler of Burma denied his request, saying, "My people are not fools enough to listen to anything a missionary might say, but I fear they might be impressed by your scars and turn to your religion."[5] Scars have a way of opening hearts.

FACING SOCIETY'S CONTEMPT

The agonies that Job and Adoniram Judson had to endure may not be ours. However, one variety of suffering is the common lot of virtually all those who profess to be God's pilgrims. I refer to the contempt or disdain by which the unbelieving world dismisses our faith.

One of the "Songs of Ascents," Psalm 123, addresses the contempt that the visible world casts toward the Christian—something that modern pilgrims don't handle particularly well.

The problem of contempt appears in Psalm 123:4, where the pilgrims observed, "Our soul is exceedingly filled with the scorn of those who are at ease, with the contempt of the proud." Believing sojourners have to swallow a lot of abuse from people who seem to have it made: "exceedingly filled with contempt . . . exceedingly filled with . . . scorn." Critics look down their proud noses and say, "You wouldn't be in this mess if you were like us. We've got it made. You've bought a lot of problems for yourself that come with your faith. That's ridiculous. Throw off those burdens of outmoded religion and walk in the bright light of modern progress. Be like us."

Scorn and contempt form the favorite weapons of every age when people are confronted with the truth. Their stings cause pilgrims to retreat from an open identification with Christ. They push us toward compromise.

When the psalmist wrote "exceedingly filled," he used a Hebrew term that commonly described eating until you just can't pack in another bite. The psalmist was up to the eyebrows with the abuse and caustic words of people who had no use for his values. Do you ever feel that way? Does it ever seem that you are all alone in your purpose to do right? Sometimes the worst pressure to conform comes from within one's family. Many believers I know have related to me how they are regarded as the black sheep in their families because they are Christians.

College students who are believers have to routinely face the disdain of teachers and classmates alike.

I experienced a little of that myself. Several years before his death, my father told me that he hoped that since I had moved to Georgia I would become a peanut farmer. When I inquired as to why that might be desirable, he told me that peanut farming, unlike the Christian ministry, was doing something useful with one's life. Contempt sometimes assumes odd forms.

College students who are believers have to routinely face the disdain of teachers and classmates alike. It does not solve the problem, but it at least tempers it to realize that such attitudes do not always emerge from a purely objective perspective. The modern university professor often has inherited a distaste for all things religious, an inheritance made more blatant by personal bias. Aldous Huxley was one of the most militant skeptics and atheists of the modern era. His poetry and scathing novels attack every value that Christianity espouses. In his maturity, he penned an autobiography in which he admitted that most of his attacks on religion were based on wishful thinking. He was an atheist because he had a deep-seated personal need for God not to be a factor in his life. This is what he said, looking back on his writing career:

> I had motives for not wanting the world to have a meaning; consequently assumed that it had not; and was able without any difficulty

to find satisfying reasons for this assumption. The philosopher who finds no meaning for this world is not concerned exclusively with the problem of pure metaphysics; he is also concerned to prove there is no valid reason why he personally should not do as he wants to. For myself, the philosophy of meaninglessness was essentially an instrument of liberation, sexual and political.[6]

This man, who as much as anybody in recent history is responsible for the sneering attitude of public universities against Christianity, came clean in this quote. What was his interest in promoting a universe without God? It freed him up to live as he pleased. So the proud tongues that throw contempt toward God's people have problems of their own, whether or not they are willing to own up to them. To be like them would mean turning one's back on the Lord.

To such accusers, we must show love. Pilgrims often forget our response must not be meeting fire with fire. To demonize them and sling insults back at them is equally to displease the Lord. "When He was reviled, [He] did not revile in return; when He suffered, He did not threaten, but committed Himself to Him who judges righteously" (1 Peter 2:23).

Those who show worldly contempt are described in Psalm 123 as being "those who are at ease" (verse 4)—people who have it made in the eyes of the world. They are also called "the proud." Unfortunately, theirs is the kind of pride that comes not from achievement, but from a wrong assessment of their station in life. The psalmist was thinking of the kind of pride discovered by a newspaper reporter as he interviewed an old rancher who had made a lot of money. The reporter asked him to what he would attribute his great success. The rancher replied, "It's been about 50 percent weather, 50 percent good luck, and the rest is brains."

How should we respond to contempt? The godly response appears in the psalmist's appeal to God: "Have mercy on us, O Lord, have mercy on us!" (verse 3). This is not a request for eternal salvation. The problem for the pilgrim psalmist was not eternity—it was the present. The pilgrims who sang Psalm 123 already knew where they were going. But they were strangling under a pile of scorn, so they appealed to God for mercy.

How does God exercise mercy? By one of three methods: (1) He lightens the load, or (2) He strengthens the back, or (3) He employs some combination of both. If you ask the average person what *mercy* means, he will almost always give you some variation of "lightening the load." But it is just as merciful, and in many ways more glorious, when God strengthens the back. Phillips Brooks, once Episcopal bishop of Boston, liked to advise young believers, "Do not pray for easy lives; pray to be stronger people! Do not pray for tasks equal to your powers; pray for powers equal to your tasks. Then doing of your work shall be no miracle, but you shall be a miracle."[7]

But once that is said, believers still face a problem of timing. We appeal, but when does God answer that appeal? So, the pilgrim psalmist turned to the question of what to do between now, the time the problem arrives, and then, when God chooses to express His mercy.

WAITING FOR DELIVERANCE

"Behold, as the eyes of servants look to the hand of their masters, as the eyes of a maid to the hand of her mistress" (Psalm 123:2). God is the master or mistress in the analogy, and we are the slaves or the maidservants. The word picture may be understood in two ways. One is to see it as a description of getting one's orders for the day. Slaves often stood around waiting for instructions. In another connection, that might be the point, but it is unlikely to be the thrust here. In Psalm 123:2 the issue is supply. Slaves had no income; they could produce no money to take care of their own needs. If they ate, it was because the master supplied the food. Christians who suffer the vicious words of skeptics and critics are unable to supply the solutions for themselves. They have to look to the Lord. In other words, they have to use pilgrim eyesight.

The verse continues, "so our eyes look to the Lord our God, until He has mercy on us." So how long are we to wait? How long do our eyes turn toward the Lord when we feel the hurt of the proud person's tongue? The answer is given here: until He has mercy on us. In other words, as long as it takes. This is exactly the halfway point in the psalm. It is also the centerpiece in the point God is trying to make to us pilgrims. Are we willing to wait for God to extend mercy?

Waiting is the believing sojourner's plan. The pilgrim headed toward Jerusalem expressed his determination to wait on the Lord, to keep his eyes on Him, in verse 1: "Unto You I lift up my eyes." He said, "I have no confidence in my own resources; I have no confidence in the gods of the current age; to You and You alone I look." The pilgrim finds his way through the maze of modern contempt by keeping his eyes toward the God of heaven. It is a view easily lost.

There have been a few times in the history of this planet when God decided to unveil His glory before men for the sake of encouraging His people during times of suffering. When Israel was on its way to the Promised Land, God did this for Moses and for the elders of Israel. The sacred text tells us that "They saw the God of Israel. And there was under His feet as it were a pavement of sapphire stone, and it was like the very heavens in its clarity. But on the nobles of the children of Israel He did not lay His hand. So they saw God, and they ate and drank" (Exodus 24:10–11). Ordinarily, a direct encounter with God in His majesty would kill a person. That's why Moses made his comment: "They saw God, and they ate and drank." The elders survived the vision because God meant it to encourage them. Such occasions have been exceptionally rare, however.

Naturally, we like to think that it would be a tremendous advantage to see a vision of God. In fact, we suspect that the select group of seventy-five people who saw the Lord at Sinai own a substantial advantage over us spiritually, and that if we were ever so fortunate as to see what they saw, we would never be the same again. We would thereafter walk with God every day. Most of these men, however, did not behave that way. They did well for a while, but later, when the water ran out, when the food was consumed, when the road proved hot and desolate, they defected. Most of them were in the group that later called for Moses' head.

The majesty of God's Person [should] comfort us when we are burdened by the contempt of pagans, by the scorn of the skeptics.

So what is the solution to the fading vision of God? It is to replace it with a fresh one. Putting our eyes on God is simpler for us than for them. We have so many doors into God's throne room in the Word of God that turning our eyes in His direction is much easier for us. We can do it whenever we choose to open His Book and learn of Him.

That is where we find our comfort and our encouragement to wait. We see the principle recognized in the second half of Psalm 123:1, where the psalmist called the Lord "You who dwell in the heavens." It is the majesty of God's person that is supposed to comfort us when we are burdened by the contempt of pagans, by the scorn of the skeptics. We are not supposed to ignore the reality of the problems we face; we are merely to see how much greater God is than those problems.

The king of Syria once sent a huge army to capture Elisha the prophet, who was visiting Dothan. The army arrived at night, and when the city awoke in the morning, the inhabitants were terrified to find themselves surrounded. Even Elisha's servant panicked and complained to the prophet, "Alas, my master! What shall we do?" (2 Kings 6:15). The prophet reassured him: "Do not fear, for those who are with us are more than those who are with them" (2 Kings 6:16).

The servant's response is not recorded. We would understand if he had wondered about the prophet's sanity. In reality, however, the servant's vision was defective, bringing Elisha to pray, " 'Lord . . . open his eyes . . .' Then the Lord opened the eyes of the young man, and he saw. And behold, the mountain was full of horses and chariots of fire all around Elisha" (2 Kings 6:17). The prophet was the safest man on the planet that day.

Elisha's prayer was as instructive as his calmness was soothing. He did not ask God to assemble the spiritual army that protected him; it was already in place. Elisha saw it; his servant did not. Elisha was not treading the ragged edge of insanity. He was dealing with what was utterly and finally real. Those around him were the deficient ones. Pilgrims who ignore the unseen spiritual world around them cannot hope to behave in a godly way when suffering comes.

What the young man needed was spiritual eyes to see what was already there. Nor does such protection apply solely to prophets and key players in God's purpose: "The angel of the Lord encamps all around those who fear Him, and delivers them" (Psalm 34:7).

The pilgrim suffers only because a benevolent God—for good and adequate reasons known only to Him—restrains His hand.

Keeping our eyes off God and His resources is the number one tool in the devil's arsenal, and the greatest enemy of the right spiritual choice is a consciousness of the routine. C. S. Lewis dramatized the issue in the first letter of his *Screwtape Letters*. A man is sitting in the Metropolitan Library in London, England. He has been a skeptic all his life. The idea of God hasn't even entered the picture of his world until now. Somehow, as he sits there reading, and thinking, and reflecting, his thoughts begin to bend toward God. The demon who writes this imaginary letter senses warning lights flashing. He's kept the man away from God for many years. He's not about to let him go now. But what's a tempter to do? How can he derail this dangerous train of thought?

Don't get him to debate it with himself, he thinks. *Don't get him to argue about it.* The Lie can never stand up to the Truth. So instead, he taps the man on the shoulder of his heart. And he whispers to him: "Aren't you really a bit hungry? Don't you think you could sort it all out better after lunch?"

He encourages the man to go out to the street and to look for a restaurant. The newspaper boys are shouting for sales. Old bus number 73 comes lumbering by, and the sights and the sounds distract him. The sense of God's accessibility is gone. The vision loses its power. The man muddles on in his skeptical mire.[8]

That loss of the vision of God is what pilgrimages—the environment of the Songs of Ascent—were designed to combat. Three times a year, every year, every Israelite was expected to send at least the head of the household to Jerusalem to worship. People were supposed to get away from the mundane and the routine and remind themselves who their God was. It had a way of making sense out of the rest of the year.

I'm sure as they walked up the hill to Jerusalem that there were skeptics along the road. There must have been people who sneered at them. Imagine taking a portion of your income and giving it to God! Imagine going such long distances just to gather in the temple grounds and eat and drink and worship with the people of God! But all the scorn and contempt in the world is no match for a fresh vision of God. That is food for the soul. That is what refreshes us and keeps us going in a hostile world.

I don't know what the attack point of your current contempt

is—in any case everybody's is different—but I do know who your God is, and I know that He hasn't changed. He still dwells in the heavens. He hears every appeal for mercy. The question is: Are you patient enough to wait until He has decided to deliver it?

Until He has delivered, suffering undeservedly is a way God opens doors to us for ministry that we can never sustain apart from suffering. Evangelist and preacher Vance Havner once observed, "God uses broken things. Broken soil to produce a crop, broken clouds to give rain, broken grain to give bread, broken bread to give strength. It is the broken alabaster box that gives forth perfume. It is Peter, weeping bitterly, who returns to greater power than ever."[9] In our brokenness, not in our power, lies our potential.

ON THE JOURNEY

1. Think back to both your greatest and worst moments in dealing with suffering in your life. How did you receive God's grace in the former situation but fail to procure it in the latter? What was your perspective in each case?

2. Ask God to give you the spiritual sight to comprehend the heavenly reality of His aid in times of suffering. Review Scripture to better comprehend this truth.

12

THE REWARDS
OF A PILGRIM

*For the Son of Man will come in the glory
of His Father with His angels, and then
He will reward each according to his works.*

—MATTHEW 16:27

*F*lorence Chadwick adjusted the strap on her swimming cap and stepped into the bone-chilling waters off Catalina Island. On this foggy Independence Day morning of 1952, she would try to become the first woman to swim the twenty-six-mile strait between the island and the California mainland. As she began her eastward swim, she heard several boat engines purring through the mist. Though she could barely see the small craft, she knew that the nearest one held her mother and her trainer. Another boat held a collection of reporters who were there to cover the event. Still another contained two men armed with rifles to drive away curious sharks.

Florence already had become the first American woman to swim the English Channel in both directions. She was well-prepared for the effort and confident that she would make it. As noon passed, she was still going strong, though certain of her direction only because an assistant was carefully monitoring a nautical compass.

After fifteen hours of constantly fighting the Pacific's waves, however, Florence began to talk of giving up. Her mother and trainer encouraged her to stay in the water. They were sure that the California coastline couldn't be far away—though nothing could be seen through the white wall of fog.

Florence continued for a while, but she had to be pulled from the water after 15 hours and 55 minutes. What defeated her was neither a muscle cramp nor a predator, but the discouragement that came from being unable to see her objective.

In reflecting on her failure, she said, "I'm not excusing myself, but if I could have seen the land I might have made it." It turned out that she was only a half mile from the coastline when she gave up.

Two months later, Florence succeeded in a second attempt during equally foggy conditions. Her success came because she kept a mental picture of the shoreline in view as she swam along. She succeeded not merely in swimming the channel, but also in breaking the men's record by two hours in the process.[1]

Pilgrims commonly experience similar troubles in moving toward their destination. We need to maintain a mental picture of where we are going. Regrettably, our perceptions of the age to come are dimmed by the fog of shoddy exegesis and the buildup of church tradition. God made us to function best when we understand where we're going and why, so we need to consider what the Scriptures teaches about our destination.

THREE STAGGERING BENEFITS

Following the Second Coming, Jesus Christ will set up His kingdom and reward pilgrims who have been faithful to their homeland and their King during the present age. At the judgment seat of Christ, believers will be examined to determine their level of faithfulness to the Lord Jesus. "Each one's work will become clear; for the Day will declare it, because it will be revealed by fire;

and the fire will test each one's work, of what sort it is. If anyone's work which he has built on it endures, he will receive a reward. If anyone's work is burned, he will suffer loss; but he himself will be saved, yet so as through fire" (1 Corinthians 3:13–15).

Biblical rewards essentially consist of three staggering benefits: (1) intimacy with Christ in the age to come; (2) sharing a portion of His royal authority in His kingdom; and (3) commendation at the judgment seat of Christ.

Intimacy with Christ in His coming kingdom is a great promise; but like many promises, it comes with a condition. On that fateful Thursday night in the Upper Room, the Savior observed, "You are those who have continued with Me in My trials. And I bestow upon you . . . that you may eat and drink at My table in My kingdom" (Luke 22:28–30). He made a promise to His closest associates on the basis of their loyalty in the midst of testing. This promise was His return for three and one-half years of faithful service rendered. The promises were made on the basis of what they had already done. The disciples couldn't invalidate it by their behavior on the night of His arrest. Many people moved in and out of the life of the Lord Jesus; the disciples stayed, and He refused to let that steadiness go unrewarded.

Without any biblical basis, many simply assume that all Christians will experience equal intimacy with the Lord Jesus in the future. That is simply not true. Equal access, maybe; but not equal intimacy. Intimacy with Christ in the age to come is paradoxically (and wonderfully) a result of intimacy with Christ now. He said, "To him who overcomes I will grant to sit with Me on My throne, as I also overcame and sat down with My Father on His throne" (Revelation 3:21). The word "overcomes" translates a Greek word commonly used for victory in battle. Jesus won His spiritual battles and calls on us to do the same. If we do, we will enjoy the closeness of those who have been comrades in arms.

Second, we will share royal authority. That's an even more amazing promise; but again, it's one with a condition. In the same passage, Jesus added a still more amazing promise of reward: "You are those who have continued with Me in My trials. And I bestow upon you a kingdom, just as My Father bestowed one upon Me, that you may . . . sit on thrones judging the twelve tribes of Israel" (Luke 22:28–30).

Again, we see the connection between faithfulness and privilege. "He who overcomes, and keeps My works until the end, to him I will give power over the nations—'He shall rule them with a rod of iron'" (Revelation 2:26–27). I will have more to say about sharing authority in the remainder of this chapter.

Third, there is the promise of commendation for faithful service to the Master. In Jesus' parable of the talents, meant to picture the judgment seat of Christ, "His lord said to him, 'Well done, good and faithful servant; you were faithful over a few things, I will make you ruler over many things. Enter into the joy of your lord'" (Matthew 25:21). The servant was commended and promised royal authority. This life offers nothing to compare to the praise the Master is supremely qualified to extend. Knowing that we are engaged in what is praiseworthy in His eyes ought to encourage us to persist in doing good. In time, His commendation will be worth whatever it costs to merit it.

ANTICIPATING OUR FUTURE HOME

These statements presuppose an ordered society in the age to come when the pilgrims occupy the visible world. Heaven itself anticipates the occasion: "There were loud voices in heaven, saying, 'The kingdoms of this world have become the kingdoms of our Lord and of His Christ, and He shall reign forever and ever!'" (Revelation 11:15). The second coming of Christ, so central to all of biblical teaching, will mark the time when the unseen homeland of the pilgrim will bring every earthly authority beneath its government.

Heaven is never the hope of the believer; the kingdom of God is.

Both Testaments ring with references to the second coming of Christ. The Old Testament contains some 1,800 references to it. The New Testament holds about 300 references to the Second Coming in its 260 chapters. To place this in perspective, it means that one of every thirty verses in the New Testament touches on the subject. Someone has calculated that for every prophecy in the

Bible about Christ's first coming there are eight anticipating His Second Coming.

Contrary to the view of pop culture, the focus of that Second Coming—what is supposed to be the hope of every Christian—is not to live with God forever in heaven. The Bible's focus from the first page to the last is that the earth will be the future home of believers. Heaven is never the hope of the believer; the kingdom of God is.

After God created man, He placed him on an earth specifically designed for man's habitation. When he fell, man twisted and ruined his relationship with both the Creator and the creation. God's design—to provide a world suited to man's nature and limitations while challenging him spiritually—was temporarily hindered. Man's defection from the divine purpose does not mean, however, that it will not eventually be fulfilled. The most dramatic scene in all the Bible describes that fulfillment. Long after the Second Coming, after the millennial age (described in Revelation 20:1–6), after all the judgments have taken place and sin is only a memory, God's Word presents an astonishing close to human history. Indeed, the closing scene of the Bible finds a new earth welcoming the new city of Jerusalem *coming down out of heaven* (Revelation 21:1–3). The new city is the capital of the final form of things— the kingdom of God.

What is more, God Himself will be there:

> I, John, saw the holy city, New Jerusalem, coming down out of heaven from God, prepared as a bride adorned for her husband. And I heard a loud voice from heaven saying, "Behold, the tabernacle of God is with men, and He will dwell with them, and they shall be His people. God Himself will be with them and be their God." (Revelation 21:2–3)

Somehow, we have managed to reverse what Scripture teaches. In the popular view, man's ultimate destiny is to go to heaven to be with God. In Scripture, God comes to earth to be with man. How Christendom managed to accomplish this astonishing reversal would require a separate book. The implications, however, are significant.

James Rue, an orthopedic surgeon and a member of the board of trustees at Tenth Presbyterian Church in Philadelphia, attended church faithfully but seldom gave any indication that his pas-

tor's sermons were stimulating him. His pastor was the respected preacher and expositor Donald Grey Barnhouse; yet for ten
years Dr. Rue never once made eye contact with Barnhouse during a sermon. Then one Sunday, Barnhouse said that eternity
would not be simply a matter of "sitting on a cloud, playing a
harp, and polishing your crown." At that, Dr. Rue for the first time
suddenly sat up straight, looked at Dr. Barnhouse with obvious
interest, and began to follow his message closely.

His attention grew even more intense as Barnhouse continued with his conception of eternal living: "Now, for example, God
is the author of all things. I read in a paper this week that there
are 37,000 varieties of wild flowers. Now these are all thoughts
of God. God thought up the flowering plants—the red ones, the
white ones, the green. He thought up the various leaves, and all
the glories of the springtime. If you are botanically minded, you
can go to God and say, 'I love your flower thoughts. I'd like to
classify a million varieties.' And God will say, 'Let there be a million varieties,' and you can go to work on them!"[2]

By this time the good doctor was fascinated. He sought out
Barnhouse at the conclusion of the message and admitted that
when it came to eternity, "I always looked forward to it with some
boredom. I think I can say for the first time in my life that I am ea-
ger to go there."[3] I suspect that Dr. Rue's private misgivings are
more widely shared than most people will admit.

THE DIVINE GOVERNMENT

The kingdom of God is in fact a kingdom. The very word *kingdom* suggests a hierarchy of administrative levels of authority:
kings, vice-regents, governors, mayors, and other features of government that kingdoms possess. The future condition of the earth
is described in John's observation, "The nations of those who are
saved shall walk in its light, and the kings of the earth bring their
glory and honor into [the new Jerusalem]" (Revelation 21:24).
Note his reference to "the kings of the earth." Pilgrims should
want to know who these people are.

They obviously are not independent kings. There is only one
supreme Ruler in the age to come. They thus have to be rulers who
exercise their authority under Jesus Christ. The kings of the earth
are people who have authority over various parts of the globe—

the new one. They will move in and out of the city—apparently for conferences and celebrations with the Lord Jesus.

Every Christian has read references in both Testaments about the kingdom of God. We know that Jesus will be King there. We also remember certain references to our reigning with Him. That, however, raises an important question: Over whom will we be reigning? If unbelievers will not be present in eternity, if rebels have been removed, who are the subjects of the kingdom of God?

It is inescapable that the subjects of the kingdom are Christians—people who are qualified to enter the kingdom solely because they put their trust in His saving work. The character of their Christian lives will not qualify them for high office in Christ's kingdom, but they are there as part of the general population of that kingdom.

These matters occupy a great deal of space in the New Testament. In Matthew 19:27, Peter spoke for the disciples when he asked Jesus a pointed question: "We have left all and followed You. Therefore what shall we have?" Modern commentators often seem quite disturbed by Peter's query, suggesting that the outspoken apostle was somehow out of line by wanting to know what lay in the future for himself and his colleagues. Jesus, however, took him seriously and issued a clear answer—an answer that included Peter and the disciples and us as well.

KINGDOM RULE FOR THE EARLY DISCIPLES

Jesus answered, "Assuredly I say to you, that in the regeneration [referring to the events following the Second Coming], when the Son of Man sits on the throne of His glory, you who have followed Me will also sit on twelve thrones, judging the twelve tribes of Israel" (Matthew 19:28). This answer, which is clear enough in the main, suffers from a translation difficulty. "Judging" in a context such as this does not primarily refer to judicial but to executive functions. The disciples are not being told that they will decide who will enter the kingdom. That prerogative belongs exclusively to Jesus (John 5:22).

Instead, they are being promised positions as rulers over the tribes of (converted) Israel in the age to come. In modern democracies, executive and judicial functions are separated, but in the world to come they will be united. Such government was apparently what the apostle Paul had in mind when he wrote, "Do you not know that we shall judge angels?" (1 Corinthians 6:3). Likewise, the judges of the Book of Judges were regional governors; that is apparently what Jesus promised Peter and the disciples as a result of their labors for Him. The reward Jesus promised must have delighted them, for they should have understood their future role not as a way of lording it over their fellow subjects, but in terms of its privileges of association with the Lord Jesus.

KINGDOM RULE FOR MODERN DISCIPLES

However, Jesus' answer expanded to include an invitation to us. Note the way He put it: "*Everyone* who has left houses or brothers or sisters or father or mother or wife or children or lands, for My name's sake, shall receive a hundredfold" (Matthew 19:29, italics added). Not a hundred percent, but a hundredfold. Invest $100 worth of funds or effort, get back $10,000 worth (or 900 percent interest over the life of the investment.)

Jesus placed qualifying for these rewards primarily in terms of sacrifice. Does this mean that pilgrims are consigned to a life of misery now in order to be great in the kingdom of God? Not at all. Mark's account added some important detail. "Assuredly, I say to you, there is no one who has left house or brothers or sisters or father or mother or wife or children or lands, for My sake and the gospel's, who shall not receive a hundredfold now in this time—houses and brothers and sisters and mothers and children and lands, with persecutions—and in the age to come, eternal life" (Mark 10:29–30).

What does He mean? Simply this: When you allow your faith to cost you the ordinary privileges, comforts, and relationships of life, you find that God has ways of replacing them—even now. If you decide to go on a mission's trip for two weeks, you will find that the family you left behind, whom you miss so terribly, is partly compensated for by the people you spend time with on the trip. Your fellow missionaries become dear to you because you are serving Christ together. At the same time, you find that the house you left behind has been replaced by a dozen houses in the place to which you go, thanks to the courtesy of like-minded pilgrims.

Earlier we considered David Livingstone's willingness to wholly trust the word of Jesus Christ implicitly. One of the few missionaries in Africa in the mid-nineteenth century, Livingstone labored under unbelievable hardship. Not long after he first arrived on the field, he was attacked by a lion and his left arm was maimed and became useless for the rest of his life. In 1862, his wife died of a fever. He lost everything that a man can lose while serving Christ on the mission field—and eventually would lose his very life in service to the Master. When he was asked at one point to reflect on his losses, he told a group of students:

> For my own part, I have never ceased to rejoice that God has appointed me to such an office. People talk of the sacrifice I have made in spending so much of my life in Africa. . . . Is that a sacrifice which brings its own blest reward in healthful activity, the consciousness of doing good, peace of mind, and a bright hope of glorious destiny hereafter? Away with the word in such a view, and with such a thought! It is emphatically no sacrifice. Say rather it is a privilege. Anxiety, sickness, suffering, or danger, now and then, with a foregoing of the common conveniences and charities of this life, may make us pause, and cause the spirit to waver, and the soul to sink; but let this only be for a moment. All these are nothing when compared with the glory which shall be revealed in and for us. I never made a sacrifice.[4]

You can mark it down as a principle of pilgrim living: *The deeper your commitment to the age to come, the less you feel deprived of anything you lose in this age.* Sacrifice in the biblical sense is seldom in the eye of the sacrificer.

---

*Things that would ordinarily seem painful
and difficult aren't when you are doing
what you love. Sacrifices don't seem sacrificial.*

It's a little like the wild story of the two devoted fishermen. When their wives decided to invite them to go shopping the next morning, the husbands looked at each other with a nod and a wink. "Sorry, we'd love to go, but we've already made plans to go fishing with each other tomorrow. We're getting up at five in the morning," one of the men said. "It's unfortunate, but I guess we won't be able to go shopping with you."

The next day, the two did awake early; and quickly they drove to the lake. They were out in their boat fishing away when a storm arose. The lake became agitated and the men experienced great difficulty keeping the boat under control. Maneuvering their way toward the marina, they ran up on a sandbar and the boat could not be driven off. Both men jumped overboard and began to push and shove with all their strength, trying to move the boat into deeper water. With his legs almost knee-deep in mud, and the waves bouncing him against the side of the boat, and his hair blowing wildly in the wind, one of the men shouted to the other with a knowing grin, "Sure beats shopping, doesn't it?"

As a fisherman myself, I've been in spots almost identical to that myself. I can vouch for the fact that it sure does beat shopping. It also makes an important point: Things that would ordinarily seem painful and difficult aren't when you are doing what you love. Sacrifices don't seem sacrificial to the one whose heart is in tune with Him who left heaven itself for us. However, He still counts them so, and rewards them generously.

Unfortunately, nothing could be clearer—nor more painful—than the fact that not all Christian disciples are willing to endure the sometimes unpleasant challenges of walking with Christ in the way Jesus described in these texts. Paul wrote, "If we endure, we shall also reign with Him" (2 Timothy 2:12). By implication, if we don't endure, we don't reign with Him. We become subjects in His kingdom by His grace; but we do not reign.

Scripture tells us about the motivation of Jesus Christ in coming to earth and dying for our sins. We are told that He did it out of love for us and in obedience to the Father's plan. But we are also told something else—that He was able to fulfill His work because He was motivated by the future. We are told to "[look] unto Jesus, the author and finisher of our faith, who *for the joy that was set before Him* endured the cross, despising the shame, and has sat down at the right hand of the throne of God" (Hebrews 12:2, italics added). The Lord Jesus looked beyond the shame of the cross to the day when His joy would be complete, and the certainty of it is made sure by His present position at the Father's right hand. "The joy that was set before Him" was not to sit at the Father's right hand presently, a merely temporary condition. As He entered heaven, the Father issued the invitation: "Sit at My right hand, til I make your enemies your footstool" (Psalm 110:1). It is in the eternal kingdom of God when "the joy that was set before Him" will be realized.

Such an anticipation of joy does not require the foregoing of present enjoyments. The Lord Jesus certainly did not exhibit a consciousness an attitude of day-to-day misery as He went about doing the Father's work. While He was "a Man of sorrows and acquainted with grief" (Isaiah 53:3), His life expressed the delights that come from constant contact with the Father, at whose right hand are lasting pleasures (Psalm 16:11).

SOME OBJECTIONS

What I have written above is only a condensation of a great deal of biblical teaching, of course. Each point deserves a fuller exposition than I can provide here. However, it will be worth our time to consider a few objections that are brought against the scenario I have presented.

The first objection is: Jesus told the disciples that He was going to prepare a place for them to be with Him, and we know He went to heaven. Therefore we will be with Him in heaven. Ask a hundred Christians where they expect to spend eternity, and at least ninety-five will reply, "Heaven." Some of those will point to Jesus' words in the Upper Room: "In My Father's house are many mansions. . . . I go to prepare a place for you. And if I go and prepare a place for you, I will come again and receive you to Myself; that where I am, there you may be also" (John 14:2–3). As far as most people are concerned, that settles that.

The matter may not be quite so simple, however. Jesus' statement allows for the possibility that the "mansions" He is preparing *could* be located in heaven eternally. It does not, however, force us to that conclusion. Jesus' intention could just as easily be: "I'm going to prepare the many dwelling places of the New Jerusalem. As soon as it is ready and the timing is right, I'm going to bring it back for you—and Me—to dwell in." Since that is precisely what the closing scenes of Revelation teach, we are on safe ground to conclude that that is what He meant. Of course, believers who die prior to the Second Coming go directly to heaven to await that grand event. However, heaven is not where they will remain.

The earthly destiny of the redeemed is also anticipated in the early chapters of the book of Revelation. John tells how the inhabitants of heaven joined together in a hymn of praise: "You are worthy . . . for You were slain, and have redeemed us to God by Your blood out of every tribe and tongue and people and nation, and have made us kings and priests to our God; and we shall reign on the earth" (Revelation 5:9–10).

Another objection is that Jesus commanded every follower to store up treasure in heaven. Indeed, the Master said, "Lay up for yourselves treasures in heaven, where neither moth nor rust destroys and where thieves do not break in and steal. For where your treasure is, there your heart will be also" (Matthew 6:20–21).

A little word study may help. The words "lay up treasures" translate a single Greek word, *thesaurizo,* from which our word *thesaurus* is drawn. The term means to "lay up something in storage," and the definition itself suggests the place of heaven in the believer's plans. But storage is, by its nature, temporary. We store up treasure in heaven so that it can be brought back with Christ, not so we can enjoy it in heaven. The closing page of Scripture contains these words of the Lord Jesus: "Behold, I am coming quickly, and My reward is with Me, to give to every one according to his work" (Revelation 22:12).

"Well," others may argue, "what about Peter's reference to 'an inheritance incorruptible and undefiled and that does not fade away, reserved in heaven for you'?" (1 Peter 1:4). The inheritance is reserved there, but it comes back with Him. Along the same lines, Paul referred to "the hope which is laid up for you in heaven" (Colossians 1:5). Heaven is where the hope is stored, not where it stays.

The final objection is that Jesus' repeated use of the phrase "kingdom of heaven" seems to suggest Christ's kingdom is indeed in heaven. The phrase "kingdom of heaven" deserves special treatment. It appears thirty-two times in the New Testament, all in the Gospel According to Matthew. The casual reader may understand this expression to mean "the kingdom which is in heaven," but more careful students will recognize that "kingdom of heaven" is merely a variant way of saying "kingdom of God." For example, Jesus said in Matthew 13:11, "It has been given to you to know the mysteries of the kingdom of heaven." In Mark 4:11, in what appears to be a record of the same speech, Jesus said, "To you it has been given to know the mystery of the kingdom of God." To suggest that the reference is to two different kingdoms seems utterly gratuitous.

One other example from Matthew is helpful. Jesus seemed to use as synonyms the phrases *kingdom of heaven* and *kingdom of God*. "Then Jesus said to His disciples, 'Assuredly, I say to you that it is hard for a rich man to enter the kingdom of heaven. And again I say to you, it is easier for a camel to go through the eye of a needle than for a rich man to enter the kingdom of God'" (Matthew 19:23–24).

LET'S ANTICIPATE OUR FUTURE REWARD

When the Lord Jesus ascended to heaven and promised to return and reward those who lived faithfully for Him, He warned them that His return would be at a time they would least expect. Two millennia have come and gone since, but it is possible to trace the gradual loss of hope in His return over time. We are now at a low point when it comes to the contemplation of true worth, according to C. S. Lewis:

> If we consider the unblushing promises of reward and the staggering nature of the rewards promised in the Gospels, it would seem that Our Lord finds our desires not too strong, but too weak. We are half-hearted creatures, fooling about with drink and sex and ambition when infinite joy is offered us, like an ignorant child who wants to go on making mud pies in a slum because he cannot imagine what is meant by the offer of a holiday at the sea. We are far too easily pleased.[5]

We are told explicitly in Hebrews 11 that "Moses, when he became of age, refused to be called the son of Pharaoh's daughter, choosing rather to suffer affliction with the people of God than to enjoy the passing pleasures of sin, esteeming the reproach of Christ greater riches than the treasures in Egypt; for *he looked to the reward*" (Hebrews 11:24–26, italics added). He knew that the commendation of the God of heaven would outweigh anything he might receive in the present age. Similarly, Abraham "waited for the city which has foundations, whose builder and maker is

God" (verse 10). We are also told that he and the other patriarchs "died in faith, not having received the promises, but having seen them afar off were assured of them, embraced them and confessed that they were strangers and pilgrims on the earth" (verse 13).

Some suggest that to exercise any interest in eternal rewards inevitably detracts from the day-to-day business of walking with God. One crude form of this objection is the statement, "You can be so heavenly minded you are of no earthly good."

However, the whole idea of laying up treasure in heaven is that we accomplish it by being of earthly good. That is, if we behave in a way that Jesus Christ would desire, by doing good to others and by building up His church, that present activity is what provides us a rich treasure for the future.

Another objection is that thinking about rewards is intrinsically selfish. Yet Moses, Abraham, and the Lord Jesus Himself are commended because they were looking beyond the immediate difficulties they faced to the reward God had in store for them. This kind of objection is based on a twisted system of virtues that makes unselfishness the highest of all possible motives. That is not biblical, as C. S. Lewis aptly observed: "The New Testament has lots to say about self-denial, but not about self-denial as an end in itself. We are told to deny ourselves and to take up our crosses in order that we may follow Christ; and nearly every description of what we shall ultimately find if we do so contains an appeal to desire."[6]

When we hear that Christ died for our sins, we don't refuse to put our trust in Him because that would be selfish. When you read the New Testament, you are constantly coming across commands that are linked with motives for obedience. Why? Because we will be better off if we do. God constantly encourages us to do what is right for ourselves by doing what is right for others. God's system of motivational ethics is simple, and based on this principle: Everything that I do that benefits someone else also benefits me. Pilgrims never face a conflict in this regard. We do not compete as Christians for a finite number of rewards. The inheritance of Jesus Christ includes "all things." By thinking about rewards myself, I do not keep anyone else from gaining every reward that he can possess.

A kind of twisted definition of "selfishness" has crept into our Christian vocabularies. The revised version insists that selfishness is being interested in our own welfare; but only a little thought reveals the folly of this kind of thinking. If we are out of line whenever we seek our own welfare, then how can we justify becoming Christians to begin with? Our concern to escape eternal condemnation becomes a selfish decision according to such a definition. The same could be said of moving out of the way of an oncoming automobile.

"Looking to the reward" is not the only motive for godly living . . . but rewards form one critical motive in Christian living— a motive that has been sorely neglected.

Contrary to this popular but unjustified definition, Scripture teaches that "God . . . gives us richly all things to enjoy" (1 Timothy 6:17). Zane Hodges explains what selfishness really is:

> Selfishness ought not to be defined simply as the pursuit of our own self-interest. Instead, it should be defined as *the pursuit of our self-interest in our own way rather than in God's way.* Since "love" is a preeminent virtue in Christianity, true selfishness often involves a pursuit of self-interest that violates the law of love. But no one who seriously pursues heavenly treasure can afford to be unloving. . . . It is not selfish to obey God by pursuing eternal rewards. Still less can someone who does so afford to be selfish in nature. For if he is, he is forfeiting the very rewards he professes to seek.[7]

Of course, "looking to the reward" is not the only motive for godly living—not by a long shot. We are to do good out of our love for Jesus Christ. We are to do good because we will be blessed right now in so doing. We are also told in Scripture to conduct our lives on the basis of godly fear; but rewards form one critical motive in Christian living—a motive that has been sorely neglected.

Equipping people for an eternity of ruling with Christ is the primary business that God is now carrying on within the church. He is bringing people into His family and then, by placing them into His service, is training them for greatness, as the late British pastor G.H. Lang observed:

At present, God is not saving the human race entire and its affairs corporate, but is selecting from it the company that are to rule the universe, superseding the existing government. He is preparing for a complete reorganizing of His entire empire, and is giving to these future rulers the severe training which is indispensable to fitting them for such responsible duties and high dignities. . . . There is manifest wisdom in a great Leader first training a body of efficient subordinates before seeking to reorganize society at large.[8]

That is a destiny that ought to thrill the most jaded. Think of it—an entire universe to rule and explore and bring under His authority! That calls for the best that regenerate human ability has to offer; all the devotion that we can bring to it, a challenge worthy of our best gifts.

At the moment, however, the people whom God has in mind to rule the future exercise little influence in the present age. You can let that discourage you if you choose, but you really shouldn't. Instead, expect it, for Jesus said it would be this way (see, for example, John 15:18; 16:2).

THE GREAT REVERSAL

The Lord Jesus said that we live in a world that is in the clutches of the Evil One at the moment, so we face spiritual limits to the effectiveness we can expect. But we are also to remember that the current situation will change at the Second Coming in an instant. We have seen such a reversal happen before, and by divine design.

We need only recall the career of the shepherd boy David. He was a nobody of nobodies. The youngest of eight sons of Jesse, he was lightly regarded by his father and brothers; but he was a young man of faith and devotion to God. One day, when Saul was ruling Israel, God sent Samuel to Bethlehem to anoint David king.

God had already decided that the current kingship would not last and had Samuel anoint David as the future king. For many years, however, he was only a king in waiting. In fact, when Saul received word of David's appointment, he began to persecute David, eventually driving him into the Jordan Valley where David lived in caves (and even outdoors) trying to survive.

While in exile, a group of people joined David. They, too, were a collection of nobodies. A great many of them were his relatives.

They were not the kind of people who were used to living in palaces. They only had two things to commend them: They were fiercely loyal to David, and they were stubborn warriors who would never retreat from a battle.

For years, David and his small band had to scramble to survive. They were poorly fed and clothed. They tried to do as much good for people at this time as they could, in the hopes of receiving a little money or a few goods to help them eke out a living. They used to hire themselves out as watchmen for people's livestock. To complicate matters still further, David refused to take matters into his own hands when he had the power to do so. Twice he had the opportunity to kill Saul, but he refused both times. He was content to wait for God to give him the throne at the proper time.

Then one day God did. All those outcasts, those offscourings of the earth, those rejects without influence, became the most important people in Israel. David made them his close advisers, his cabinet members, his generals, his emissaries to other nations. Their willingness to put themselves out for David's sake when the going was rough caused their elevation to high authority.

Those events did not happen by accident. They are preserved in Scripture because they model the exact situation of David's greater Son, the Lord Jesus Christ. He was rejected by those who should have hailed Him King and enthroned Him. Now He is a King in exile. He lives at a distance from the place that is rightfully His. He awaits the day when the Father will make His enemies a footstool for His feet.

At the moment, however, He is training a body of efficient subordinates who will be able to rule with Him and extend His influence over the whole earth. When that training is concluded —and His Father approves the timing—He will return to claim His throne; and when He does, He will exalt those who were so trained: people who were willing to be faithful and loyal to Him during His exile.

That is a destiny truly glorious—a destiny to which you and I, dear pilgrim, are called today. What He wants from you and me is to be faithful to Him, to do as much good as we can today, to call others to join His company. Finally, He wants us to wait patiently for the day—The Day when His friends join Him in extending divine rule over the universe.

ON THE JOURNEY

1. What personal benefits or choices have you given up to serve God more effectively? Beyond a greater sense of His commendation, have you ever received alternate blessings in your life as a result of your sacrifice?

2. Is your productivity and sense of accomplishment built upon the rewards you receive in the here and now or the treasures you are storing in heaven? How satisfied are you with your motivations and goals?

13

THE SATISFIED
PILGRIM

*The settled happiness and security which we all desire, God
withholds from us by the very nature of the world: but joy,
pleasure, and merriment He has scattered broadcast. We are
never safe, but we have plenty of fun, and some ecstasy. . . .
Our Father refreshes us on the journey with some pleasant
inns, but will not encourage us to mistake them for home.*

—C. S. LEWIS[1]

*P*sychiatrist Thomas Szasz captured modern man's disillu-
sionment when he wrote, "Happiness is an imaginary condition, formerly attributed by the living to the dead, now usually
attributed by adults to children and by children to adults."[2] In
spite of the doctor's opinion, people begin to think about the great
possibilities of future joy when they are very young, and with good
reason. We hear from those around us that one thing or another
will make us truly happy people. We are told that wealth will make
us happy; or that love or marriage will do it; or travel, or learning, or something else will.

Then, after a while, we begin to see that those conventional solutions to our aspirations never measure up. No matter how much wealth we have, it doesn't satisfy our deepest cravings. No matter how good our marriage, it doesn't quench the fires of our innermost longings. Brief moments of exhilaration enter our experience and provide just enough encouragement to make us desire more. Like a mirage, however, the joy satisfaction that we seek seems to retreat into the distance as we approach.

The satisfaction we yearn for comes only when we continue, step-by-step, on life's greatest journey. Pilgrims, homeward bound, can daily find satisfaction in the journey itself.

MUNDANE DETOURS

Yet many adults take every other road in the pursuit of what they are sure will satisfy them. The roads are indeed diverse. Take, for example, the odyssey of a southern Californian named Larry Walters. Larry, a truck driver by trade, always wanted to fly. Gaining a pilot's license and an airplane are expensive avocations, however, and he lacked the money to chase his dream in a conventional way. One day in 1982, however, he decided to pursue it unconventionally.

Larry obtained forty-two surplus weather balloons and filled them with helium. He had friends tie the balloons to his "aircraft"—an aluminum lawn chair, which he christened "Inspiration I." Larry strapped on a parachute and attached a six-pack of beer and a bag full of peanut butter and jelly sandwiches to the chair. He then loaded a pellet gun so that he could shoot out the balloons when it was time to come down. He figured that he would rise a few hundred feet, an ample altitude for surveying the neighborhood. However, when his friends released Larry and his balloons, Inspiration I shot up 16,000 feet, right through the approach corridor to Los Angeles International Airport.

Cold and scared, Larry stayed airborne for better than two hours, forcing the airport to shut down its runways for much of the afternoon. At his descent, his balloons draped over power lines and blacked out a Long Beach neighborhood for twenty minutes.

The adventure earned Walters a $1,500 fine from the Federal Aviation Administration as well as the year's top "award" from the Bonehead Club of Dallas, Texas. It would also have garnered him the altitude record for gas-filled clustered balloons, but the prize could not be officially recorded because he was unlicensed and unsanctioned. The escapade also put him on the lecture circuit for a brief time, and secured him appearances on *The Tonight Show* and *Late Night with David Letterman*. When asked by the press why he did it, Larry answered: "Well, you can't just sit there."[3]

The world's beautiful people . . .
suffer disproportionately from the
boredom of arriving at the summit and
finding the mountaintop disappointing.

In this search for satisfaction, boredom often interferes. Personal satisfaction seems to elude everyone. Today's news often carries reports of celebrities and notables who have discovered for themselves the inadequacies of today's happiness prescriptions. The world's beautiful people, in fact, seem to suffer disproportionately from the boredom of arriving at the summit and finding the mountaintop disappointing. As I began to write this chapter, the news services were carrying the story of two top athletes who had recently died. One was a National Football League all-pro who met his death via a heroin overdose. The other was a National Hockey League player who perished in an auto accident. The latter's blood alcohol level was over three times that of his state's definition of "drunk."

Pro tennis player Boris Becker rose to be number one in the world a few years ago, yet admitted that he was suicidal even as his achievements and fame were peaking. He said, "I had won Wimbledon twice before, once as the youngest player. I was rich. I had all the material possessions I needed. . . . It's the old song of movie stars and pop stars who commit suicide. They have everything, and yet they are so unhappy. I had no inner peace. I was a puppet on a string." Jack Higgins, internationally famous novelist, was asked what he would like to have known when he was younger. He replied, "That when you get to the top, there's nothing there."[4]

Muhammad Ali, the most famous boxer of the twentieth century and arguably its best-known athlete, constantly enjoyed stardom at the center of a circle of adoring admirers and hangers-on.

Now out of the spotlight and suffering from a degenerative illness, Ali evaluates his fame by saying, "I had the world, and it wasn't nothin'."[5]

The litany is heard loudly among rock musicians too. "Grunge music" star Kurt Cobain often sang of how he despised himself and wanted to die. Such aspirations existed in spite of his international renown and millionaire status. Perhaps the world shouldn't have been surprised when he took his own life with a shotgun blast. When Pearl Jam lead singer Eddie Vedder heard of Cobain's suicide, he trashed his hotel room in frustration and lamented, "People think you are some kind of grand person just because you can put your feelings into songs." Vedder observed that fans of rock stars "write letters and come to the shows . . . hoping we can fix everything for them. But we can't. What they don't understand is that you can't save somebody from drowning if you're treading water yourself."[6]

FAMILIAR PATHS

Leisure time has expanded even as transcendent values have retreated. Idleness, frustration, and lack of focus seem to generate much of the world's activities. This rampant emptiness accounts for the strangeness of what passes for art, music, fashion, and entertainment in the world. How else can phenomena like radio shock jock Howard Stern, basketball star/cross-dresser Dennis Rodman, and Jerry Springer's bazaar of the bizarre be understood?

A list of the supposedly shortest books in the Library of Congress made its way around the Internet not long ago. Among them: *My Plan to Find the Real Killers,* by O.J. Simpson; *Things I Wouldn't Do for Money,* by Dennis Rodman; and *My Best Motivational Speeches,* by Dr. Jack Kevorkian. Here's one that may be even shorter: *Pleasures That Ultimately Satisfy.* The author's name isn't important; any human being could write it.

Man's emptiness is nothing new, transcending chronological and philosophical as well as political borders. Our inner vacuum aches to be filled. Even a committed atheist like Bertrand Russell knew of it:

One is a ghost, floating through the world without any real contact. Even when one feels nearest to other people, something in one seems obstinately to belong to God, and to refuse to enter into any earthly communion—at least that is how I should express it if I thought there was a god. . . . There *must* be something more important, one feels, though I don't *believe* there is. (Italics in the original.)[7]

Today's sophisticates . . . hope that some not-yet explored nuance of experience will fill their emptiness and make sense out of their world.

The Athenian sophisticates of Paul's day also knew about emptiness: "All the Athenians and the foreigners who were there spent their time in nothing else but either to tell or to hear some new thing" (Acts 17:21). And so it is with today's sophisticates: They continually push the envelope, hoping against hope that some not-yet explored nuance of experience will fill their emptiness and make sense out of their world.

Several years ago, ABC News described a new work of modern art: a chair with an attached shotgun. In order to "appreciate" this masterpiece, the aesthete is required to sit in the chair and look directly into the business end of the shotgun barrel. Adding spice to the exhibit was the knowledge that the "artist" had loaded the gun and attached a timing device set to fire it at some point during the next hundred years. The report noted that people were waiting in line to take a chance at not being the victim.

The author of Ecclesiastes, a man who had done it all, summarized the frustrated longings of humanity when he wrote, "All things are full of labor; man cannot express it. The eye is not satisfied with seeing, nor the ear filled with hearing" (Ecclesiastes 1:8). He knew experientially the limitations of "life under the sun," that is, life without God: "Whatever my eyes desired I did not keep from them. I did not withhold my heart from any pleasure, for my heart rejoiced in all my labor; . . . Then I looked on all the works that my hands had done and on the labor in which I had toiled; and indeed all was vanity and grasping for the wind" (Ecclesiastes 2:10–11). In other words, all his efforts at finding satisfaction were a waste of time.

The dead ends that so consistently confront the world's pleasure seekers have not gone unnoticed. C. S. Lewis observed that when people try to explain the world's dissatisfactions, they generally arrive at one of two conclusions, both of which are wrong.

THE FOOL'S CONCLUSION

Some reach what might be called the fool's conclusion. The fool puts the blame for his boredom on the poor quality of what he has been seeking. He concludes, when his marriage is disappointing, that it's his wife's fault; so he looks for another wife. The travel wasn't quite what he had hoped, so he goes somewhere new. His hobby wasn't nearly as good as he had thought it might be, so he seeks another hobby. He goes through life chasing fantasies without finding their corresponding realities, and always for him it is because what he has is never good enough.[8]

The rich and famous seem to speak the fool's answer most often. (They at least have the wherewithal to continually seek new versions of their dreams.) Rarely do they recognize their foolish responses. Well-known political cartoonist Ralph Barton committed suicide, leaving a note pinned to his pillow: "I have had few difficulties, many friends, great successes; I have gone from wife to wife, and from house to house, visited great countries of the world, but I am fed up with inventing devices to fill up 24 hours of the day."[9] Like Hamlet in more ways than one, Barton would have agreed with the melancholy Dane, who once mused: "How weary, stale, flat, and unprofitable/Seem to me all the uses of this world!"[10]

THE CYNIC'S CONCLUSION

A second deficient answer comes from the cynic. He tries many things to make himself a satisfied individual. None of them work, so he concludes that the quest itself is the problem. As a result, he settles down and tries not to expect too much. Among other things, such an attitude of reduced expectations forms a key part of Buddhism, but a lot of nominal Christians approach life this way, too. The older they get, the more certain they are of this point of view. They say, "When I was young I thought that I could find the end of the rainbow, but I know better now."[11]

This is certainly a better solution than the fool's answer, because it doesn't destroy one's life; but it can make a person bitter and cause him to exhibit a superior, priggish attitude toward others. The cynic's answer might be workable were it not for the fact that God intends us to live forever—and certainly not in a cynical state. Our capacity for entertaining a dream is not at fault. It's the dream itself—and our method of gaining it.

THE PILGRIM WAY

However, it is not enough to reject false answers; we must start out on the journey of knowing the true answers, or to be more precise, the journey of knowing God through Jesus Christ. That is the essence of life's greatest journey. Our satisfaction will not be complete and permanent in this life, but along the pilgrim journey we can satisfy much of our spiritual thirst; that partial slaking will prove sufficient to encourage us to continue down the pilgrim way. As we walk, we learn that nothing in this world can compare to the pleasures of simply knowing the One with whom we are walking. Pilgrims are supposed to love Him increasingly the closer they draw to the City of God.

What the world yearns for is not what we have, but it is what we know we will ultimately have. If we would represent our homeland and our King properly, we must walk the pilgrim road.

How, then, do we walk the pilgrim path so that others will be attracted? Here are four guiding principles for walking as pilgrims on life's greatest journey:

1. See the destination.
2. Know the limits.
3. Feed the need within.
4. Seek God diligently.

First, we must see the destination. Philosopher and mathematician Blaise Pascal wrote, "There once was in man a true happiness of which now remain to him only the mark and empty trace, which he in vain tries to fill from all his surroundings, seeking from things absent the help he does not obtain in things present. But these are all inadequate, because the infinite abyss can only be filled by an infinite and immutable object, that is to say, by God

Himself."[12] Pilgrims cannot settle, as the age would have us do, for less than the great King.

God intends for us to find our satisfaction in Him. David said, "One thing I have desired of the Lord, that will I seek: that I may dwell in the house of the Lord all the days of my life, to behold the beauty of the Lord, and to inquire in His temple" (Psalm 27:4). He said again, "My soul longs, yes, even faints, for the courts of the Lord; my heart and my flesh cry out for the living God" (Psalm 84:2).

During this great pilgrim journey, our daily destination is closeness with God; our final destination is His very presence when we are reunited with Him.

David had the same daily destination: "As the deer pants for the water brooks, so pants my soul for You, O God. My soul thirsts for God, for the living God. When shall I come and appear before God?" (Psalm 42:1–2). This craving of the presence of God forms a recurring theme in the Psalter.

David's desire to "dwell in the house of the Lord" needs to be understood against the backdrop of Old Testament worship. He could not have been referring to any earthly tabernacle or temple, for he was not a priest. Consequently, he had no ability to take up permanent or even frequent residence in the earthly place of worship designed by God. Therefore, he must have had something else—an unseen "house of the Lord" which was accessible to himself and to all pilgrims. We worship God "in spirit," in a realm which is real though unseen; there it is that our inmost desires must be sought.

Jesus told the Samaritan woman, "Whoever drinks of this water will thirst again, but whoever drinks of the water that I shall give him will never thirst. But the water that I shall give him will become in him a fountain] of water springing up into everlasting life" (John 4:13–14). He contrasted the well that lay outside of her village with the "fountain" that He could implant within her. Wells can be destroyed by filling them with dirt; springs cannot. Pushing dirt into a spring merely deflects it—in time it will find another way out. When pilgrims conform to the world's values, they forfeit the everlasting Spring for the muddy dregs of what is fading away—what can never last and never satisfy.

Second, we must know the limits. Because we are fallen and live in a fallen world, our longings can only be partially satisfied until God Himself is accessible to us—and they will never be satisfied if we conform to the world and exclude Him from our search. Wisdom dictates that we grant to the simple pleasures of our earthly pilgrimage the place they deserve.

We must recognize the limits of the world's pleasures. They cannot satisfy our pilgrim yearning, but they have an important role nonetheless. "Probably earthly pleasures were never meant to satisfy it, but only to arouse it, to suggest the real thing," Lewis wisely wrote. "If that is so, I must take care, on the one hand, never to despise, or be unthankful for, these earthly blessings, and on the other, never to mistake them for the something else of which they are only a kind of copy, or echo, or mirage."[13]

When we know the limits of earthly pleasures, the things of this world will loosen their grip on us. I remember hearing the account of an evangelist who was preaching in New York City. As a gesture of kindness, his hosts gave him a tour of the city, including some of its most upscale stores. When he returned to his room, he got on his knees and thanked God for the hospitality of his hosts, for the wondrous sights he had seen during the day, and above all for the fact that he had not seen one thing that he wanted.

Third, as pilgrims we must feed the need within. We all have certain desires placed within by our Maker. For all of these a valid, divinely designed satisfaction exists. That is how we feed the need. We have needs to have purpose and challenges in life; needs to learn and to love. The many desires He has given us can be satisfied in illegitimate ways, of course; but the point is that the longings are planted by the Creator. In a sense, they make us what we are.

Lewis observed of our spiritual hunger: "I must keep alive in myself the desire for my true country. . . . I must never let it get snowed under or turned aside; I must make it the main object of life to press on to that other country and to help others to do the same."[14]

So we feed the needs, but always—first and foremost—we feed our deepest spiritual need. Jenny Lind, known in her time as the Swedish Nightingale, gained the world's accolades on the operatic stage; but at the height of her fame she abandoned her operatic career at age twenty-nine. A friend once found her sitting with a Bible on her lap, looking out into the glory of a sunset. They talked for a while, and soon Jenny's friend asked, "How is it that you ever came to abandon the stage at the height of your success?"

Because, she said, pointing to the Scriptures, "Every day it made me think less of this and [glancing at the sunset] nothing at all of that."[15]

Pilgrims need to be conscious of the way the world distracts us from what is eternally important and, like Miss Lind, turn away from them. At the same time, we should turn to the teaching of God's Word to encourage us along the pilgrim road. With David, we need to appeal to God by praying, "I am a stranger in the earth; do not hide Your commandments from me" (Psalm 119:19).

Fourth, as pilgrims, we should seek God diligently. David wrote in Psalm 24 about "ascending" as a pilgrim to approach the God who owns the world: "Who may ascend into the hill of the Lord? Or who may stand in His holy place?" (Psalm 24:3). The Psalm then proceeds to describe how God's people are to walk the pilgrim ascent to Him and with Him. We see this especially in Psalm 24:6, which says, "This is Jacob, the generation [or "family"] of those who seek Him, who seek Your face." Even though God created everything, and all men ought to seek Him, David wrote there was only one family on earth who was doing so—the family of Jacob.

Seeking God is distinct from conversion. Being introduced to Jesus Christ doesn't require doing anything other than believing in Him. It doesn't require moral qualifications; in fact, it requires abandoning any pretense of being qualified in oneself.

However, though seeking God is distinct from conversion, it is dependent on conversion. That is, only converted people may apply. Conversion happens once. Seeking God never stops, because God is too deep ever to be known completely.

According to guideline one—seeing the destination—we take steps to draw close to God in a world that regards Him as unimportant (or at least less important than the tasks of daily living). In guideline four—seeking Him diligently—we learn His priorities and seek to please Him, for, as we will see, pleasing Him—through holy living guided by holy motives—is key to approaching God.

HOW TO SEEK GOD DILIGENTLY

David described in Psalm 24 two positive qualifications and two negative ones for approaching God. First, the person who truly seeks God *does the right things.* He has clean hands. Verse three asks, "Who may ascend into the hill of the Lord? Or who may stand in His holy place?" Verse four provides four answers to these questions, beginning with, "He who has clean hands."

Having clean hands means that you live as one who respects the holiness of God and demonstrate that respect by means of personal integrity. It means that you show in your dealings with people that you care what God thinks of you.

David, the author of these words, discovered this the hard way. After he had conquered the city of Jerusalem and made it his capital, he decided to bring the ark of the covenant into the city. Until that time it had been carted from one place to another on purely pragmatic grounds. Jerusalem had recently become the permanent center of Israelite civilization, so it seemed logical to bring the ark, the symbol of God's covenant presence with His people, into the city.

David assembled the people and secured the services of an ox cart. He set the ark on it and brought it out of the house where it had been resting and started it toward Jerusalem. As they approached the city, one of the oxen stumbled and the ark began to topple from the cart. A man named Uzzah, who was driving the oxen, extended his hand to steady the ark. Even though it seemed like a good idea at the time, it wasn't. The ark was the holiest place under heaven. God had said that it was the place in particular where He dwelt on the earth. What seemed like a good idea in fact was irreverence—a casual and presumptuous approach to holy things—and God took Uzzah's life because he touched the ark and showed disrespect for God's holiness (2 Samuel 6:7).

David became upset at the event and abandoned plans to bring the ark into Jerusalem. He left it at the house of a man named Obed-Edom. For three months it was there, and God singled out Obed-Edom for blessing because the ark was there.

People told David about it, and he concluded, "We ought to bring the ark into Jerusalem after all. This time, however, we will do it the way God said to do it." So, he ordered the Levites to carry the ark in the way the Scripture directed that it be done. He probably wrote Psalm 24 for the occasion. The references to opening the gates of the city and the entrance of the King of glory could well refer to that celebration.

The first attempt to move the ark reminded David in a graphic way that God is a holy God. He can only be approached on His terms. If you don't do it His way, don't do it. When Paul told the church to pray, he said, "I desire therefore that the men pray everywhere, lifting up holy hands" (1 Timothy 2:8). He went on to define "holy hands" as those "without wrath and doubting." Holy hands are hands not fouled by anger and hostility toward people. If you profess with a loud voice that you are a churchgoer and stand for right principles, you need to be sure that people see that in a positive way. If you are a bear to work with, tone down your claims of godliness until your colleagues see that you are a person who bears the marks of God's kindness and gentleness.

The person who seeks God [does] the right things [and does them] for the right reasons.

David possessed a zeal for God in his desire to see the ark brought into Jerusalem, but one that was not informed by the truth. His objective was excellent; his methods were not. God in His mercy often overlooks zealous acts performed in ignorance, but not always. Uzzah's death sent David into a temporary tailspin, until God's blessing of Obed-Edom showed that it was not the presence of the ark that caused the trouble; it was the negligence of those who were handling it—David in particular.

The person who seeks God must also do the right things for the right reasons. That's what Psalm 24:4 means when it continues "and a pure heart." You might say that God is concerned with interior decoration as well as landscaping.

A lot of bad reasons exist for doing the right thing. Some would say: "Do what is right, because if you do what is wrong, you'll get caught." That is true enough, but if that's your only reason to do right, you may find that if the odds of discovery are low enough, or if the temptation is large enough, you will yield.

It's an infamous story, one I've heard several times. Many years ago, George Bernard Shaw engaged a young woman in conversation at a gathering of British nobility. She was impressed by the opulence and wealth of the people in the room. He pointed out a member of the House of Lords and said to her, "There's Lord—.

He is worth a hundred million pounds. If he offered you half of it, would you sleep with him?"

Blushing slightly, the young lady said, "I suppose I would."

Just then he called her attention to a hobo who could be seen through the window picking among the garbage. He said, "Do you see that man? If he offered you five pounds, would you sleep with him?"

The young lady became huffy, and asked, "Of course not! What do you think I am?"

Shaw replied, "Madam, we have already established that. We are now merely quibbling over price."

Sometimes people do what is right because they believe it will benefit them. That's true, too. Righteousness does profit in the long run if it is accompanied by contentment (1 Timothy 6:6). In the short term, however, it often doesn't work out that way. People become disillusioned and often cease to do right because they are not immediately benefited by doing so.

A pure heart seeks to do right because God would have it that way. A God seeker is one who lives to see God glorified.

People actually try to fool God into thinking that He is occupying their affections when He isn't. I know— I have tried it myself on occasion.

The apostle Paul was thrown into prison in Rome for crimes he didn't commit. It would have been easy for him to become discouraged and fall into despair, but he refused. Instead, he wrote the Philippian church, thanking them for their prayers on his behalf. He said, "For I know that this will turn out for my deliverance through your prayer and the supply of the Spirit of Jesus Christ, according to my earnest expectation and hope that in nothing I shall be ashamed, but with all boldness, as always, so now also Christ will be magnified in my body, whether by life or by death" (Philippians 1:19–20). What is important is that people think more of Christ whatever happens.

The last two qualifications for approaching God are negative. The person who seeks God allows no competition for his affections. That's what Psalm 24:4 means when it continues, "Who has not lifted up his soul to an idol." He does not offer his inner self to a substitute deity. Unmixed motives are essential when seeking God. Jesus said, "You cannot serve God and mammon" (Matthew 6:24). We can fool other people into thinking that we are interested in pursuing the truth, but we can't fool God. On the contrary, we are supposed to lift up our souls in worship to the true God: "To You, O Lord, I lift up my soul. O my God, I trust in You; let me not be ashamed; let not my enemies triumph over me" (Psalm 25:1–2).

People actually try to fool God into thinking that He is occupying their affections when He isn't. I know—I have tried it myself on occasion. It doesn't work. God is not mocked. We come off looking and feeling ridiculous, because He always knows what's inside and can expose our hypocrisy in amazing ways.

One of David's descendants, King Asa, on the strength of what Oded the prophet told him, began to genuinely seek God. "He took courage, and removed the abominable idols from all the land of Judah and Benjamin and from the cities which he had taken in the mountains of Ephraim; and he restored the altar of the Lord that was before the vestibule of the Lord" (2 Chronicles 15:8). Asa knew that as long as there were idols in the land—competition with the true God for the hearts of Judah—God would not allow Himself to be found. In the same way, the pilgrim must know and banish from his affections what would inhibit his passion for the living God.

The final qualification for approaching God is this: A person who approaches God's hill must permit himself no dishonesty. Stated positively, he will display integrity in all his dealings. Psalm 24:4 concludes, "Nor sworn deceitfully." He does not misrepresent himself to get what he wants rather than depend on God. He knows that his credibility with God is worth more than momentarily obtaining a possession.

Pilgrims cannot afford to be like the teenager who once called the dentist's office and in a tentative voice told the secretary, "I need to make an appointment." The secretary answered, "The dentist is out of town. Can you call back again later?" The teenager, in a much brighter tone, responded, "I'd be delighted to. When will he be out of town again?"

Our deceptions often mask a simple unwillingness to let our faith cost us any discomfort. Asa and the people of Judah, by contrast, offered to the Lord the equivalent of a hundred years' salary: "They offered to the Lord at that time seven hundred bulls and seven thousand sheep" (2 Chronicles 15:11). Just think of the alternative uses of that wealth that people might have proposed. Think of all the missionaries you could send to the Gentiles with the money from seven hundred bulls and seven thousand sheep! The God seeker knows, however, that delight in God outstrips all motivations, even the noblest ones. The soul that seeks God is glad that it can offer up willingly to God what it holds in trust.

One of the costliest parts of seeking God for Asa was the breach it brought into his own family. His grandmother had become an idolater. As leader of the people of God, Asa had to put his zeal for God to the test when he found out that a holder of high office in his own family was bowing down to idols. Asa was equal to it: "He removed . . . his grandmother from being queen mother, because she had made an obscene image of Asherah. And Asa cut down her obscene image and burned it by the Brook Kidron" (1 Kings 15:13). Seeking God sometimes requires allowing a breach in the family to continue when the alternative means tolerating a rival authority.

Indeed, one of the basic lessons of pilgrim living is that there can be only one Sovereign in any believer's life. He alone has the right to command us because He made us. He made us for Himself, and only in walking with Him can we find the satisfaction of genuine delights: "You will show me the path of life; in Your presence is fullness of joy; at Your right hand are pleasures forevermore" (Psalm 16:11). Finding true delight is among the rewards—both in this world and the world to come—of life's greatest journey.

ON THE JOURNEY

1. What event, person, or possession in this life has given you the sense of greatest happiness? Why could that experience not be sustained or fully satisfied? How has your greatest spiritual experience differed from it?

2. Is there anything at present that fills a place in your heart that only God should occupy? Ask God how you can remove it and allow Him to completely fill the vacuum.

Epilogue
JOY IN THE JOURNEY

Y ou and I, upon joining God's family, became pilgrims on life's greatest journey. You may be a reluctant pilgrim, still admiring or perhaps even dabbling in the world's pleasures. Or you may be a seeking pilgrim, trying to follow the Master on the pilgrim path, committed to pleasing Him regardless of whether rewards appear or not. If you are in the first category, I hope this book has helped you see that being a seeking pilgrim is worth your effort. Honoring God has rewards in abundance—though not at every turn and often not in ways we may imagine. We call this life's greatest journey because God's good plans always are fulfilling to us and honoring to Him.

And so to all seeking pilgrims, let me summarize the packing list—what you must take on your journey—and give a word of consolation and reality.

We actually looked at the pilgrim's packing list at the end of the last chapter, when we studied Psalm 24:3–4, which describes how pilgrims can seek God diligently. Here King David has provided believers with a packing list containing four items: clean hands, a pure heart, unmixed intentions, and personal integrity (or an absence of deception). Review pages 220–25 to learn how to pack these four items.

Having all these qualities, however, merely means that we are properly equipped for the journey. They guarantee neither a life filled with euphoria nor a near-term fulfillment of our longings, for it is the journey itself that is critical. God imputes righteousness to the believer in Christ when he believes. From that moment, he possesses a righteous standing before God. His character, however, is shaped along the pilgrim road. There is a sense in which it is true that you take into eternity the capacities for joy that you develop along the pilgrim way.

Expand your enjoyment of Christ now by walking faithfully with Him—that is the very process by which you shape your soul for never-ending pleasures in the age to come. The Lord Jesus Himself "for the joy that was set before Him endured the cross" (Hebrews 12:2).

That future joy also can sustain us during the hard times. In the early years of the twentieth century, a missionary couple by the name of Morrison left Africa. They were returning to New York to retire. They had been working in Africa for years and had no pension; their health was broken, and they were defeated, discouraged, and fearful.

The Morrisons discovered they were booked on the same ship as President Teddy Roosevelt, who was returning from one of his big-game hunting expeditions. No one paid any attention to the husband and wife; instead, the couple watched the fanfare that accompanied the president's entourage, with passengers trying to catch a glimpse of the great man.

As the ship moved across the ocean, the old missionary said to his wife, "Something is wrong. Why should we have given our lives in faithful service for God in Africa all these many years and have no one care a thing about us? Here this man comes back from a hunting trip and everybody makes much over him, but nobody gives a hoot about us."

"Dear, you shouldn't feel that way," his wife said.

"I can't help it; it just doesn't seem right."

When the ship docked in New York, a band was waiting to greet the president. The mayor and other dignitaries were there. The papers were full of the president's arrival, but no one noticed this missionary couple. They slipped off the ship and found a cheap flat on the East Side, hoping the next day to see what they could do to make a living in the city.

That night the man's spirit broke. He said to his wife, "I can't take this; God is not treating us fairly." His wife encouraged him to commit the matter to prayer; perhaps God would grant him wisdom to see things from a different perspective.

A short time later he came out from the bedroom, but now his face was completely different. His wife asked, "Dear, what happened?"

"I told the Lord how bitter I was that the president should receive this tremendous homecoming, when no one even met us as we returned home. And when I finished, it suddenly occurred to me: We're not home yet!"[1]

It is easy to forget that we are not home yet. Being fully appreciated and fulfilled are experiences that belong fundamentally to the age to come. We have a taste of them now, and we can communicate that taste to others. But our ultimate satisfactions and greatest joys await the time when Jesus Christ is present with us.

Until then, we can savor each pleasure that He places on the path, delight in the dignity of being one of His pilgrims, and live distinctively as people who know the true virtues of our homeland.

NOTES

Chapter 1: Leaning and Meaning

1. Quoted in Cal Thomas and Ed Dobson, *Blinded by Might: Can the Religious Right Save America?* (Grand Rapids: Zondervan, 1999), 96.

2. Joel Belz, "Analyzing the Salt," *World,* 28 November 1998, 7.

3. A. Cleveland Coxe, ed., *The Church Fathers: The Ante-Nicene Fathers,* vol. 1, *The Apostolic Fathers,* "The Epistle of Mathetes to Diognetus." AGES Software, Albany, Oregon. On *Theological Journal Library CD, version 2,* CD-ROM, Galaxie Software, 1998.

4. Sinclair Ferguson, "The Resident Alien," *Moody,* September–October 1996, 30.

5. C. S. Lewis, *Mere Christianity* (New York: Macmillan, 1963), 52.

6. Ibid., 118.

Chapter 2: Blended Pilgrims

1. George Barna, *What Americans Believe* (Ventura, Calif.: Regal, 1991), 247.

2. "Gallup Poll," *Signs of the Times,* November 1991, 6; quoted on the Biblical Studies Foundation web site. Available at www.bible.org/illus/c/c-56.htm.

3. George Barna, quoted in Marv Knox, "Poll Shows Bible Widely Revered but Mostly Ignored by Americans," *Fellowship Extra* [on-line]. Available at www.cbf-online.org/fellowship/9702bible.html.

4. Charles R. Swindoll, *Come Before Winter* (Portland, Ore.: Multnomah, 1985), 77.

5. George Barna, *If Things Are So Good Why Do I Feel So Bad?* (Chicago: Moody, 1994), 90–91.

6. Barna, *What Americans Believe,* 206.

7. According to an Evangelical Press News Service report quoted in "Problems and Sufferings?" [on-line]. Available at www.livingwaters.net/problems.htm.

8. Barna, *What Americans Believe,* 212.

9. Quoted in Charles Colson, *Against the Night* (Ann Arbor, Mich.: Servants, 1989), 93.

10. Quoted in Erwin Lutzer, "Pastor to Pastor," *Moody Monthly,* n. d., 76, as cited in "Worldliness," at the Biblical Studies Foundation web site. Available at www.bible.org/illus/w/w-52.htm.

11. Joel Belz, "Analyzing the Salt," *World,* 28 November 1998, 7.

12. Quoted in "Divorce," Raymond McHenry, ed., *In Other Words,* Fall 1999 (computer disk). Available from Raymond McHenry, 6130 Barrington, Beaumont, TX 77706.

13. Josh McDowell and Bob Hostetler, *Right from Wrong* (Dallas: Word, 1994), 8–9.

14. George Gallup, "Vital Signs," *Leadership,* Fall 1987, 17.

15. Quoted in Robertson McQuilkin, "Digging Deeper," *Moody,* May 1993, 34.

16. Ibid.

17. Barna, *What Americans Believe,* 85.

18. Walt Russell, "What It Means to Me," *Christianity Today,* 26 October 1992, 30.

19. G. K. Chesterton, *Autobiography* (London: Hutchinson, 1937), 223–24.

20. Quoted in Warren Wiersbe, *The Integrity Crisis* (Nashville: Nelson, 1988), 40.

21. William R. Levesque, "Witness: Numbers Fabricated," *The St. Petersburg Times,* 4 February 1999, A1.

22. Glenna Whitley, "The Second Coming of Billy Weber," *D Magazine,* July 1989, 94; quoted in Joe E. Trull and James E. Carter, *Ministerial Ethics* (Nashville: Broadman & Holman, 1993), 9.

23. Trull and Carter, *Ministerial Ethics,* 9.

Chapter 3: The Values of a Pilgrim

1. Patrick Henry, Last Will and Testament, "Quotes." Available at www.muffet.com/lds/quotes.html.

2. Charles Swindoll, *Rising Above the Level of Mediocrity* (Waco, Tex.: Word, 1987), 225–26.

3. Michael P. Green, ed., *Illustrations for Biblical Preaching* (Grand Rapids: Baker, 1989), 220.

4. Mike Yaconelli, "Evangelical Gigolo," *The Wittenberg Door,* June–July 1980, 32.

5. Green, ed., *Illustrations for Biblical Preaching,* 72.

6. Quoted in *The Elizabeth Elliot Newsletter,* May/June 1999, 2. Published by Servant Publications in Ann Arbor, Mich.

7. Carl G. Johnson, ed., *My Favorite Illustration* (Grand Rapids: Baker, 1972), 64.

Chapter 4: The Vision of a Pilgrim

1. David B. Barrett, ed., *World Christian Encyclopedia* (Nairobi: Oxford Univ., 1982), 689.

2. C. S. Lewis, *Mere Christianity* (New York: Macmillan, 1960), 119.

3. James S. Hewett, ed., "It Is Finished," *Parables, Etc.,* July 1988 [computer disk service]. Available through The AutoIllustrator, P.O. Box 5056, Greeley, CO 80631.

Chapter 5: The Ethics of a Pilgrim

1. Quoted in Charles Colson, *Against the Night* (Ann Arbor, Mich.: Servant, 1989), 123.

2. Jay Grelen, "ECFA Suspends Mission over Fundraising Letters," *World,* 1 November 1997, 8.

3. Jay Grelen, "But It's For a Good Cause . . . ", *World,* 27 September 1997, 13.

4. Ibid.

5. Quoted in Gene Edward Veith, "Christ and Culture," *World,* 23 May 1998, 28–29.

6. Ibid, 29.

7. Joseph Sobran, "Pensees: Notes for the Reactionary of Tomorrow," *National Review,* 31 December 1985, 50.

8. Michael P. Green, ed., *Illustrations for Biblical Preaching* (Grand Rapids: Baker, 1989), 194.

9. *Today in the Word,* 28 March 1993; daily devotional of Moody Bible Institute, Chicago.

10. Charles Swindoll, *Rise and Shine* (Portland, Ore.: Multnomah, 1989), 200–202.

11. Ibid., 206.

12. Ted Engstrom, *Integrity: Character from the Inside Out* (Wheaton: Harold Shaw, 1997), quoted in "Integrity," Biblical Studies Foundation web site [on-line]. Available at www.bible.org/illus/i/i-64.htm.

13. Colson, *Against the Night*, 151–52.

Chapter 6: The Road Map of a Pilgrim

1. Quoted in "Bible," Biblical Studies Foundation web site [on-line]. Available at www.bible.org/illus/b/b-38.htm.

2. From the *Newsletter of the International Bible Society,* quoted in James S. Hewett, ed., *Parables, Etc.,* September 1987 [computer disk]. Available through The AutoIllustrator, P.O. Box 5056, Greely, CO 80631.

3. Lewis Carroll, *Alice Through the Looking Glass* (London: Macmillan, 1880), 100.

4. Alan Bloom, *The Closing of the American Mind* (New York: Simon & Schuster, 1987), 26.

5. Ibid., 25.

6. From *Fyodor Dostoyevsky: A Study* (1921), quoted in "A Lengthy Biography," Biblical Studies Foundation web site [on-line]. Available at www.bible.org/illus/d/d-100.htm.

7. Roy Hoover, "The Jesus Seminar" in Robert W. Funk, ed., *The Five Gospels: The Search for the Authentic Words of Jesus* (New York: Macmillan, 1993), 34–35.

8. C. S. Lewis, Letters, quoted in Clyde S. Kilby, ed., *A Mind Awake: An Anthology of C.S. Lewis* (New York: Harcourt, Brace, 1980), 162.

9. Doug McIntosh, *God Up Close: How to Meditate on His Word* (Chicago: Moody, 1998).

Chapter 7: The Work of a Pilgrim

1. Dorothy Sayers, *Creed or Chaos?* (New York: Harcourt, Brace, 1949), 56.

2. Adapted from a version of this story appearing in "Fresh Sermon Illustrations" [on-line]. Available at www.wsbaptist.com/fsi/archives/ 990615.htm.

3. "Keep the Workday Holy," *Our Daily Bread,* 5 September 1994; daily devotional of RBC Ministries, Grand Rapids, Mich.

4. Charles Colson, *Kingdoms in Conflict* (Grand Rapids: Zondervan, 1987), 68.

5. Leon Wood, *A Commentary on Daniel* (Grand Rapids: Zondervan, 1973), 36–37.

6. Many Bible students have described this remarkable prophecy in detail. For a good discussion, see Harold H. Hoehner, *Chronological Aspects of the Life of Christ* (Grand Rapids: Zondervan, 1977), 115–139.

7. William Barclay, *The Letters to the Galatians and Ephesians* (Philadelphia: Westminster, 1976), 179.

8. Harry A. Ironside, *Illustrations of Bible Truth* (Chicago: Moody, 1945), 33–35.

9. *Our Daily Bread,* 5 September 1994.

10. Not in the sense of being sorrowful that they were Christians, of course. The Greek word *apologia* means "a courtroom defense."

Chapter 8: The Politics of a Pilgrim

1. Richard John Neuhaus, "Against Christian Politics," *First Things,* May 1996, 73.

2. Taken from interviews conducted by the Chinese Church Research Center in Hong Kong; quoted in Carl Lawrence, *The Church in China* (Minneapolis: Bethany, 1985), 36–37.

3. Cal Thomas, "Not of This World," *Newsweek,* 29 March 1999, 60.

4. Jon Allen, "Personal Integrity," *Illustration Digest,* September–October 1989, 4–5. Available through *Illustration Digest,* P.O. Box 170, Winslow, AR 72959.

5. H. Richard Niebuhr, *Christ and Culture* (San Francisco: Harpercollins, 1986).

6. Hugh Kerr, ed., *Compendium of Luther's Theology* (Philadelphia: Westminster, 1966), 218.

7. Greg Bahnsen, *Theonomy in Christian Ethics;* quoted in Hal Lindsey, *The Road to Holocaust* (New York: Bantam, 1989), 33.

8. Rousas J. Rushdoony, "Government and the Christian," *The Rutherford Institute,* July–August 1984, 1.

9. C. S. Lewis, *God in the Dock: Essays on Theology and Ethics* (Grand Rapids: Eerdmans, 1970), 198.

10. Gene Edward Veith, "Christ and Culture," *World,* 23 May 1998, 29.

11. Brannon Howse, "The People and Agenda of Multicultural Education," *Understanding the Times,* January 1997, 3; cited in Josh McDowell and Bob Hostetler, *The New Tolerance* (Wheaton, Ill. Tyndale, 1998), 53.

12. Tim Crater, *Associated Ministries Newsletter,* 25 April 1999, 1.

13. Joseph Sobran, "Pensees: Notes for the Reactionary of Tomorrow," *National Review,* 31 December 1985, 48.

14. As quoted in William Barclay, *The Gospel of Mark* (Philadelphia: Westminster, 1975), 12.

15. Ibid., 13.

16. Cal Thomas and Ed Dobson, *Blinded by Might: Can the Religious Right Save America?* (Grand Rapids: Zondervan, 1999), 92–93.

17. Warren W. Wiersbe, *The Integrity Crisis* (Nashville: Nelson, 1988), 75–76.

18. Thomas and Dobson, *Blinded by Might,* 92.

19. Quoted in Michael S. Horton, *Beyond Culture Wars* (Chicago: Moody, 1994), 37.

Chapter 9: The Wealth of a Pilgrim

1. Quoted in "David Livingstone's Text," James S. Hewett, ed., *Parables, Etc.*, February 1984 [computer disk]. Available through The AutoIllustrator, P.O. Box 5056, Greeley, CO 80631.

2. Quoted in William Barclay, *The Letters to the Philippians, Colossians, and Thessalonians* (Philadelphia: Westminster, 1975), 85.

3. T. R. Glover, quoted in Barclay, *Philippians, Colossians, and Thessalonians*, 85.

4. William Shakespeare, *King Henry the Sixth*, 3.3.1., from *The Complete Works of William Shakespeare*, [CD- ROM] Creative Multimedia Corporation, 225 SW Broadway, Suite 600, Portland, OR 97205.

Chapter 10: The Temptations of a Pilgrim

1. Quoted in Wayne A. Detzler, *New Testament Words in Today's Language* (Wheaton, Ill.: Victor, 1986), 369.

2. Timothy D. Crater, "The Filling of the Spirit in the Greek New Testament" Unpublished thesis, Dallas Theological Seminary, 1971, 32–48.

3. Clarence Edward Macartney, *Facing Life and Getting the Best of It* (New York: Abingdon, 1940), 36.

4. Jon Allen, ed., "Drug News," *Illustration Digest*, March–April 1989, 6. Available through *Illustration Digest*, P.O. Box 170, Winslow, AR 72959.

5. Dietrich Bonhoeffer, *Creation and Fall*, quoted in *Bible Illustrator*, January 1991 [computer disk.]. Available by subscription from Parsons Technology, 1700 Progress Drive, Hiawatha, IA 52233.

6. The story of Augustine's conversion through the influence of Ambrose and his mother's prayers appears in Susan B. Anthony, ed., *The Confessions* (New York: Vintage, 1998).

Chapter 11: The Suffering of a Pilgrim

1. Frank Boreham, *When Scripture Changes Lives* (Waynesboro, Ga.: OM LIT, 1994), 102. Some of the material on Adoniram Judson was adapted from Ruth A. Tucker, *From Jerusalem to Irian Jaya: A Biographical History of Christian Missions* (Grand Rapids: Zondervan, 1983), 121–131.

2. Boreham, *When Scripture Changes Lives*, 103.

3. Peter would never have referred to the inherited culture of Jewish Christians as that of "aimless conduct received by tradition from your fathers" (1 Peter 1:18).

4. Philip Yancey, *Where Is God When It Hurts?* (Grand Rapids: Zondervan, 1977), 28.

5. Courtney Anderson, *To the Golden Shore* (Boston: Little, Brown & Company, 1956), quoted in James S. Hewett, ed., "Judson's Scars," *Pastor's Story File*, August 1984, [computer disk]. Available through The AutoIllustrator, P.O. Box 5056, Greeley, CO 80631.

6. Aldous Huxley, *Ends and Means* (New York: Garland, 1937), 270.

7. Quoted in "Reflections," *Leadership* (vol. 6, no. 3) as cited in James S. Hewett, ed., *Pastor's Story File,* April 1989 [computer disk]. Available through The AutoIllustrator, P.O. Box 5056, Greeley, CO 80631.

8. C. S. Lewis, "The Screwtape Letters" in *The Best of C. S. Lewis* (New York: Christianity Today, 1969), 16.

9. Vance Havner, quoted in James S. Hewett, ed., *Parables, Etc.,* September 1982, [computer disk]. Available through The AutoIllustrator, P.O. Box 5056, Greeley, CO 80631.

Chapter 12: The Rewards of a Pilgrim

1. Michael P. Green, ed., *Illustrations for Biblical Preaching* (Grand Rapids: Baker, 1982), 165–66.

2. Donald Grey Barnhouse, *The Love Life: A Study on the Gospel of John* (Glendale, Calif.: Regal, 1973), 216.

3. Ibid., 217.

4. Quoted in Samuel Zwemer, "The Glory of the Impossible," *Perspectives on the World Christian Movement,* Ralph Winter and Stephen Hawthorne, eds. (Pasadena, Calif.: William Carey Library, 1981), 259.

5. C. S. Lewis, *The Weight of Glory and Other Addresses* (New York: Simon & Schuster, 1980), 26.

6. Ibid., 25.

7. Zane C. Hodges, "The Doctrine of Rewards, Part 2," *Grace in Focus,* November–December 1994, 3–4.

8. G. H. Lang, *The Epistle to the Hebrews* (Miami Springs, Fla.: Conley & Schoettle, 1985), 52–53.

Chapter 13: The Satisfied Pilgrim

1. C.S. Lewis, *The Problem of Pain* (New York: Macmillan, 1962), 115.

2. "Join the Happy Minority," *Our Daily Bread,* 11 October 1994; daily devotional of RBC Ministries, Grand Rapids, Mich.

3. Robert Fulghum, *All I Really Needed to Know I Learned in Kindergarten* (New York: Villard, 1988), 139; Myrna Oliver, "Soared to Fame on Lawn Chair," Los Angeles Times, 24 November 1993, C11.

4. "What's Missing?" *Our Daily Bread,* 9 July 1994.

5. *Today in the Word,* October 1990, 11; quoted in "Fame," Biblical Studies Fellowship web site. [on-line] Available at www.bible.org/illus/f/f-12.htm; internet.

6. Tom Sirotnak, *Warriors* (Nashville: Broadman & Holman, 1995), 24.

7. Bertrand Russell, *The Autobiography of Bertrand Russell* (Boston: Little, Brown, 1968), 121.

8. C. S. Lewis, *Mere Christianity* (New York: Macmillan, 1963), 119.

9. Quoted in Josh McDowell, *The Resurrection Factor* (Nashville: Nelson, 1993), 1.

10. William Shakespeare, *Hamlet*, 1.2.(lines), from The Complete Works of William Shakespeare. [CD-ROM] Creative Multimedia Corporation, 225 SW Broadway, Suite 600, Portland, OR 97205.

11. Lewis, *Mere Christianity*, 120.

12. Blaise Pascal, *Pensees*, translation with an introduction by A. J. Krailsheimer, (New York: Penguin Books 1966), 425.

13. Lewis, *Mere Christianity*, 121.

14. Ibid.

15. *Webster's Biographical Dictionary* (Springfield, Mass.: G. & C. Merriam, 1976), 901.

Epilogue: Joy in the Journey

1. Condensed from Ray E. Stedman, "The Nature of Prayer," (sermon). Delivered on 16 February 1964 at Peninsula Bible Church, Palo Alto, California [on-line] Available on at www.pbc.org/dp/stedman/jprayer/0057.html.

Know God More Deeply

HOW TO MEDITATE
ON HIS WORD

God UpClose

Doug
McIntosh

God Up Close
How to Meditate on His Word

You *can* know God more deeply by meditating on His Word. The Bible contains remarkable claims of what happens when believers meditate on God's Word. When we meditate—or delight in God's truth—we are prosperous (Joshua 1:8), we gain understanding (Psalm 19:7), we are given life (Psalm 119:93), and so much more!
Best of all, meditating on Scripture familiarizes us with God's ways and precepts so that we can meet Him on a more personal, intimate level.

Quality Paperback 0-8024-7079-3

MOODY
The Name You Can Trust
1-800-678-8812   www.MoodyPress.org

Moody Press, a ministry of Moody Bible Institute,
is designed for education, evangelization, and edification.
If we may assist you in knowing more about Christ
and the Christian life, please write us without obligation:
Moody Press, c/o MLM, Chicago, Illinois 60610.